THE GREEK CHORUS

The Greek Chorus

T. B. L. WEBSTER

METHUEN & CO LTD
11 NEW FETTER LANE LONDON EC4

First published 1970 by Methuen & Co Ltd
11 New Fetter Lane   London EC4
© 1970 by T. B. L. Webster
Printed in Great Britain by
Richard Clay (The Chaucer Press), Ltd
Bungay, Suffolk

416 16350 5

Distributed in the U.S.A.
by Barnes & Noble Inc.

Contents

LIST OF ILLUSTRATIONS   *page* vii
LIST OF ABBREVIATIONS   ix
INTRODUCTION   xi

I. THE ARCHAEOLOGICAL MATERIAL   I

   1. Introduction   I
   2. Down to the time of Homer   4
   3. Seventh Century   8
   4. Archaic   11
   5. Ripe Archaic   17
   6. Early Classical   23
   7. Classical   26
   8. Free Period   30
   9. Later   31

II. LITERARY SOURCES   46

   1. Down to the time of Homer   46
   2. Seventh century   56
   3. Archaic period, 600–530 B.C.   67
   4. Ripe Archaic period, 530–480 B.C.   80
   5. Early Classical period, 480–450 B.C.   95
   6. Classical period, 450–425 B.C.   132
   7. Free period, 425–370 B.C.   151
   8. Later   192

III. CONCLUSION   200
   GLOSSARY OF METRICAL TERMS   213
   INDEX   217

Illustrations

1. Geometric fragment from Argos: Athens, National Museum (p. 7, no. 44).
From *Imago*, 1969.

2. Corinthian skyphos: Paris, Louvre CA 3004 (p. 11, no. 76)
From *Rylands Bulletin*, 36 (1954), 584, fig. 1.

3. Attic black-figure kylix by the Heidelberg painter: Amsterdam 3356 (p. 14, no. 102).
From Allard Pierson Stichting, Amsterdam.

4. Shoulder-picture of Attic black-figure lekythos by the Amasis painter: New York 31.11.10 (p. 16, no. 122).
Photograph: Metropolitan Museum.

5. Shoulder-picture of Attic black-figure lekythos by the Amasis painter: New York 56.11.1. (p. 16, no. 123).
Photograph: Metropolitan Museum.

6. Attic black-figure neck-amphora: Berlin 1966. 1 (p. 20, no. 159).
Photograph: Staatliche Museen.

7. Attic red-figure cup: Oxford 305 (p. 22, no. 192).
Photograph: Ashmolean Museum.

8. Attic red-figure pelike by Phiale painter: Boston 98.883 (p. 27, no. 237).
Photograph: Museum of Fine Arts.

9. Attic red-figure bell-krater by Polion: New York 26.78.66 (p. 28, no. 244).
Photograph: Metropolitan Museum.

10. Attic red-figure kalyx-krater by the Dinos painter: Oxford 1937.983 (p. 28, no. 250).
Photograph: Ashmolean Museum.

11. Attic marble relief: Athens, Acropolis Museum, 1338 (p. 32, no. 288c).
Photograph: German Archaeological Institute.

Acknowledgements are due to the editors of *Imago*, the John Rylands Library, the Allard Pierson Stichting, Amsterdam, the Metropolitan Museum, New York, the Staatliche Museen, Berlin, the Ashmolean Museum, Oxford, the Museum of Fine Arts, Boston, and the German Archaeological Institute, Athens, for photographs and permission to reproduce.

Abbreviations

(other than standard abbreviations for journals)

A.B.V.	J. D. Beazley, *Attic Black-figure Vase-painters*
A.R.V.	J. D. Beazley, *Attic Red-figure Vase-painters* (2nd edition)
B.H.T.	M. Bieber, *The History of the Greek and Roman Theater* (2nd edition)
C.V.	*Corpus Vasorum Antiquorum*
D	E. Diehl, *Anthologia Lyrica Graeca*
K	T. Kock, *Comicorum Atticorum Fragmenta*
K.i.B.	F. Winter, *Kunstgeschichte in Bildern*
L.C.S.	A. D. Trendall, *Red-figured Vases of Campania, Lucania, Sicily*
L.M.	A. M. Dale, *The Lyric Metres of Greek Drama* (2nd edition)
L–P	E. Lobel and D. L. Page, *Poetarum Lesbiorum Fragmenta*
M.T.S.	*B.I.C.S.*, Suppl. no. 20
M. to H.	T. B. L. Webster, *From Mycenae to Homer*
M.u.Z.	(i) E. Pfuhl, *Malerei und Zeichnung der Griechen* (ii) A. Rumpf, *Malerei und Zeichnung*
N	A. Nauck, *Tragicorum Graecorum Fragmenta* (2nd edition)
N.C.	H. G. H. Payne, *Necrocorinthia*
P.C.D.	A. W. Pickard-Cambridge, *Dithyramb, Tragedy and Comedy* (2nd edition)

Abbreviations

P.C.F.   A. W. Pickard-Cambridge, *Dramatic Festivals of Athens* (2nd edition)

P.M.G.   D. L. Page, *Poetae Melici Graecae*

Trendall–Webster   A. D. Trendall and T. B. L. Webster, *Illustrations of Greek Drama* (forthcoming)

Introduction

Much has been written about the poetry sung by the Greek chorus. But most books, while admitting that it was sung and danced, say little about that side of the performance. This is an attempt to trace the history of the dance of the chorus rather than its words, in so far as we can apprehend it from the metre, which controlled the feet of the dancers as well as organizing the words of the song, and in so far as we can see it on Greek vases and reliefs. I have learnt much from Miss Lawler's many papers and from her excellent book, *The Dance in Ancient Greece* (1964), but she is primarily concerned with ancient technical terms, secondarily with pictures, and comparatively little with metre. Ancient sources give us a great deal of information about the choral poets and about cult dances in different places, but on the actual movements of the dance they are not very helpful. Too many of the terms are either unexplained or explained in so many ways that the result is confusion, or they only refer to particular postures without saying how these were connected together, and in any case the technical treatises are so late that they are probably much more influenced by the solo dances of the Hellenistic and Roman pantomimos than by the tradition of archaic and classical choral dance.

Other books on Greek dance have interpreted the pictures in terms of modern dance-steps; this is attractive but carries with it the obvious danger that the modern steps belong to a completely different dance tradition which may be largely misleading. This seems to me to vitiate a recent large work by G. Prudhommeau called *La Danse Grecque Antique* (1965). Having found modern dance-steps and positions in ancient representations, the author then allots them metrical values and so is able to give the choreography of Greek texts. Thus Aeschylus, *Agamemnon* 1448, φεῦ, τίc ἂν ἐν τάχει is analysed as dactyl, spondee [*sic*], and long syllable, and given the appropriate steps for these values.

Quite apart from the false quantity, the metrical analysis is wrong; the phrase is an indivisible dochmiac, and there is no reason to suppose that the opening of a dochmiac when it took this metrical shape was danced in the same way as the dactyls of a hexameter. Was it danced differently when it opened with what the authoress would call an iamb or a spondee or a tribrach? We shall never be able to construct the choreography of ancient choruses from their texts any more than we can reconstruct their music.

What the pictures can do for us is to show us what different kinds of choruses looked like at different times. The pictures are not films or even photographs of the performance. They are what the artist remembered of the dance, translated into the prevailing conventions of his art and fitted into the space at his disposal. When the dance was uniform, the figures could all be represented in the same position; when the dance went through a number of memorable postures, it is possible that the artist showed this by putting different figures in different postures so that his single frieze showed no actual moment but a number of different moments. The figures have to be interpreted, but if we do not ask too much we can learn from them what different kinds of choruses looked like, what types of dance persisted over a long period, what new forms of dance were introduced at different times. Where we know the sort of text that the chorus in a picture sang as they danced, the picture tells us something about the text; we can visualize the chorus and we can state the tempo of their dance. In some cases where the connection between picture and text is particularly close we can say that these dance-steps go with this metre, and then this suggestion can be tried out on other examples.

I have put the archaeological evidence first as a separate chapter. It seemed less confusing to keep it separate than to weave it in with the history of the chorus as derived from literary sources and metre. It is also convenient to have clearly separated the questions which the archaeological evidence poses to the literary sources, such as can they provide a suitable dance at this place or this time? What name can be given to this new step and what metrical change can be associated with it? Is this song likely to have been danced in the tempo suggested by the picture? The first chapter, then, is a history of the visible appearance of the chorus with references to literary sources wherever desirable. The second chapter is a history of choral performances with the emphasis on the metre as controlling the dance as well as the words, and with references to the visual appearance wherever possible.

Choral poetry was a unity of song, dance and music, and the poet was responsible for all three. We have only the vaguest idea about the music, but we need not therefore confine ourselves to the words; we can also study the metre in its double function of organizing words and dance. Metrics is often regarded as an excessively difficult study, chiefly remarkable for the disagreements of the expert metricians. But although, as in every live branch of scholarship, there will always be furious disagreement, at the fairly general level at which this book is written there is a great deal of common ground which is readily intelligible, and I believe that the conception of metric as primarily dance, which can in some cases be visualized, is an aid to comprehension.

The first requirement of such a history of Greek choral metric is consistency. The same principles and the same terminology must be applied over the whole range from Homer to the late Hellenistic period. It was, in fact, because I had access to such a consistent system that I conceived the possibility of writing this book. My wife, A. M. Dale, left, when she died, not only *The Lyric Metres of Greek Drama* and a number of published articles on Greek metre, which cover a great deal of choral lyric from Alkman to drama and have been reissued by the Cambridge University Press as *Collected Papers of A. M. Dale*, but also notebooks with analyses of all the choruses and solo lyrics of tragedy and comedy. It was when I was preparing these for eventual publication as supplements to the *Bulletin of the Institute of Classical Studies* (*London*) that I first conceived the idea of this book. When I indexed the metrical units of tragedy (metrical units are what in an ideal edition would occupy a single line of text), I became interested in finding how many of the very large number of metrical units used by the tragic poets, over two hundred, were in fact traditional. Finally, when I was teaching metric at Stanford, I felt more and more the need to visualize these choruses, and I found in fact that there was more material for this than I expected.

I make no apology for following my wife's metrical interpretations exclusively, because it was essential in my view that, as far as possible, a single sensitive ear should be responsible for all the analyses. For all tragedy and comedy and a good deal of earlier lyric I had her guidance. Where I had not, I have tried to follow her principles, but here error may have come in. But for the most part I have simply put into chronological order what she had treated systematically under different types of metre.

I have tried to make the book useful to those who are not familiar with metrical terminology (and I hope to some of the many interested in Greek poetry who do not know Greek) by adding a glossary of metrical terms. But there is one more general matter that should be explained here. Wherever possible, I have expressed metrical units in my wife's *ds* terminology instead of the traditional longs and shorts. It is vastly easier to print, write, speak and remember than longs and shorts, and its use makes the rhythmical variations and repetitions in a long stanza immediately apparent. My wife's description can be found in *Collected Papers*, 63, and *Lyric Metres of Greek Drama*, 177. The following account is slightly modified from that: *s* is single-short enclosed between two longs; *d* is double-short enclosed between two longs. If further elements are simply added, a vertical line is placed between them: *s′s* is two cretics. If the rhythm is prolonged, the letters are written straight on: *dd* is a dactylic hemiepes, *sds* is a glyconic. A headless unit is shown by ʌ: an anapaestic dimeter can be shown as ʌ*dddd* and an ionic dimeter as ʌ*dx*ʌ*dx*. *x* in this and in other cases is used for anceps: thus an iambic trimeter is *xsxsxs*. Some forms of syncopated iambic and trochaic, and in particular some forms of dochmiac, are difficult or impossible to represent. But the majority of lines, particularly the long and complicated lines of the Pindaric victor-ode are readily apprehended in this form.

As texts, I have used Page, *Poetae Melici Graeci* (*P.M.G.*), wherever possible (the running numbers are repeated in Page, *Lyra Graeca Selecta,* which also gives most of the Sappho and Alkaios that I have quoted with the running numbers of Lobel–Page), Snell's texts of Bacchylides and Pindar, and the Oxford texts of the dramatists.

The Archaeological Material

1 · INTRODUCTION

A considerable number of vases, a smaller number of reliefs, and a few other objects illustrate Greek choral dances from the Minoan to the Roman period. Before any useful comparison of these illustrations with literary sources can be made, they must be roughly classified by date, types of chorus, and by the actual dance figures represented. For dating I have followed a simple division into eleven periods which allows a reasonably easy equation between history of art and history of poetry.

    I Minoan–Mycenaean
    II Protogeometric and Early and Middle Geometric (which has no illustrations of choruses)
    III Late Geometric
    IV Seventh century (including Proto-Attic and Corinthian down to the end of Early Corinthian)
    V Archaic (to 530 B.C. including Attic black-figure to Exekias and the Amasis painter, Middle and Late Corinthian)
    VI Ripe Archaic (530–475 B.C., including later black-figure and the painters in Beazley, *Attic Red-figure Vase-painters*[2], down to and including Makron, p. 482)
    VII Early Classical (475–450 B.C., Hermonax to the Lewis painter, *A.R.V.*, 483–984)
    VIII Classical (450–425 B.C., *A.R.V.*, 986–1311)
    IX Free (425–370 B.C.)
    X Late Classical (370–325 B.C.)
    XI Hellenistic

It is probably impossible to find any classification of types of chorus which will exclude all overlap, and the following classification is far from perfect. I have kept it because it grew fairly naturally out of the material:

(*a*) Exarchon (leader) of dancers, himself dancing.
(*b*) Dancers linked to each other by holding wrists: 1. mixed, 2. women, 3. men.
(*c*) Pyrrhiche.
(*d*) Slow dances: 1. processional, *a*. men, *b*. women, 2. laments, *a*. men, *b*. women.
(*e*) Maenad and satyr dances:

    1. Ordinary (mixed or satyrs alone or maenads alone)
    2. Satyr-play choruses
    3. Old satyrs
    4. 'Lenaian' satyrs and maenads
    5. Maenads with winged sleeves
    6. Maenads on points
    7. Maenads in tragedy
    8. 'Anacreontes'.

(*f*) Tragic choruses and singers, other than maenads.
(*g*) Women, not included above: 1. races, 2. dances.
(*h*) Men, not included above:

    1. Comic choruses, including sixth-century Attic forerunners
    2. Komasts, including Corinthian and other padded dancers
    3. Victory choruses
    4. Miscellaneous.

In order to be able to trace dance postures across from one type of chorus to another and from one period to another it was necessary to have some fairly simple notation which is easy to remember. Equation with preserved ancient names of dances may to some extent be possible later, but the names cover a very small number of the postures, they are preserved in late sources, and to some extent they derive from solo dancers rather than from choruses. Equation with modern dance postures is likely to be misleading because the modern postures belong to quite a different tradition of dancing. Movements of the feet are primary and can be denoted with capital letters. Movements of the arms come next and are denoted by small letters. Movements of the torso can be denoted with Greek letters; they are difficult to interpret because they are particularly affected by the artistic convention within which the artist is working (sideways-bending cannot be shown if the figure is drawn in profile), but for a preliminary survey it was sufficient to note only a pronounced forward bend (α) and a pronounced backward lean (β). For foot movements, A. Seeberg (*S.O.*, 41, 1966, 72) provided a fruitful beginning with his classification of Corinthian padded dancers into three basic postures, which can be followed into quite different types of chorus at many times.

A   Both knees bent and feet close together. To this can be added, because here too the knees are both bent and the feet are on the same level:

    AJ Jump

    AK Headstand

    AT Dancing on points.

B   Forward kick, one knee raised, the other leg bent.

C   Backward kick, the other leg bent. To these can be added two variants:

    CC Backward kick, the other leg straight

    BC One leg bent, the foot of the other fairly near the buttock, perhaps an intermediate position between B and C or between C and B, but very characteristic and recognizable.

D   Run. Noted by Seeberg as often occurring with A, B, C.

P   Goose-step or Prance. One knee raised, the other leg straight or nearly straight, which distinguishes it from B.

L   Lunge. One leg stiff, the other bent at the knee, both feet on the ground.

W Walk. Legs fairly close together, heels on or nearly on the ground.

S   Stride. Legs wider apart, at least one heel raised off the ground, knees bent. Distinction here is not entirely easy, and in particular cases may be doubtful. Essentially the walk is a slower, processional posture, and the stride a quicker, dance posture.

Arm movements are only noted when they are characteristic. Very often movement of either or both arms is conditioned by something carried, torch, thyrsos, drinking vessel, lyre, spear, or shield, and these arm positions are only noted when they seem to be part of the dance as such.

c Clapping hands

d Arm straight downwards, or

(d) Diagonally downwards

e Arm extended forwards, or

(e) Arm extended backwards

g Arm extended forward in greeting, slightly bent

k Arm bent with hand on hip

(k) Arm bent with hand near hip level

l Arms linked, usually by hand clasping partner's wrist

m Arms muffled in himation: often it can be seen that one arm is akimbo, k

s Hand raised to forehead, or

(s) Hand raised to level of forehead

u Arm extended upwards

w Winged sleeves

x Hand slapping shoulder

2 · DOWN TO THE TIME OF HOMER

How far Minoan choral dances were taken over by the Mycenaeans and transmitted by them to the classical Greeks is a question which cannot be satisfactorily answered. But two rather different instances can be quoted in which continuity is virtually certain. One is the so-called Harvester vase (1) from Hagia Triada, which is a steatite Minoan vessel of the sixteenth century B.C. The men are going out to harvest led by a dignitary, perhaps a priest. They sing as they do a kind of goose-step, and are interrupted by a stooping dancer, who breaks through the files and shouts at them. Forsdyke has seen here the ancestor of the exchanges between the choruses of classical comedy and an interlocutor, which will occupy us later. The actual step is clearly a marching step and the men must sing in marching rhythm. It recurs in a notable series of satyrs carrying lyres, which runs from the late sixth to the late fifth century (2), a chorus of men carrying lyres of the mid-sixth century (3), and occasionally a dancing satyr (4).

The other instance is the connection between the dances of Minoan women and the dances of Maenads in classical representations. It was natural to suggest this because of the connection of Ariadne with Crete and dancing on the one hand and with Dionysos on the other. With the recent discoveries on Keos (5) the plausibility of direct transmission is increased, particularly as in the fifth century Keos still remembered its Minoan settlement. Large statues of Minoan/Mycenaean dancing ladies have been found in a Mycenaean shrine which in classical times was dedicated to Dionysos. The Minoan gold ring (6) of about 1500 B.C. from Isopata near Knossos has a dance of four women in a flowery meadow. A little figure in the same dress appears in the distance; it is uncertain whether she is the leader of the dancers or the epiphany of the goddess whom they are invoking. Two of the women bend back with arms raised straight in greeting; two bend forward with forearms raised. Both postures with the same striding gait can be found in later dancing maenads (7).

Pictures of choruses next appear in the late geometric period roughly the last third of the eighth century B.C. These have been studied in two dissertations of 1963 to which I am much indebted: Renate Tölle, *Frühgriechische Reigentanz* (Hamburg), and R. Crowhurst, *Representations of performance of Greek choral lyric* (unpublished). Here we can distinguish, besides the numerous linked dances of men and women holding each other by the wrist, laments, pyrrhics, choruses of men, choruses of women, solo dancers, and perhaps maenads and komasts.

A few of the linked dances seem to be mixed. On an Attic oinochoe in Tübingen (8) sixteen women walk with arms sunk and linking hands, and nine men walk with arms raised and linking hands. But the painter evidently thinks of a single dance, because the last man lowers his hand to touch the last woman's hand and the first man is placed beyond the lyre-player (who is thought of as leading the women) so that the first woman can raise her hand to join his. On a cup in Athens (9) three men, one certainly and the other two probably carrying a lyre, divide the dancers into three groups, all walking with sunk hands: (a) two women linked, (b) three women and four men, all linked, (c) four women linked and four women separate. On an amphora in Copenhagen (10) seven women on one side of the neck and seven men on the other walk with lowered linked hands holding identical sprays: they probably belong to a single mixed dance. Outside Athens, a deep cup from Tegea (11) is decorated with a dance of linked women who walk and linked men who flex both knees: they appear all to be holding a rope; there is, as far as I know, no reference in literature to such a dance, but a possible ancestor can be seen in a fourteenth-century fresco (12) from Mycenae with a procession of ass-headed daemons (or masked humans?).

Dances of women walking with linked hands either raised or lowered are very common. They are known from Sparta, Tegea, Tiryns, Delos, Corinth, Argos, Mycenae, as well as Athens (13). Only a few variants on the normal scheme need be noted. On a kantharos in Copenhagen (14) two women with hydriai on their heads with linked hands from which sprays depend walk towards a lyre-player. On a kantharos in Dresden (15) three women with lowered linked hands walk towards a lyre-player; the first holds a wreath. The men's dance on the other side of this vase is interpreted by Tölle as a pyrrhic (see below), and possibly the two dances were performed at the same festival. A clue to the women's dance may be given by a cup in Athens (16), where four women with linked hands, the first holding a wreath, walk towards a woman, presumably a goddess, seated on a throne with a footstool. It is tempting to connect this, the pyrrhic, and the women with hydriai with an early festival of Athena of which elements survived into the later Panathenaia. On a hydria in Markopoulon (17) a normal dance of thirteen women is preceded by a smaller woman, not linked to the rest, on a higher base line: she is presumably a soloist who leads the chorus, rather than a goddess, and this may be relevant to the interpretation of the Minoan ring from Isopata (6).

There were also dances of men walking with linked hands, usually raised rather than lowered. These occur in Attica (18) and elsewhere (19). It is not always easy to distinguish between walking and striding; but when one or both heels are raised, I have called the movement striding, and it must be recognized as a quicker dance movement than walking (20). Normally the men are drawn naked, but occasionally the painter shows that they are wearing short chitons (21). Twice the linked male dancers are given a leader, both times represented on a smaller scale: on a pourer (22) in the Kerameikos he raises both his hands; on an oinochoe in Boston (23) he stands on his head.

In laments women normally walk and tear their heads with both hands (24) and this attitude is found already on Mycenaean larnakes. Sometimes, however, only one hand tears the head, one is raised towards it (25) or is propped on the hip (26) or is raised in a gesture of greeting (27). The men mourners on the big, early vases (28) walk with both hands to their heads like the women. Later, however, they walk (29) or stride (30) with one hand raised to their heads and the other arm lowered, more or less straight and sometimes holding a spray. Short chitons are sometimes indicated, and sometimes are easily mistaken for a shield (31). They may wear swords and they sometimes carry spears (32).

The men's dance on the Dresden kantharos (33) is interpreted by Tölle as a pyrrhic: the outside figures wear swords and hold spears; the inside figures appear to be unarmed, but their raised arms are in much the same position as the shield-arms of later pyrrhicists; all four have a wide stride. Tölle also sees pyrrhicists on the two striding figures armed with spears and Dipylon shields on the Copenhagen kantharos (34). A fragment in the Vlastos collection (35) has striding legs with raised heels and pairs of spears; this also is probably a pyrrhic. Unlike all these, walking warriors with helmets, shields, and two spears on a cup in Munich (36) link hands, but this also must be a variant of the pyrrhic.

A few other male dances can be distinguished. On a fragment from the Acropolis (37) a man has one foot on a small platform between a tripod and a flautist; this platform is found again in later dance scenes. On a stemmed krater in Athens (38) the striding figures with raised heels and flying hair take part in a dance rather than a race, because they do not run. A dancer with raised knee and outstretched hands from Artemis Orthia (39) anticipates posture B. On several vases the dancers are clapping their hands either above their heads or in front of their bodies; their legs either stride (40) or one foot is raised backwards (41) or both knees are flexed (42). Three of these clapping dances are led by a jumping figure (43). The jumper also appears on a fragment in Argos (44, fig 1), only the striding legs of the figure behind are preserved, and he is separated off by a swan. The jumper is preceded by an ordinary file of linked women, which probably ran round the vase, as the skirt and legs of a woman can just be seen behind the striding man, who may be a lyre-player.

The other early pictures of dancers are unique. On the handle of an oinochoe in Copenhagen (45) is a woman with flexed knees and two

7

branches in lowered hands, the only possible example of a women's dance without linked hands. A pyxis in Vienna (46) has two women with linked hands and flexed knees: their skirts are remarkably rendered by wavy lines, which it is tempting to regard as a survival of Mycenaean–Minoan frilled skirts; unfortunately the statement that the vase was found in Keos, where continuity between Minoan–Mycenaean ecstatic women's dances and the classical cult of Dionysos is assured, is suspect and the style points to Boeotia. Certainly the dance is wilder than any other early dance of women, and it is possible that these are the first surviving Greek (as distinct from Minoan–Mycenaean) maenads. Padded dancers appear on a fragment from Miletos (47); their lowered hands perhaps cross each other rather than link, and probably their legs are in posture B with one knee raised forward, but the style is rough and it is difficult to be certain.

3 · SEVENTH CENTURY

The earliest Proto-Attic vases were certainly made in the eighth century, but there is no break between them and their successors; similarly, the earliest black-figure was probably produced before 600 B.C. For the purposes of this section, therefore, seventh century means Proto-Attic down to the establishment of canonical black-figure, and Middle and Late Proto-Corinthian, Transitional and Early Corinthian. In this period the padded dancers begin to appear in their canonical form in Corinth. They have been studied in detail by Axel Seeberg (48). Here it will suffice to note that the commonest postures, A with both knees flexed, B with one knee raised, C with one foot raised backwards, BC intermediate between B and C, and D the run, all appear in the late seventh century, and on a kothon in Würzburg (49) one dancer is sailing above the ground in a sort of ecstatic jump.

A new form of chorus with a great future is the procession; the figures walk, usually wrapped in a himation, but, as they are often attended by a musician, they must be reckoned as a form of chorus. Fragments of early Proto-Attic from the Agora (50) have women in procession wearing chiton and himation; on one they carry sprays. On a late Proto-Corinthian hydria (51) similar women move away from a dinos, a large mixing bowl, which may perhaps be a prize for their dance. On an early Corinthian neck-amphora in Philadelphia (52) the processing women are separated by a woman bearing a tray of offerings from an ordinary chorus of women, who walk with lowered linked hands to the accompaniment of a flautist. Men, bearded and holding sprays, form the procession on an early Proto-Attic fragment from the Agora (53). On a middle Proto-Attic stand (54) eight men with sticks are led by two other figures of which only the legs remain; they have been interpreted as flute-player and lyre-player. Eretrian vases (55) also have women processing with sprays.

On the Corinthian amphora in Philadelphia and on the Proto-Corinthian hydria (56) a traditional chorus of linked walking women is associated with a procession. On a Corinthian alabastron (57) two linked women are associated with a string of padded dancers in attitude A. On a Corinthian olpe (58) the dance of linked women may be in honour of Artemis, lady of beasts, who also appears on the vase. Many choruses are simply traditional (59), but one Proto-Attic hydria (60) emphasizes the fact that the women are singing, and on another (61) the linked women are led by a man, who strides ahead of them clapping his hands.

As earlier, it is not always easy to decide whether a male and female chorus belong together or not. On the Analatos painter's hydria (62) men with linked lowered arms holding sprays are separated by a lyre-player from women similarly walking with linked arms and sprays; this must be a mixed dance, whether it is contemporary or mythical. On a later amphora by the same painter in the Louvre (63) a flute-player separates two pairs of man and woman with hands linked, holding sprays. A fragmentary hydria in the same tradition from the Agora (64) has two women and a man with linked hands and sprays, then a lyre-player, then three figures with linked hands and sprays; the first and third are women, but the second is missing and if it too was a woman, this may be a dance of women with a male leader rather than a mixed dance.

A unique mixed dance decorates an oinochoe of about 680, found in Etruria but apparently decorated by a Euboean (64a): three men alternate with two women; their arms cross but are not certainly linked; the women wear Minoan dress, and the men wear breastplates; the outside men hold oars, and one of the women holds a large wreath; the women walk, the outside men are in posture C and the central man strides. Mr Coldstream identifies the dance by the crane between the first man and woman as the Geranos (crane) danced by the Athenian boys and girls after Theseus had killed the Minotaur. Certainly the dance is very like the dance seen later on the François vase (114). But there Theseus has a lyre and presumably the lyre is traditional in the story. It is the presence of the lyre-player that makes it attractive to see the same story on the Analatos painter's hydria in Athens (62) but not on his vase in the Louvre with a flute-player (63). The difference in tempo between the women and the men can be paralleled on other vases. It is very interesting that the Euboean artist like the Boeotian artist of no. 46 remembers Minoan dress. A quite different mixed dance appears on a fragment from Crete (65) where women dance with children between them, holding their hands; some texts mention dances where women and girls dance together.

Where the men and women do not occur in the same frieze, it is better not to speak of mixed dances, although it is still possible that both dances occurred at the same festival. Thus a Proto-Attic vase in Berlin (66) has on the neck, below a chorus of nine linked women led by a lyre-player, a chorus of twelve boys striding and clapping their hands, led by a flautist. And an amphora in Oxford (67) has women walking with lowered hands on one side of the neck and men striding with lowered hands on the other. Neither of the choruses on this Oxford amphora have their hands linked. Another chorus of women walking without linking their arms occurs on a krater in Berlin (68). They wear chiton and himation but their arms are bare, and this distinguishes them from the processional choruses discussed above. The men's chorus on the Oxford amphora has a variant on another amphora in Oxford (69) of the same date; here the men stride with raised heels; one arm is lowered, the other is bent so that the hand is level with the hip.

A fragment in Eleusis by the Analatos painter (70) has an ordinary chorus of men walking with linked lowered hands. But a later Proto-Attic chorus (71) of bearded men strides with raised heels and linked raised hands; the leader has his foot on a podium or platform like the dancer on the earlier fragment from the Acropolis (72). The striding men with two spears and shields or elaborate chitons on an amphora from the Agora (73) are probably dancing a pyrrhic. The helmeted men striding with one hand to their heads and the other lowered on a fragment in the Vlastos collection (74) are performing a normal lament. A new scheme appears on a Proto-Attic vase in Mainz (75): the women walk muffled in their cloaks, one hand raised, and the torso bent forwards.

4 · ARCHAIC

In this period, which runs from the beginning of black-figure to the beginning of red-figure, five new types of chorus appear and the old choruses of men with linked arms seem to have been dropped. The new types are (i) choruses of satyrs and maenads, (ii) a special type, which can be called Anacreontes, (iii) choruses which can be called pre-dramatic since they contain some element which can be identified with later comedy, (iv) choruses which celebrate an athletic victory, (v) women's races. We shall have to notice how far new types of chorus take over traditional dance steps from existing choruses and how far they develop their own, and how much also the traditional choruses introduce new steps.

The padded dancers provide many steps for new choruses, particularly for the choruses of satyrs and maenads, and the Anacreontes. In this period padded dancers appear in Corinthian, Attic, Boeotian, Laconian, and Chalkidian. They are so numerous that only a few interesting examples can be quoted. A Corinthian skyphos (76, fig. 2) gives the names of the fertility spirits whom the dancers represent; the attitudes are the normal A, B, BC, C; one, with both knees flexed and the forearm raised upright is repeated by an Attic satyr – it may be labelled A(s). The satyr-like figure with fruits in both his raised hands on the amphoriskos with the return of Hephaistos (77) is in the same attitude – A(ss) – as one of the Anacreontes. Attic satyrs and maenads commonly run, attitude D. This too is often found among the padded dancers; two interesting runners in view of later developments are a padded dancer with a lyre (78) and a man dressed as a hairy satyr (79), who is perhaps the leader of the dancers, like the curious figure with an artificial phallos, who, however, walks with a greeting gesture (80).

When Corinthian padded dancers dance with women (81), the women are naked; where their names are preserved they seem to be the female counterparts of the beings represented by the padded men. Whether the Corinthians actually used naked women or whether the painters painted what the dancers represented instead of the dancers themselves, we cannot say. In Attica it is clear that men wore padded white tights to represent women in these dances (82). The Attic painters move gradually away from reality; the dancers become slim, the men are painted naked and the women wear short chitons, but the dance steps are basically the same (e.g. nos. 84–5).

One of the earliest Attic vases (83) has a jumping figure rare in Corinthian, a figure with flexed knees and arm stretched downwards – Ad – which recurs as a satyr posture, and a figure with one knee raised and one arm straight forward – Be – which recurs both as a satyr and as a maenad posture. A variant of this with the other hand near the hip is also found both on an early komast (84) and on a satyr. Two other satyr postures are seen in komasts near the middle of the century: Bg, one knee raised and both hands raised in greeting (84a), and Ag, both knees flexed and one hand raised in greeting (85).

Sometimes the later Attic komasts show little of their ancestry. On an amphora by the Swinger (86) two pairs, all ivy-crowned and all bearded except one, dance on either side of a seated lyre-player: the step is a stride with one hand near the hip and the other raised in greeting. On a chous by the Amasis painter (87) two men dance on either side of a flautist. They are in typical komast postures, except that they are just finishing, instead of being in the middle of, a backward kick (C) and the painter has represented their belly contortions more realistically than usual. The third dancer, who wears a himation muffling his left arm and holds a long ivy-spray in his right hand, seems out of context, and his step is a stride, not a komast step. This collocation is not unique (88); either the clothed dancer is the exarchon of the komasts or he belongs to a different kind of performance.

Laconian (89) and Chalkidian komasts (90) show few if any variations on the usual postures. Boeotian komasts are more exciting. The artists were evidently much impressed by the high kick and combined it with a forward- or backward-leaning torso and various gestures of the hands including the greeting gesture (91). On one kantharos (92) such revels are accompanied not only by the normal flautist in posture A but also by a running lyrist, as on the Corinthian alabastron already quoted (93).

The link between the dances performed by the padded dancers, who are ordinary men disguised by padding and standard costume, and the dances performed by satyrs and maenads, who must in the main be creations of the imagination, is particularly clear on the Chalkidian neck-amphora (94); the satyrs and maenads on the main frieze repeat the A, B, C postures of the padded dancers on the shoulder. In Attic the running posture D, often with one forearm raised and sometimes touching the brow, dominates the satyr pictures, so that it gives the impression that satyrs and maenads are not so much dancing in one place like the komasts but moving from one place to another. This is not true of an early cup by the Heidelberg painter (95), where on one side they dance while Dionysos and Ariadne stand and watch, but on the other Dionysos himself joins the dance. The parallels on komast vases have already been noted: A for the fluting satyrs, Ad for a satyr, Be for a maenad, B(s) for satyrs and maenads. The satyr next Ariadne and the maenad next Dionysos are in posture A with one hand raised and the other arm down. This posture Ad(s) occurs on an Argive geometric fragment which may represent a very early komast (96).

The dancing Dionysos has one knee raised, torso bent forward, one hand near his hip, and the other arm diagonally down, Bd(k), a step which a later maenad also performs (97). But on two vases from the end of this period, a band-cup (98) and a Nikosthenic amphora (99), besides satyrs and maenads in the old postures such as Ag, A(s), B(d), Be(k), B(ks), which have been noted in the komasts, many run, usually with one hand raised. On one side of the band-cup they run up to Dionysos and Ariadne instead of dancing in their presence: on the other they are proceeding with Hephaistos, who is being brought back on his mule. On the Nikosthenic amphora satyrs and maenads alternate right round the vase. On each side of the band-cup the number of runners equals the number of those who perform the older steps; on the Nikosthenic amphora there are six runners to eight older postures.

I have called the satyrs and maenads 'in the main creations of the imagination', but the earliest maenads with their very short chitons (e.g. no. 95) are not unlike the men dressed as women who dance with Attic padded dancers (e.g. no. 82), and the Attic women who performed as maenads at the 'Lenaia' or at Delphi may have provided a model for the slightly later maenads with long chitons. For the satyrs there are the men dressed as hairy satyrs on Corinthian vases (no. 79), and perhaps the smooth satyr is not difficult to imagine from this. The Attic vases with padded dancers representing both satyrs (or satyr-like beings) and nymphs or maenads are our only evidence for a performance uniting the two, but in the later dithyramb (Pratinas, *P.M.G.* 708) and the fifth-century satyr-play (Aeschylus, *P.Oxy.* 2245; Euripides, *Cyclops*, 63 ff.) the satyrs speak of themselves as habitually dancing with nymphs or maenads.

Most of the pictures of 'Anakreon and his boon-companions' belong to the ripe archaic and early classical periods, but Lydos painted a forerunner (100). Both Anakreon and the two komasts move more slowly than the normal komasts; they stride and Anakreon has one hand on his hip. Two other vases may be included here, because like the Anacreontes the men wear female costume. On the hydria (101) four men (in costume singularly like the Lydos Anakreon) advance towards a flute-player; one knee is raised, they lean backwards, and their hands are on or near their hips (Bkkβ). On the cup (102, fig. 3) a similar party occurs on both sides, but a trio instead of a quartet. But each side of the cup also has another trio; one is in posture A with both hands raised like the satyr-like figure on the Corinthian amphoriskos (103). The other party is in attitude B but leans forward with one hand raised in greeting and the other lowered towards the knee, not, I think, pulling up the chiton like the marble korai (cf. Lawler, *T.A.P.A.* 74, 1943, 64); the posture recurs later in komasts and maenads. The song must have told of the journey of the advancing trio, how a party were surprised at them on the way and another party greeted their arrival, but what the audience saw was presumably three stages in the dance of a single chorus.

The main group of Anacreontes are rightly taken to be a dance at a symposion and not a public performance. The performance on the hydria and the cup is much more obviously drilled. If, as I think, there is some connection between these and the rest, these may represent a 'stage version' of the Anacreontes; a number of these choruses on black-figure vases prefigure the choruses of Old Comedy. We do not know of any comedy called *Anakreontes* but Kratinos wrote an *Archilochoi* and Telekleides wrote a *Hesiodoi*. Presumably the plural titles mean that the actor and the chorus wore the same mask, so that the title might be translated 'Archilochos, etc., and his boon-companions'.

The other predramatic chorus on a vase of this period is the Christchurch Titans (104); they are the ancestors of Kratinos' *Ploutoi*, who announce themselves as Titans when they enter (105). We have no evidence that they entered on stilts, but the anapaestic dimeters which they sing would be a perfectly possible metre for a marching entry on stilts. The curious pointed caps of the Christchurch Titans are Eastern; Titans visited their brother Prometheus when he was punished in the Caucasus, but the hats may signify no more than foreign, outlandish. Perhaps also the men who attend Dionysos and Ariadne on an amphora in New York (106) belong to a pre-dramatic chorus; they have one hand on their hips under large cloaks.

It is difficult to know how to interpret a neck-amphora in Paris (107) with four lyre-players in long chitons and himatia, three bearded and one beardless (this combination of one unbearded and three bearded is found also on komast vases); the first and third prance, the second and fourth walk. This combination of steps is found also in the series of lyre-playing satyrs, which starts in the next period. They look like a chorus, and again a possible descendant is provided by Magnes' *Barbitistai* (lyre-players).

Two Corinthian choruses have nothing to do with drama. On an aryballos (108) a flute-player Polyterpos plays while Pyrrhias, described as leading the dance *prochoreuomenos*, jumps with his hands above his head in front of four boys in pairs, who smack their hands on their thighs; both knees are slightly flexed. This continues the tradition of earlier dancers with jumping leaders. A fragment from Aigina (109) again gives a flute-player and two paired dancers, probably boys wearing chitons, but the break makes it impossible to say anything more about them. The same overlap of pairs is seen on an Attic amphora (110) where two pairs of Muses walk playing the castagnets behind Apollo, who plays the lyre as he leads them to Zeus.

Epinikia appear now for the first time. The earliest picture is on a cup (111) by the C painter; the victor carries the tripod on his head. From either side three bearded men in long chiton and himation walk with either *rhyta* or *phialai* in their hands while the flute-player plays. Beazley suggests that they sing Archilochos' hymn to Herakles, which is in alternating iambic trimeters and catalectic iambic dimeters. On a rather later amphora (112) the movement is more lively; four naked youths stride on either side of the victor who carries his tripod; this is perhaps the komos at the site of the victory rather than the welcome home shown by the C painter.

We have seen before choruses of men and women dancing with linked hands, which, we have said, may have belonged to the same dance or at least to the same festival. But I only know one certain and one possible instance (113) where men and women alternate in the chain. Now on the François vase, certainly on another fragment and probably on a third (114) Klitias painted the dance of the Athenian youths and maidens rescued from the Minotaur. Boys and girls walk alternately with lowered linked hands; on the François vase, where nearly the whole scene is preserved, Theseus leads them striding with his lyre and they are greeted by Ariadne's nurse and Ariadne.

Linked dances of women walking continue in the old tradition in Attic and Corinthian (115). The Corinthian linked dancers have interesting associations, once with padded dancers (116), and once with padded dancers and with men walking in procession (117). Presumably the artist is showing different parts of the same festival. The Attic linked dances show interesting differences of pace: the women on a pyxis stride, leaning forwards (118); the women on a Little Master cup run (119); the women on a Siana cup run towards an altar dragging a little boy with them (120); perhaps we should recall the earlier Cretan fragment with women and children (121). The Amasis painter painted two lekythoi with linked dances, and in both of them the pace changes: on one (122), which has a loom scene as the main picture, four women walk and four women run towards a seated goddess holding a wreath; on the other (123), which has a wedding procession as main picture, three women walk towards a seated flute-player, then three women walk towards a seated lyre-player, who is approached by three women running from the other direction. Here (as on the cup with Anacreontes) we have different moments in the same dance (figs. 4-5).

The women who run with linked arms can be distinguished from a new class, women racing. Klitias (124) paints Nereids racing, and a marble fragment of the geison of a pediment from Teichioussa near Miletos (125) has women racing with flowers in their hands.

The Corinthian procession of men which belongs to the same festival as the padded dancers and the linked women has already been quoted (126). Processions of women in a sacrifice scene occur several times in Corinthian (127). An Attic stamnos (128) has five women in a row, muffled in cloaks. A rather special class in Attic (129) and Boeotian (130) is formed by the Athenian boys and girls who watch Theseus killing the Minotaur. Probably the five women on the stamnos in fact belong here, as the front of the vase shows Theseus and the Minotaur. The case for thinking of them as performing a processional dance rests on the Munich cup, where one file is led by Ariadne's nurse who dances for joy, striding with torso well forward and both hands raised in greeting, a posture known from later maenads. More certainly a processional dance can be seen on an Attic amphora (131) where three youths muffled in their himatia with one hand on hip and the other holding a *tainia* walk behind a flute-player, who wears formal dress. As they have ivy-wreaths in their hair, they are perhaps performing a dithyramb rather than a victory song. So also two bearded muffled men by the Amasis painter (132) are probably dithyramb singers; one holds a long ivy-spray and stands before a flute-player; the other is crowned with ivy, and a goat separates him from a lyre-player.

Two plaques by Sakonides (133) and Exekias (134) give pictures of laments: the singers all walk; the women and some of the men raise one hand to their heads and some of the men raise their hands in greeting.

5 · RIPE ARCHAIC

In this period new choruses are formed by satyrs with lyres, satyrs and maenads performing an act of worship (grouped together as 'Lenaian' without any implication as to the festival which they are celebrating), maenads with winged sleeves (though this is a striking innovation in costume rather than a new dance), and once perhaps a chorus of tragic or pre-tragic maenads.

The most exciting maenad dances are those which contain maenads with winged sleeves (135). In general it is true to say that the running posture is less common both for satyrs and for maenads than in the archaic period. The old komast steps survive, particularly B and C. A good example is a black-figure neck-amphora in Cambridge (136). On a small late black-figure neck-amphora in London (137) the satyr has one knee raised, torso forward, one arm greeting and the other straight down, and the maenads stride, one with the back foot off the ground and one hand raised, one with one hand raised and the other on her hip.

Mountains are twice shown in pictures of maenads with winged sleeves, and so the painter is presumably thinking of the Oreibasia. On a skyphos by the Brygos painter (138) a single maenad dances between two peaks, feet striding, body bent right forward, both arms extended, one forwards and one upwards. On a cup by the Briseis painter (139) a peak is shown at each handle; the maenads either stride or stride with the back foot lifted (associated with the stride this is rather different from the komasts' posture C – there the foot is kicked much higher); arms are extended forwards, backwards and downwards, body bent forwards; among them Dionysos dances, leg kicked right back, body bent forwards, one arm extended backwards holding a snake, and one forwards with ivy-sprays (the same kind of wild dance as on the much earlier cup by the Heidelberg painter). A satyr also holds posture C, with one arm forwards and one upwards. These are very exciting dances emphasized by the bending of the body forwards or backwards and by the extended arms. In them the satyrs twice (140), though still in posture C, come very near to the lunge which strikes the eye of the painters in the next period.

Maenads with winged sleeves occur at least twice on 'Lenaian' vases. Before discussing Frickenhaus' series of these (141), a few other religious performances may be noted. On a black-figure lekythos (142) three satyrs dance round a rising phallos and a fourth moves away from them playing the lyre. It is curious that two themes are repeated from an earlier Corinthian alabastron (143), on which padded dancers perform round the rising head of Dionysos, the lyre-player, and the central pair, with one dancer catching hold of the foot of the other. Nearer the 'Lenaian' vases are pictures of dances round satyr-masks. Here the dancing of the satyrs and maenads is excited but on the whole traditional (144).

On the 'Lenaian' vases the performance takes place round the mask of Dionysos which is usually fixed to a column. The first (145) in Frickenhaus' list is, I think, unique in having the mask in a cave; the maenad dances away with an oinochoe in one hand and a wineskin in the other. The maenads on the early vases in Frickenhaus' list either 'stride' with gestures of greeting (146) – at least twice they have winged sleeves (147) – or 'walk' muffled in their himatia (148). Even on the wonderful cup by Makron (149) they all stride, generally with one arm extended forward, sometimes with body bent forward.

Miss Philippaki has argued (150) that this was a festival held in private houses. She bases the conclusion on the appearance of a chair behind one of the women and an alabastron hanging on the wall. But the chair may rather indicate that these are ordinary Athenian women performing as maenads rather than mythical maenads. This is strongly indicated by a small white lekythos of this period (151); here the maenad, equipped with phiale and thyrsos, seems to be rising from the chair in her room – marked by the mirror on the wall – to go to the festival. Men taking part in a chorus as maenads may appear on a black-figure pyxis (152). Their chitons are full long for men, and they have fawnskins, which would suit maenads; they 'walk' to the flute-player with one hand raised. It is possible that a tragic chorus of maenads produced by Thespis would look like this.

The majority of Beazley's Anakreon vases (153) belong to this period. They dance a fluid dance, sometimes striding, sometimes walking, the body often bent backwards and sometimes forward, the arms often extended forwards or downwards, sometimes carrying parasols or drinking vessels; and the lyre-player, once inscribed Anakreon, usually takes part. The postures can often be paralleled among the wing-sleeved maenads and the Lenaian maenads, and a cup by Douris (154) with wing-sleeved maenads and satyrs on the outside has an Anakreon dancing with another man on the inside.

Four black-figure vases are on the edge of this group. On a cup in Naples (155) a man in woman's dress with a parasol strides leaning forward, with his free hand near his hip; above his head a small female head shows that he is playing the part of a woman. On a black-figure lekythos (156) three Anakreons stride leaning backwards, and in the background three small women stride leaning forwards; it is unclear what the difference in scale means; is it possible that the painter means that the men imagine themselves to be maenads? Less interestingly, Anakreons can be recognized on a black-figure stamnos (157) where one walks playing the lyre while another dances with both knees flexed, and on a skyphos (158), where a man in ivy-wreath and himation holds posture B, leaning forward and with one hand near his hip, in front of a flautist.

Choruses of satyrs with lyres like the lyre-playing men noted above (107) appear now for the first time, although we have seen a kind of pre-echo in earlier prancing figures and earlier lyre-playing komasts and satyrs. On a black-figure neck-amphora of about 530 (159, fig. 6) one prancing satyr is followed by two walking satyrs, all playing the lyre. They occur again on an early fifth-century black-figure lekythos (160), leaving a herm behind them, passing a block or podium (cf. above n. 37), and approaching a flaming altar. The first walks, the second prances and the third strides in front, leaning forward. A contemporary black-figure lekythos (161) has five satyrs walking with lyres: they are old hairy satyrs and have white hair and beards.

A number of comic choruses have been preserved. In this period we cannot say for certain whether they are dramatic or pre-dramatic: comedy started officially at the City Dionysia in 486, and probably earlier at the Lenaia (162). Many of the choruses are mounted, and therefore we can say nothing of their steps, the knights, the dolphin-riders, and the ostrich-riders (163). But we can say that the Oltos dolphin-riders came on to anapaests because 'on a dolphin', an anapaestic metron, comes out of their mouths, and anapaestic dimeters are a good marching metre for an entrance (Aeschylus used it for his mounted Nereids). The ostrich riders are met by a little Pan, who strides, leaning backwards with his arms akimbo under a muffling himation. We have noticed this muffling himation over the arms before (164); now it occurs again on two vases with running soldiers (165), who are also to be reckoned as a comic chorus. This is a specially elaborate himation worn by characters whom one would not expect to wear it. The normal long himation swathes the Berlin chorus of cocks (166), who walk on behind their flute-player like a processional chorus, and the old men on a skyphos in Thebes who run on carrying

20

torches (167). The other side of this skyphos has old men standing on their heads and waving their legs to a flute-player, a posture noted before in Corinthian and geometric (168). The London cocks (169) run with arms extended to spread their wings.

In all these it is justifiable to see comic or pre-comic choruses entering. Three other pictures are more doubtful. A trio of running Minotaurs (170) with both arms akimbo probably belongs here. A trio of soldiers (171) each carrying a helmeted head as he strides leaning forward may possibly be a comic chorus. The dance on a red-figured krater (172) with men muffled in short himatia, two of them wearing masks with grotesque ears, is perhaps comedy; it is certainly not an entry but a dance 'on stage'. The man on the left flexes both knees in posture A, the man in the middle does a back kick in posture C, the man on the right steps forward from posture A (this variant is not uncommon in Attic komasts).

The komast vases continue in this period. Perhaps the most interesting is the unique picture of komasts dancing with women in very short chitons on a Caeretan hydria (173). The postures are the normal A, B, BC, C, but associated with very individual arm movements which sometimes repeat or nearly repeat the postures of the Anacreontes, for instance B with the torso forward and the arms greeting and A with the torso leaning backward and both forearms raised. Among the Attic komast vases the Rome mastos cup (174) shows very clearly that the women's parts were taken by boys, because some of the boys have women's heads above their heads. The Berkeley vase with komasts (175) is a Panathenaic amphora with a fighting Athena on the front, and therefore raises the question of whether the komasts did not have something to do with the Panathenaic festival. The Agora skyphoi (176) are firmly associated with Dionysos by the goats under the handle. On the Cambridge mastoid cup (177) and the Heidelberg skyphos (178) the komasts have ivy-wreaths. The wildest Attic komasts are on a psykter by Smikros (178a) and combine high-kicks with belly slaps – B(kk) and C(ks).

The only linked dances that continue are dances of women. On Clazomenian vases (179) they walk, bending slightly backwards. On an Attic fragment (180) from an Artemis sanctuary in Athens they stride. A red-figure nuptial lebes (181) has striding women with linked hands shown in a double row: they are either Muses or, perhaps more likely, the Delian women dancing with Apollo.

Women's races are also still represented in Attica (182) and in Magna Graecia (183). The Brauron girls (184) dance as well as racing, striding towards a flaming altar with hands raised in greeting. A dance of women apparently dressed as Amazons is painted by the Beldam painter (185); the leader has one arm raised in greeting, the other hand on her hip; she leans slightly backwards. The same posture occurs in a Muse, one of four dancing with Apollo on a lekythos by the Sappho painter (186) – two other vases (187) repeat the walking Muses, who appeared earlier. On a neck-amphora in Copenhagen (188) four women dance very gaily towards a boy, all have one hand on their hips, all stride except one who lifts one foot off the ground (B); all except one lean well forward. Rather similar attitudes are taken by three women dancing with three bearded lyre-players (189). Running women but without linked hands appear on an Attic skyphos (190).

The processional dances are interesting in this period. On a skyphos (191) four women walk to the right with one forearm raised to the left. The tradition of men walking muffled in their himatia often with one hand on the hip is continued by a cup in Oxford (192, fig. 7); two boys are singing for a flute-player in front of a herm. On a cup in New York (193) four boys sing to a flute-player in front of a row of columns, and the other side of the cup has a similar scene. It is natural to combine this with the Oxford cup and suppose that the performance took place at the Stoa of the Herms, which will then also be the place indicated by the herm on the Taranto lekythos with the prancing satyrs (194). A single boy with arm raised in greeting corresponds to a Nike on the other side of an amphora of Panathenaic shape in London (195), so that this chorus also may have performed at the Panathenaia. But a muffled boy singing on a platform with a flute-player (196) is perhaps rather a solo singer.

A number of pyrrhicists appear in this period. They normally stride with the knees well flexed, very often with a shield on the extended left arm and a spear in the lowered right hand (197). The Beldam painter (198) catches a moment when they are all crouching: the formal dress of the flute-player shows that they are pyrrhicists and not warriors. It is difficult to explain pyrrhicists holding a scabbard in one hand and a sword in the other, who have girls' heads above their heads, unless we are meant to see an allusion to the fact that girls danced the pyrrhic (199).

6 · EARLY CLASSICAL

The important new evidence in this period is the illustration of satyr-plays and tragedies. The dances of maenads and satyrs are still represented and many of the maenads have winged sleeves. The running posture has practically vanished; the old komast steps A, B, C are much less common than before. The common postures are striding legs with torso bent forwards or backwards and arms either extended forwards or backwards or with one or both hands on or near the hips. In satyrs particularly angular positions are emphasized, and this is particularly obvious in the new lunge with one leg extended and the other knee, whether forward or backward, sharply bent (200). It is very possible that these new postures are inspired by the satyr-play, and this would account also for the appearance of the lunge in the ordinary komos of young Athenians (201).

The 'Lenaian' maenads continue, and it is not entirely easy to formulate the difference between the ripe archaic and the early classical and classical pictures. It is easy to contrast Makron's Lenaian maenads (202) striding with bodies leaning forward, arms extended or waving thyrsuses, with the quiet maenads of the Villa Giulia painter (203) and his contemporaries (204), who walk as often as they stride, and in contrast to the Makron maenads, who wear swirling chitons, have large himatia which conceal most of their chitons and sometimes cover their arms. But it must be remembered that on ripe archaic black-figured lekythoi (205) Lenaian maenads walking, muffled in himatia, are as common as maenads striding with greeting arms; and on the Villa Giulia painter's Oxford stamnos, while four maenads move gently near the table while wine is dispensed, the fifth strides away with torso thrown back, one forearm raised and the other arm stretched stiffly downwards (like some of the Anacreontes that we have noticed). Early classical painters are more interested in the quiet dance while the wine is poured out, ripe archaic painters are more interested in the wilder dance which follows. Occasionally early classical vases follow the older tradition (206).

The latest of the Anakreon vases (207) belong to this period and on the whole continue the old steps. The lyre-player usually strides or walks with torso bent back. The dancers stride with one arm often stretched down and one hand on or near the hip. The himation often muffles one or both arms.

The two earliest satyrs who are fixed as stage-satyrs by their loincloths belong to the earliest decades of the fifth century, and it cannot be chance that they coincide chronologically with Pratinas. One (208) wears a breastplate (?) and has a spear; he strides leaning forward, one arm extended, the other holding his spear near his hip. The other (209) by Makron strides turning his body round and clutching his flanks just above his hips, either belly-slapping or a variant of the arms or arm akimbo, which is very common in the satyr-play. In our period we have six satyr-play vases which can be taken in chronological order.

Satyrs building a couch are possibly the chorus of Aeschylus' *Thalamopoioi* (210). Two stride like the Makron satyr. One has both knees flexed (A), body leaning back, and one hand just above his hip. The leader kicks back one foot (C), and leans right forward with the left arm straight out and the right arm straight down. This is an excited dance. Next is a satyr lyre-player (211) walking to accompany Dionysos in the Return of Hephaistos. He seems to have stepped out of the choruses of lyre-playing satyrs (212) into the satyr-play. The chorus of Pans on the Niobid painter's kalyx-krater (213) is probably best explained as an alternative chorus for a satyr-play (perhaps with a rising of Persephone). The four Pans are all in typical satyr-play postures; the central pair both lunge, one with hand on hip and the other arm extended, the other with one arm down and the other greeting. The outside pair stride, one leaning forward and greeting and the other leaning back with hands raised. On a volute-krater (214), which may illustrate Sophocles' *Pandora*, five satyrs dance as Pandora rises from the earth. The outside ones stride, as the outside Pans, and the left-hand one also greets; the right-hand one has his hand to his brow in astonishment. The satyr to the left of the goddess is in the same attitude as Makron's satyr, but his arms are both extended. The two to her right both lunge, one with right arm extended, the other with both hands on hips. Only fragments survive of a satyr-play showing the Release of

Hera (215) but it looks as if both satyrs lunge, one forward and the other repeating the satyr to the right of Pandora.

The choruses of dramatic maenads belong to tragedy, but it is best to keep them together because they exhibit certain common characteristics and certain analogies with other maenad vases. The earliest, a fragment from the Agora (216), only shows that the maenad is striding. The Ferrara maenad (217) with one knee raised, torso forward, one arm extended forward, the other back, recalls the greeting trio of the Amsterdam Anacreontes (218). The Berlin maenads (219) are slightly later. The one with profile face lunges with one arm extended and the other down like a satyr; the one with full face has the same arm positions, but strides like Makron's satyr. Both these positions of the legs, lunging and striding with one leg almost stiff recur in the maenad chorus on the Niobid painter's kalyx-krater (220); four of the maenads have one or both arms extended and two have hands on their hips.

The British Museum Phineus (221) is shown to be dramatic by the fact that Phineus wears a mask; two Harpies run off with arms extended carrying food from Phineus' table; this must surely be a lyric or at least recitative exit from Aeschylus' *Phineus*, produced with the *Persae*. The scene in the *Persae* itself in which Dareios rises from his tomb was illustrated on a hydria by the Leningrad painter (222). The fragments are desperately unclear, but two members of the chorus to left and right are leaning backwards, one with his hand to his cap in the gesture of surprise; another (?) is certainly striding, and one is cowering below the pyre with raised frightened hands (presumably he looked back towards the pyre). The woman dancing away in a picture of Euripides' *Peliades* (223) is surely one of the chorus: she strides with one arm diagonally downwards and the other forearm half raised. This is more like the fluid movement of the contemporary Lenaian maenads by the same Villa Giulia painter than the staccato movement of the tragic maenads considered above.

The Villa Giulia painter (224) also painted women striding with lowered linked hands. Thus this old tradition goes on, and the two other tempi, walking (225) and running (226) are also found at this time. On the Sotades' painter's astragalos (227) the three girls coming towards Hephaistos (?), who summons and greets them, stride with linked hands. The rest, three with winged-sleeves, dance outside, but because they are dancing in the air (they are probably Aurai, as one of them holds a formal flower) the painter has put them on tiptoe; this precedes by some years the earliest maenads to dance on points.

As before, some vases have pictures of single members of processional choruses, boys muffled in their himatia, one striding instead of walking, as on one vase (228). On the other side of this vase, and on a vase by the same painter in Oxford (229), there is a warrior who can reasonably be interpreted as a pyrrhicist (230). It is tempting to suppose that both dances belonged to the same festival, probably the Panathenaia. Another muffled boy (231) is on the back of a vase with a wing-sleeved maenad running towards a thyrsos planted in the ground; if the thyrsos takes the place of the idol of Dionysos she may be a 'Lenaian' maenad and the muffled boy may have sung a dithyramb at the same festival.

Finally in this period a very curious scene on a column-krater in Basel (232): six young men in pairs, their right feet raised off the ground, their left knees flexed, both arms raised in greeting, dance before an altar which is adorned with wreaths of myrtle and diadems, and behind which stands a bearded muffled figure with open mouth. They themselves wear diadems and a sort of jersey, decorated and fringed over their short chitons. The attitude rather recalls ripe-archaic maenad dances, particularly if the step is interpreted as nearer to a 'stride' than to the archaic forward kick (B). The enigmatic figure singing behind the altar may perhaps be interpreted as the leader of a men's processional chorus which took part in the same festival, unless this is a scene from tragedy (the young men's faces look rather like masks) and the chorus are summoning or rather greeting a ghost, like Dareios in the *Persae* or Achilles in Sophocles' *Polyxene*, but this ghost is a Greek, *not* a Persian, and a civilian, *not* a soldier like Achilles.

7 · CLASSICAL

Many classical satyr and maenad dances are dull, and both sexes seem to have lost their fire. But two new developments towards the end of the period look forward to the new excitement which is clear enough to us in the choruses of Euripides' *Bacchae*: dancing with tambourines and dancing on points. Two maenads on a bell-krater by the Dinos painter (233) hold tambourines in outstretched arms. One raises her knee in the old komos posture B, the other strides with torso leaning back; so also the third who holds her himation with one hand extended, the other back over her head. The first maenad on points, and here there is no question of floating on air like the Sotades' painter's Aurai (234), is on a squat lekythos by the Eretria painter in Berlin (235); she performs a solo with body leaning back and both arms raised in greeting, before the seated audience of Dionysos and his thiasos. Maenads on a bell-krater by the Pothos painter (236) have also caught the new excitement; one runs with one arm extended, the other dances in attitude B with torso leaning forward, and an ivy-spray in each hand, one raised and one lowered. This attitude is very close to the attitude of the dramatic maenad by the Phiale painter (237, fig. 8) – certainly dramatic because the painter has added a companion, a boy in the same clothes but with his mask still on the ground. Probably the Pothos painter's maenad should be described as lunging like the Phiale painter's maenad, but she has already taken one foot off the ground as in attitude B. The satyr in front of her is certainly in attitude B and raises one hand to his brow. It is not certain whether the maenad striding with one hand on her hip and the other forearm raised, both in winged sleeves, in a scene depicting the madness of Lykourgos (238) is a tragic choreut or not; it is natural to think of Aeschylus' *Edonoi*, where the chorus was male; a subsidiary chorus of maenads is, of course, possible but the painter may rather have been inspired by a description in a messenger speech. Another maenad by the Phiale painter (239) is interesting because it repeats the position of the Anakreon by Psiax (240) in reverse. On the other side a woman walks or rather strides leaning forward, muffled in her cloak with one hand on her hip. Nothing marks her as a maenad, and the painter may have been thinking of a female chorus of tragedy. He may, however, have thought rather of a Lenaian maenad and contrasted the rather tame reality of an Athenian woman performing as a maenad with the mythical ideal on the other side where the maenad dances to the fluting satyr.

The 'Lenaian' maenads now too show considerable variation as before. Many of them walk (241). The Phiale painter (242) makes one walk, but two stride, one leaning forward with forearm raised. The best known of all the Lenaian vases is the stamnos by the Dinos painter (243); here all the maenads stride, two bend forward with tambourines (so that it was possibly in the 'Lenaian' dances and not in the maenad choruses of tragedy that the tambourine first appeared), and one is muffled in her himation, leaning back with one hand on her hip and the other holding the thyrsos. These vases show a change of tempo within the dance like the earlier lekythoi by the Amasis painter (122–3).

Satyrs with lyres appear again once (244, fig. 9), and they are inscribed 'singers (victorious) at the Panathenaia'. They are evidently men dressed up as old satyrs and they move towards a flute-player in formal costume, who has lowered his flutes. As on the earlier vases, one prances and the other two walk, but their movements now are remarkably wavering and uncertain, as if the rhythm were far less firm and definite than it was in the late sixth century, which is exactly what we should expect from our knowledge of metric.

We have a number of satyrs either in dramatic costume or occurring in pictures of satyr-plays. A satyr in dramatic costume (245) performs for Hephaistos in the presence of Dionysos. He lunges with one hand on his hip and the other arm extended like one of the Niobid painter's Pans (246). The satyr in a picture of Sophocles' *Amykos* (247) raises one knee, bends forward, and greets with his hands in a traditional satyr and komast posture. A series of vases (248) (which actually ends in the next period) illustrates a satyr-play which is almost certainly Aeschylus' *Prometheus Pyrkaeus*; conceivably a revival was celebrated by a famous picture. At any rate the attitudes taken by the satyrs holding torches to receive Prometheus' fire turn up again and again, and we have only to note the most interesting. The earliest of the vases (249) alone has the drawers of the stage satyr, but this fixes the whole series as dramatic. He has one knee raised and both arms extended in different directions, posture Be(e). On the Dinos painter's version (250, fig. 10) the satyr Komos has the old posture C, Sikinnis lunges leaning back with one hand raised, Simos lunges with one arm extended. All these four postures recur in other pictures of the series with variations of the arm movements, and in addition on the Berlin lekanis (251) posture A with both knees flexed, torso bent back, and hands greeting, and the stiff-legged stride of the Makron satyr (252), and on a column krater in Athens (253) a satyr runs slapping his back, and another strides leaning back and slapping his shoulder. This series is the richest illustration of a single chorus that we possess.

For tragedy we have a Fury running in pursuit of Orestes to Delphi (254). The audience did not see this in the *Oresteia*, but the artist may have been inspired by their pursuit of Orestes from Delphi or their arrival in Athens. The Lykaon painter painted the death of Aktaion after Aeschylus' *Toxotides* (255), a messenger speech, of course, but the running figure of Lyssa, inspiring the hounds, must surely have been a recitative trochaic entry or exit like the scene with Lyssa and Iris in Euripides' *Hercules*. The earliest pictures of Thetis and the Nereids riding dolphins and sea-monsters when they bring Achilles his new arms belong to this period. The obvious source is Aeschylus' *Nereids*, and we can suppose that Aeschylus was inspired by the old dolphin-rider choruses: his Nereids (255a) arrived to anapaests like Oltos' dolphin-riders.

Sophocles' *Thamyras* is illustrated on two vases, one with his pride (256) and the other with his fall (257). On the first Thamyras' mother dances to crown him with a wreath: one knee is raised, her right hand is raised in greeting, and her left hand is near her hip. On the second she strides with torso bent forward and her hands tearing her hair; on the other side of Thamyras the Muse, representing the chorus, walks muffled in her himation, just like the figures that we have observed in processional choruses. The *Nausikaa* was also an early play in which Sophocles distinguished himself playing ball. He must therefore himself have acted Nausikaa, and the ball scene was what we should call a lyric dialogue between Nausikaa and the chorus. On a lid by Aison (257a) two members of the chorus are shown running towards Nausikaa as Odysseus emerges from the bush. There must therefore have been a lively dance before and an agitated dance after Odysseus awoke. A single vase (258) shows an actor taking the part of Perseus in a comedy which in this scene at least parodied Sophocles' *Andromeda*. He enters taking posture B with one hand raised to his brow. This again must be a lyric or at least recitative entry.

What we have called the processional scheme has a peculiarly interesting application on a bell-krater by the Kleophon painter (259): on either side of an ivy-decorated erection a poet and a flute-player with four members of a chorus, all muffled in elaborate himatia, three of them with one hand on their hips and one holding an ivy-spray in his other hand. The poet is named Phrynichos, and the other men have names which are known from contemporary Athenian records. They all wear ivy-wreaths, and therefore their identification as dithyramb singers is compelling. It is not quite so certain that the occasion was the Anthesteria. But the likeness of costume and stance makes it highly probable that the boy-singers on the earlier cups (260) are also singing the dithyramb. One other vase (261) is worth mentioning here: on one side of a stele a boy muffled in himation and with one hand on hip like the dithyramb-singers, and on the other side a woman with a torch, similarly walking muffled in her himation and with the other hand on her hip. This should be an evening chorus of women in the same festival as the boy's chorus.

8 · FREE PERIOD

For this period the material is virtually restricted to satyr and maenad dances, satyr-play choruses, and comedy. The chance of preservation has much to do with this since we find interesting choruses of linked women, processional choruses, and pyrrhicists much later. The two significant omissions are the Lenaian maenads and the maenads with winged-sleeves. The festival celebrated by the Lenaian women must have continued, but it looks as if Athenians no longer commissioned special vases with pictures of it. The absence of winged-sleeves suggests a change of fashion in some performance in which men or women performed as maenads. In the satyr and maenad dances the satyrs lunge as before and the maenads dance on points with or without tambourines (262).

The satyrs in the picture of Euripides' *Cyclops* (263) kick up their back-legs in the old posture C, but their hands are lowered in the same gesture as Lyssa when she urges on Aktaion's hounds (264); they are urging on Odysseus' sailors to blind the Cyclops and this fixes the reference to ll. 656 ff. The Pronomos vase (265) shows cast and satyr-chorus of the *Hesione* (?) by Demetrios: only one satyr dances, and he is in posture B with one arm extended and the other akimbo. This is exactly repeated by a satyr choreut on a contemporary rhyton (266). The satyrs in attendance on Dionysos and Ariadne on the back of the

Pronomos vase are in well-known postures. One lunges with one arm extended like Simos on the Prometheus vase (267). Two are in posture B, but with torso bent forward with one arm raised and the other greeting, much like the *Amykos* satyr (268). The satyr on another contemporary Attic Dinos (269) lunges with one arm extended and the other hand on his hip like the earlier satyr dancing for Hephaistos (270) and reversing the posture of one of the Niobid painter's Pans (271). A rather later satyr in terracotta (272) has both arms akimbo and both knees slightly flexed, posture A. The one satyr who is already dancing among the early-Apulian Tarporley painter's satyr choreuts (273) leans back with arms akimbo and one leg kicked up behind. This is unique but something like it occurs on the Berlin lekanis with the *Prometheus Pyrkaeus* (274).

We have more illustrations of comic dancing from this period. A child in comic costume and middle-aged mask (275) dances off with a torch and both knees flexed (A) followed by a child carrying a large cake. In front of Herakles' centaur-chariot (276) dances a wreathed slave with two torches in posture B. Both of these are figures from the *exodos* of comedy. On a bell-krater in Heidelberg (277) two chorus-men take part in a female chorus: one is dancing off in posture C with a torch in one hand and raising his mask on to his forehead with the other. The other chorus-man is dancing a chorus in the play, muffled in his himation like the Kleophon painter's dithyramb-singers (278). Among the remarkable polychrome oinochoai found in the Agora three are relevant here: the man who rows an enormous blue fish (? suspended between stilts) is probably a member of the chorus (279); the pair carrying an enormous cake (280) run on to the stage or into the orchestra; Dionysos and Phor (a thief?) (281) dance towards each other with hands raised in greeting, Dionysos raises his foot from posture A to posture C, Phor is in posture B.

9 · LATER

The few pictures of choruses from later periods are chiefly interesting as showing continuity. Thus the two marble reliefs from the Agora (282), both probably from the third quarter of the fourth century, show comic choruses with the left knee raised and the heel near the buttock, one of the original komast postures, BC. Three new satyr-plays are illustrated, but it must, of course, be remembered that the plays themselves may be earlier. The two satyrs who steal Herakles' arms while he holds up the world for Atlas are in postures B and C (283). When the satyrs greet the sun after his eclipse (284), three lunge, one raises his foot backwards in attitude C, and their arms are in the well-known positions of greeting, spying, astonishment. In a Perseus play the satyrs were frightened by the Gorgoneion and this is repre-sented on several vases (285); the satyrs lunge, kick forwards or kick backwards, their hands go to their brows or their hips or are raised in astonishment, all attitudes that we have seen before. The satyr dancing away to the right of Perseus with raised frightened hands but looking back gives a possible explanation for the raised hands on the Attic hydria which illustrates Aeschylus' *Persae* (286): he may also have looked back at the pyre. A late fourth-century terracotta relief from the Agora (287) has a traditional dance of women who stride with lowered linked hands. Three reliefs from Athens (288), dated about 350, 346, and 323 B.C. have pyrrhicists in the striding dance with shield arm extended and spear arm lowered. The first of these is a combined dedication for the Panathenaia and the City Dionysia but the representation, if any, of the latter chorus has not survived. The third (fig. 11) is also a double dedication for a victory with pyrrhicists and for a victory with a chorus of men; the name of the festival (or festivals) has not survived, but the chorus of men (as well as the pyrrhicists) are preserved: they walk muffled in their cloaks like the dithyramb-singers of the Kleophon painter (289).

NOTES

1 Harvester vase, Heraklion Museum. *M. to H.* 50, fig. 16; Matz, *Crete and Early Greece*, App. 15–16; Forsdyke, *J.W.I.* 17, 1954, 1; Lawler, *Dance in Ancient Greece*, figs. 9–11.

2 Cf. above, p. 20.

3 Attic black-figure neck-amphora, Paris, Louvre E861, Devambez, *Greek Painting*, 79. See below, n. 107.

4 E.g. Athens, N.M. 9690, *A.B.V.* 505; Metzger, *Imagerie*, 49, pl. 26, 1–3. See below, n. 142.

The Archaeological Material

5 See J. M. Caskey, *Hesperia*, 35, 1966, 363.

6 Heraklion Museum. *M. to H.* 50 f., fig. 13; Matz, op. cit., 129, pl. 33a.

7 The women bending back: cf. Athens, N.M. 464, *A.B.V.* 553; *B.H.T.*[2] fig. 73. The women bending forward: perhaps Warsaw 142465, *A.R.V.*[2] 1019; *P.C.F.*[2] fig. 20a.

8 Tübingen 2657. Tölle, no. 1; Crowhurst, no. 46; Davison, *Y.C.S.* 16, 1961, 83, fig. 127 (the Burly painter).

9 N.M. 874. Tölle, no. 8; *C.V.* Athens, 2, pl. 54–5 (interpreted as Thargelia); Davison, fig. 134 (the Burly workshop).

10 Copenhagen 9378. Tölle, no. 25; Crowhurst, no. 27; K. Friis-Johansen, *Thésée et la danse à Délos*, 1945, fig. 5–6; Coldstream, *Geometric Pottery*, 59.

11 Tegea, Tölle, no. 121, pl. 25; *B.C.H.* 44, 1921, 407.

12 Athens, N.M. 2665. M. Robertson, *Greek Painting*, 31.

13 Typical examples: Sparta, Dawkins, *Artemis Orthia*, fig. 37D; Tölle, no. 117. Tegea: *B.C.H.* 45, 1921, 407, fig. 54; Tölle, no. 122. Tiryns: Tölle, no. 108. Delos: *Delos*, XV, pl. 43, 56; Tölle, no. 131. Corinth: *A.J.A.* 1930, 412; Coldstream, pl. 30; Tölle, no. 113. Argos: Waldstein, *Heraion*, pl. 57; *K.i.B.* 112, 11; Tölle, no. 92, 101. Mycenae: J. M. Cook, *B.S.A.* 48, 1953, 37, pl. 17, A 4, etc.; Tölle, no. 104. Athens: e.g. Munich 6228, *C.V.* 3, pl. 109–10; Tölle, no. 13; Crowhurst, no. 1.

14 N.M. 727. *M. to H.* fig. 24; *B.S.A.* 50, 1955, 48; Davison, 83, fig. 128 (the Burly painter); Tölle, no. 6; Crowhurst, no. 11.

15 Dresden 1699. Hampe, *Sagenbilder*, pl. 23; Tölle, no. 5; Crowhurst, no. 68.

16 N.M. 784. *K.i.B.* 112, 9; Tölle, no. 7; Crowhurst, no. 10. Cf. the dance on the skirts of the bell-doll from Boeotia, Louvre CA 623, Richter, *Korai*, figs. 5–8.

17 Tölle, no. 16, pl. 6a.

18 E.g. Attic, Berlin 4506. Neugebauer, *Führer*, pl. 2; Tölle, no. 2; Crowhurst, no. 33.

19 E.g. Argos, Tölle, nos. 83–4; Amyklai: *K.i.B.* 110, 7.

20 Amsterdam 1215. *C.V.* Pays Bas, 1, pl. 23, 1; Tölle, no. 3. Agora P 1730. Burr, *Hesperia*, 2, 1933, 580, no. 162, fig. 42; Tölle, no. 36; Crowhurst, no. 44. Amyklai: *K.i.B.* 110, 7; Tölle, no. 119.

21 New York 25.78.50. Davison, 43, 145, fig. 37 (Workshop of 894); Tölle, no. 63; Crowhurst, no. 35.

22 Kerameikos 812. *Kerameikos*, V, pl. 117; Tölle, no. 10.

23 Boston 25.43. Fairbanks, no. 269c, pl. 23; Tölle, no. 11; Coldstream, 75.

24 E.g. Attic: Berlin 1963.13. Greifenhagen, *Führer*, pl. 34. Agora P 4990. Brann, *Agora*, VIII, no. 336, pl. 19; Davison, 43, fig. 36 (Workshop of 894); *M. to H.* pl. 23; Tölle, no. 40. Boeotian: Louvre A 575; Pfuhl, *M.u.Z.* fig. 17; Tölle, no. 124. Mycenaean larnakes from Tanagra. E. Vermeule, *J.H.S.* 85, 1965, 123 ff., nos. 1, 3, 4, 4a.

25 Kerameikos 1370. *Kerameikos*, V, 247, pl. 40, 153; Tölle, no. 359.

26 Athens, N.M. 810. Davison 43, fig. 38 (Workshop of 894); *M.D.A.I.(A).* 1890, pl. 10; *K.i.B.* 112, 8, 13; Tölle, no. 30, Beilage I.

27 Louvre A 575 (see n. 24).

28 E.g. Athens, N.M. 804; *M. to H.* pl. 21; Davison, fig. 1. (Dipylon master); 990, *M. to H.* pl. 22; Davison, fig. 25 (Hirschfeld painter). But it is impossible here to distinguish male from female mourners.

29 E.g. Agora P 4990, see above, n. 24.

30 E.g. Kerameikos 1370, see above, n. 25.

31 E.g. Markopoulon, amphora, Tölle, no. 38, pls. 11–12.

32 E.g. Agora P 4990, see above n. 24.

33 See above, n. 15.

34 See above, n. 14. Note that a duel is part of the armed dance in Xenophon, *Anab.* VI, 1, 5.

35 Tölle, no. 37, pl. 16b.

36 *C.V.* 3, pl. 124, 3–4; Tölle, no. 9.

37 Athens, N.M. 291. Graef–Langlotz, no. 303, pl. 11; Tölle, no. 51. Cf. below, n. 71, 160.

38 See above, n. 26.

39 Dawkins, *Artemis Orthia*, 63, fig. 37H; Tölle, no. 118.

40 Copenhagen 727, see n. 14. Toronto C 951. Davison, fig. 119 (Stathatou hand); Tölle, no. 27; Crowhurst, no. 36.

41 Athens, N.M. 14447. Tölle, no. 4, pl. 3; Crowhurst, no. 32. Düsseldorf. Tölle, no. 26, pl. 8, with flautist. Delos: *Delos*, XV, 38, no. 11, fig. 2; Tölle, no. 132.

42 Argos. *M.D.A.I.(A).* 57, 1932, 134, fig. 3; Tölle, no. 102.

43 Athens, N.M. 14447; Copenhagen 727; Delos.

44 Argos, see above, n. 13. Tölle, no. 101.

45 Copenhagen, Ny Carlsberg 3153. *M. to H.* pl. 27; Davison, fig. 131 (the Burly workshop); Tölle, no. 12, pl. 4.

46 Vienna, IV 3458. Tölle, no. 130, pl. 26b; Hampe, *Frühgriechische Sagenbilder*, pl. 29; Coldstream, 205. For the Minoan dress, cf. below, n. 64a.

47 Balat. *P.C.D.²* 140, 315, no. 109, pl. 15b; Tölle, no. 133. Possibly compare a fragment from Argos, Tölle, no. 103, *A.J.A.* 1939, 435.

48 A. Seeberg, *B.I.C.S.* Suppl., forthcoming. The dance postures are summarized by him in *S.O.* 41, 1966, 72.

49 Würzburg 118. Langlotz, pl. 9, 12; Payne, *N.C.* no. 724, fig. 44b; Seeberg, no. 215; *P.C.D.²* no. 37.

50 Agora, P 3617. *Agora*, VIII, no. 422 (Mesogeia Workshop); Tölle, no. 60. P 26411. *Agora*, VIII, no. 417.

51 Kraiker, *Aigina*, no. 342; Payne, *N.C.* 210, n. 3.

52 Philadelphia. *A.J.A.* 38, 1934, 523, pl. 32. Cf. p. 17, no. 127, for procession of women with flute-player, Berlin 3929.

34

53 Agora, P 13285. *Agora*, VIII, no. 442.

54 Berlin A 41. *C.V.* Germany, 2, pl. 30; *D.B.F.* 105, n. 27.

55 *B.S.A.* 47, 1952, pls. 5 and 6, C 2–4, 6; Pfuhl, *M.u.Z.* fig. 101.

56 Cf. above, nos. 51–2.

57 Rhodes. Buschor, *Satyrtänze*, 17, fig. 7; Seeberg, no. 223. Cf. also p. 16, n. 117 below.

58 Louvre E 603. Payne, *N.C.*, no. 768A; Jucker, *A.K.* 6, 1963, 60, pl. 21, 2–7.

59 E.g. Attic: Vlastos collection, hydria, Mesogeia painter, J. M. Cook, *B.S.A.* 35, pl. 45, 46a; Tölle, no. 57; *Agora*, VIII, no. 472. Berlin A 1, *C.V.* Germany, 2, pl. 1; Tölle, no. 126. Corinth: proto-Corinthian hydria. *Perachora*, II, no. 1297. Early Corinthian, Madrid 10788, Payne, *N.C.* no. 767; Pfuhl, *M.u.Z.* fig. 67. Boeotia: skirt of bell-doll, Louvre B 53, Higgins, *Greek Terracottas*, pl. 9d.

60 Athens, N.M. 18435. Tölle, no. 55; Crowhurst, no. 14; *M.D.A.I.(A)*. 76, 1951, 65, no. 3, Beilage 38.

61 Berlin 313R. Mesogeia painter. Davison, fig. 64; *C.V.* Germany, 2, pl. 86, 88; Tölle, no. 52; Crowhurst, no. 30; J. M. Cook, *B.S.A.* 35, pl. 43.

62 Athens, N.M. 313. J. M. Cook, *B.S.A.* 35, pl. 38b, 39; Davison, fig. 61; Tölle, no. 47; Crowhurst, no. 48.

63 Louvre. J. M. Cook, *B.S.A.* 35, 173; Buschor, *Gr. Vasen*, fig. 43; K. Friis-Johansen, *Thésee*, fig. 8; Tölle, no. 50; Crowhurst, no. 49.

64 Agora P 10.154. *Agora*, VIII, no. 384; Tölle, no. 48; Crowhurst, no. 28.

64a British Museum 49.5–18.18. J. N. Coldstream, *B.I.C.S.* 15, 1968, 90.

65 Heraklion 3205. *B.S.A.* 12, 1905–6, 47, fig. 24; Tölle, no. 133. For women and girls dancing together compare *Hymn to Aphrodite*, 116; Euripides, *Tro.* 332, *I.T.* 1144.

66 Berlin A 1, *C.V.* Germany, 2, pl. 1; Tölle, no. 126.

67 Oxford 1936.599. Davison, fig. 60; J. M. Cook, *B.S.A.* 35, 169; Tölle no. 28.

68 Berlin A 34. *C.V.* 2, pl. 22; *A.B.V.* 1, 1 (painter of Berlin A 34). Cf. Athens, N.M., from Anagyrous, Richter, *Korai*, pl. 8a.

69 Oxford 1935.19. Davison, fig. 59; J. M. Cook, *B.S.A.* 35, 169, pl. 38a; 42, 150; Tölle, no. 56.

70 Eleusis 841. J. M. Cook, *B.S.A.* 35, 175, fig. 1; Tölle, no. 34; Crowhurst, no. 10.

71 Berlin A 46. *C.V.* 2, pl. 37, 1–2.

72 Cf. above, n. 37.

73 Agora P 24032. *Agora*, VIII, no. 415.

74 Vlastos collection. Tölle, no. 46d, pl. 16d.

75 Mainz 156. *C.V.* 1, pl. 25.

76 Louvre CA 3004. *P.C.D.*² no. 40; Seeberg, no. 202; *G.T.P.* pl. 5a; Trendall-Webster.

77 Athens N.M. 1092 (664). Payne, *N.C.* no. 1073; *P.C.D.*² no. 38, fig. 5; *B.H.T.*² fig. 130; Seeberg, no. IV; *J.H.S.* 85, 1965, 103, pl. 24. *S.O.* 41, 1966, 73. Trendall–Webster.

78 Louvre S 1104. Payne, *N.C.* no. 461; *C.V.* 9, pl. 33, 1–6; Seeberg, no. 216; *P.C.D.*² no. 35; Metzger, *Imagerie*, 49, pl. 25, 1. The flautist on this vase holds his flutes but does not play.

79 Brussels A 83. *P.C.D.*² no. 44; Payne, *N.C.* no. 1258; Seeberg, no. VI, cf. *S.O.* 41, 1966, 68.

80 Oslo, Jensen Collection. *P.C.D.*² no. 46, pl. 10c; Seeberg, no. V; *C.V.* Norway, I, pl. 3, 3–4.

81 E.g. Dresden ZV 1604. *P.C.D.*² no. 48; Payne, *N.C.* no. 1477; Seeberg, no. 232; Buschor, *Gr.V.* fig. 80.

82 E.g. Berlin 1966.17. Trendall–Webster. (Attributed by A. Greifenhagen to the K.Y. painter.)

83 Athens N.M. 12688. *P.C.D.*² no. 10, pl. 3; *A.B.V.* 30, 680 (K.Y. painter).

84 Palazzolo. *P.C.D.*² no. 12, fig. 2; *A.B.V.* 34/1 (Palazzolo painter).

84a Taranto. *Arch. Reports*, 1960–1, 39, fig. 4 (Heidelberg painter).

85 Florence 70955. *P.C.D.*² no. 14; Rumpf, *Sakonides*, pl. 2–3; *A.B.V.* 110/32 (Lydos).

86 New York 41.162.184. *A.B.V.* 305/22; *C.V.* Gallatin, pl. 36, 1.

87 Oxford 1965.122. *A.B.V.* 154/45; *J.H.S.* 51, 1931, 262, fig. 6–8; Karouzou, *Amasis painter*, pl. 42, 3; *P.C.F.*² fig. 61.

88 Cf. Karouzou, no. 49, pl. 40, 8–9. Compare the mantled youth in Oxford with Dionysos on Boston 01.8026, Karouzou, pl. 37.

89 Cf. Seeberg, *S.O.* 41, 1966, 72.

90 Leiden 1626. *P.C.D.*² no. 71; Rumpf, *Chalkidische Vasen*, no. 2.

91 Munich 419. *A.B.V.* 30, 6; *C.V.* pl. 270, 3–4; Pfuhl, *M.u.Z.* fig. 171.

92 Bonn 334. *A.B.V.* 30, 11; Ure, *A.A.* 1933, 18, figs, 13–14.

93 See above, n. 78.

94 See above, n. 90. Cf. also Brussels A 135. *P.C.D.*² no. 70; Rumpf, no. 13.

95 Copenhagen, N.M. 5179. *A.B.V.* 64/24; *C.V.* 3, pl. 113, 2.

96 Fragment from Argos, quoted above, n. 47.

97 See below, n. 188 (woman or maenad) and n. 239 (Dionysos).

98 New York 17.230.5. Beazley, *D.B.F.* 56, pl. 24–5; *C.V.* 2, pl. 19.

99 British Museum B 296. *A.B.V.* 219, Painter N; *C.V.* pl. 72, 2.

100 Rhodes 12200. *A.B.V.* 115; *C.V.* Rhodes, pl. 19, 1–2.

101 Swedish private collection, *Münzen und Medaillen*, Auction 34, no. 121.

102 Amsterdam 3356. *A.B.V.*, 66; *C.V.* Pays Bas, pl. 2; *P.C.D.*² no. 21; *G.T.P.* pl. 3; Trendall–Webster.

103 See n. 77.

104 Christchurch, University of Canterbury, Logie Collection. By the Swinger. *P.C.D.*² no. 24; Brommer, *Antike Kunst*, 11, 1968, 50; Trendall–Webster.

105 Page, *G.L.P.* no. 38.

106 Metropolitan Museum (Gift of Eugene Holman 1959). *P.C.D.*[2] 153, no. 28.

107 Louvre E 861. Devambez, *Greek Painting*, 79. See above, n. 3.

108 Corinth. Roebuck, *Hesperia*, 24, 1955, 158; Guarducci, *Annuario*, 37–8, 1960, 280 f.; A. Boegehold, *A.J.A.* 69, 1965, 259; L. Threatte, *Glotta*, 45, 1967, 186.

109 Kraiker, *Aigina*, no. 539, pl. 40.

110 Copenhagen, N.M. 3241. *C.V.* 3, pl. 102, 2; Crowhurst, no. 165.

111 Heidelberg S1. *A.B.V.* 51, 1; *D.B.F.* 22; Crowhurst, no. 171. Perhaps cf. Siana cup in Cleveland, 1966. Perhaps also the Amasis painter's lekythos, *A.B.V.* 155, 63.

112 Copenhagen, N.M. 109. *C.V.* 3, pl. 101, 2; *A.B.V.* 135 (Group E); Crowhurst, no. 174.

113 See above, n. 63–4.

114 François vase. Florence 4209. *A.B.V.* 76, 1; K. Friis Johansen, *Thésee et la danse à Délos*, figs. 1–2. Fragments: Athens, Acr. 596, 597a–e, 598; Graef pl. 24, 29; *A.B.V.* 77; *D.B.F.* pl. 12, 4–5; K. Friis Johansen, fig. 7.

115 Attic: Heidelberg 208. *A.B.V.* 45 (Polos painter); *C.V.* pl. 32, 3. Corinthian: Paris, Cab. Med. *C.V.* 1, pl. 15–16; Payne, *N.C.* no. 944. Beziers, Jucker, *A.K.* 6, 1963, 47, pl. 17, 2. Lawler, fig. 37. Perachora. *Perachora*, II, nos. 1951–2 etc. And see below, nos. 116–118.

116 Dresden Z.V. 1604, above, n. 81. Cf. also above, n. 57.

117 Berlin 4856. Payne, *N.C.* no. 876; Seeberg, no. 193; Jucker, op. cit., pl. 22, 2–7.

118 Brauron. L. Kahil, *A.K.* Beiheft, 1, 5, no. 3, pl. 1, 4.

119 Tarquinia. Lawler, frontispiece; Beazley, *J.H.S.* 52, 1932, 181, fig. 14; Crowhurst, no. 146.

120 British Museum 1906.12–15.1 *A.B.V.* 90/7 (Burgon group); Lane, *Greek pottery*, pl. 38b; Ashmole, *J.H.S.* 66, 1946, 8.

121 Cf. above, n. 65.

122 New York 31.11.10. *A.B.V.* 154; Karouzou, *Amasis painter*, pl. 43; Crowhurst, no. 167.

123 New York 56.11.1. Lawler, 117, fig. 48; von Bothmer, *A.K.* 3, 1960, pl. 7.

124 Athens, Acr. 594; *A.B.V.* 77; *D.B.F.* pl. 12, 1–2; Rumpf, *M.u.Z.* pl. 9, 9.

125 British Museum B 585. Picard, *Manuel*, I, 375; Crowhurst, no. 125; Richter, *Sculpture and Sculptors*, fig. 466; Lawler, *T.A.P.A.* 76 f., 1943, 65.

126 Cf. above, n. 117.

127 E.g. Oslo 6909, *C.V.* pl. 4, 2. Berlin 3929, Payne, *N.C.* no. 669, pl. 23, 3; Richter, *Korai*, pl. 7b. Paris, Cab. Med., Payne, *N.C.* no. 878; *C.V.*, 1, pl. 17. Perachora, *Perachora* II, 1781, 2228, 2066.

128 Paris, Niarchos. B. Philippaki, *Stamnos*, pl. 1, 1–2.

129 E.g. Munich 2243. *A.B.V.* 163 (Glaukytes and Archikles); *D.B.F.* 55–6, 111; K. Friis Johansen, *Thésée*, fig. 22.

130 Louvre. Skyphos. *Enc. Phot.* 280, 19; K. Friis Johansen, *Thésée*, fig. 21.

131 Emmerich Gallery Catalogue, 22, iv, 1964, no. 13.

132 Würzburg 333. *A.B.V.* 153; Karouzou, *Amasis painter*, pl. 42, 3. Orvieto 1001. *A.B.V.* 153.

133 Athens, Vlastos. *A.B.V.* 113; *D.B.F.*, pl. 19; Rumpf, *Sakonides*, pl. 14.

134 Berlin 1811–26, etc. *A.B.V.* 146. Technau, *Exekias*, pl. 14–18; Rumpf, *M.u.Z.* pl. 12, 1–4.

135 Studied by Lawler in *M.A.A.R.* 6, 1927, 29; Beazley in *A.K.* I, 1958, 5; Edwards, *J.H.S.* 80, 1960, 82.

136 G 47. *C.V.* 1, pl. 10, 2; *A.B.V.* 314.

137 B 296. *C.V.* pl. 70, 10; *A.B.V.* 596.

138 New York 29.131.4. *A.R.V.*² 381; *B.H.T.*² fig. 20.

139 British Museum E 75. *A.R.V.*² 406; Lawler, fig. 24. For the Dionysos, cf. above, n. 95.

140 Cab. Med. 576. Pfuhl, *M.u.Z.* fig. 427; Lawler, fig. 29. Cambitoglou, *Brygos painter*, 17, pl. 7: note the likeness of the lyre-playing Dionysos to Anakreon. Munich 2645; Lawler, fig. 28. Both *A.R.V.*² 371, Brygos painter.

141 Frickenhaus, *Lenäenvasen*, 72nd Winckelmanns Programm, Berlin 1912, Additions *P.C.F.*² 30, n. 2. Add now Philippaki, *Stamnos*, XIX.

142 Athens, N.M. 9690. *A.B.V.* 505; Metzger, *Imagerie*, 49, pl. 26, 1 3.

143 See above, n. 78.

144 E.g. Palermo, Haspels, *A.B.L.* pl. 23, 3; Athens, Vlastos collection, *A.B.L.* pl. 25, 6; Munich 1874, *A.B.L.* pl. 31, 1.

145 Berlin 1930. *A.B.V.* 573, Haimon group; *M.D.A.I.(A).* 53, 1928, 89.

146 E.g. nos. 3, 7, 10, bf. lekythoi, Athens 464, *A.B.V.* 553; *B.H.T.*² fig. 73.

147 Sydney, rf. fragment, *P.C.D.*² no. 7, pl. 2a. Stockholm *A.B.V.* 560; Nilsson, *Gesch.* pl. 37, 3.

148 E.g. nos. 6 and 9, bf. lekythoi.

149 Berlin 2290. *A.R.V.*² 462 (Makron); *C.V.* 2, pl. 87; *P.C.F.*² fig. 17; Lawler, fig. 5.

150 *Stamnoi*, xix.

151 G. Schneider-Herrmann, *B.A.V.B.* 42, 1967, 75.

152 Eleusis 1212. *P.C.D.*² no. 20, pl. VIa; Buschor, *Satyrtänze*, 65, takes as a forerunner of the tragic chorus.

153 *Attic rf. vase-paintings in Boston*, ii, 58. Note particularly, no. 1. Meggen. Black-figure white-ground plate. *A.B.V.* 294 (Psiax); Richter, *A.R.V.S.* fig. 36. No. 2. Copenhagen N M. 13365 (inscribed). *C.V.* 8, pl. 333; *A.R.V.*² 185 (Kleophrades ptr.). No. 6. Madrid 11009. *C.V.* pl. 6–8. The notes coming out of Anakreon's mouth on no. 2 probably imply that the rest of the party will sing in unison, cf. *P.C.F.*² 262.

The Archaeological Material

154 Munich 2647. Beazley, no. 10; *A.R.V.²* 438; *J.D.A.I.* 31, pl. 3, 84–5.

155 Naples 81138. *C.V.* pl. 27; Brommer, *Antike u. Abendland*, 4, 42, fig. 1; Webster, *W-S*, 69, 1956, 113.

156 New York 41.162.13. *C.V.* Gallatin, pl. 7, 8; *A.B.V.* 538; *A.B.L.* 241 (Haimon painter). Perhaps cf. *C.V.* Bucarest, pl. 21, 3–6.

157 Philippaki,*Stamnos*, pl. 10. *A.B.V.* 344, Beaure painter.

158 Heidelberg 279. *C.V.* 1, pl. 42, 7–8.

159 Berlin 1966, 1. *A.B.V.* 285, Circle of Antimenes painter; Greifenhagen, *Führer*, pl. 52; Gerhard, *A.V.* pl. 52; Buschor, *Satyrtänze*, 85; Roos, *Orchestik*, 220 f.; Beazley, *Hesperia*, 24, 1955, 314. Cf. above, n. 109.

160 Taranto 6250. Lo Porto, *N.Sc.*, 18, 1964, 269, fig. 86; Trendall–Webster.

161 London B 560. *A.B.V.* 495 (Class of Athens 581); Corbett, *J.H.S.* 85, 1965, pl. 6a; *P.C.D.²* no. 2.

162 Cf. *P.C.F.²* 40.

163 Knights: Berlin 1697. *A.B.V.* 297; *P.C.D.²* no. 23; *B.H.T.²* fig. 126. Dolphin-riders: Schimmel. *A.R.V.²* 1622 (Oltos); Sifakis, *B.I.C.S.* 14, 1967, 66. Selinunte, *Arch. Reports*, 1966–7, 40, fig. 19. Fogg, *C.V.* Robinson, pl. 37. Boston 20.18. *A.B.V.* 617 (Heron group); *P.C.D.²* no. 25; *B.H.T.²* fig. 125. The reverse shows ostrich-riders. Trendall–Webster.

164 Cf. above, n. 106.

165 Brooklyn 09.35. *P.C.D.²* no. 30. Würzburg 344. *P.C.D.²* no. 29; *A.B.V.* 434 (Group of Vatican G 48); Brommer, *A.A.* 1942, 67. Nicosia, Cyprus. *Cyprus Report*, 2, 1934, pl. 9, 2; Beazley, *Attic Vases in Cyprus*, 37.

166 Berlin 1830. *P.C.D.²* no. 27; *B.H.T.²* fig. 124.

167 Thebes B.E. 342. Trendall–Webster.

168 Cf. above, p. 6, n. 23; a Corinthian padded dancer stands on his head on Athens, N.M. 3444, Payne, *N.C.* no. 1004.

169 British Museum B 509. *A.B.V.* 473 (Gela painter); *B.H.T.²* fig. 123; *P.C.D.* no. 26; Lawler, fig. 20–1; Trendall–Webster.

170 British Museum B 308. *C.V.* pl. 81/1; Lawler, fig. 27.

171 British Museum B 658. *A.B.V.* 586 (Beldam painter); *A.B.L.* 266; Brommer, *A.A.* 1942, 76, fig. 6–8.

172 Tarquinia RC 8261. *A.R.V.²* 260 (Syriskos painter); *B.H.T.²* fig. 180; Roos, *Orchestik*, 157; Lawler, 87, fig. 34.

173 Louvre, Campana 10227. *P.C.D.²* no. 84; Devambez, *Mon. Piot*, 41, 1946, 35.

174 Rome, Museo Industriale. *P.C.D.²* no. 18; *B.H.T.²* fig. 182.

175 Berkeley 8/3380. *A.B.V.* 339; *C.V.* pl. 23, 3.

176 Athens, Agora P 1544, 1547. *A.B.V.* 518 (Theseus painter); *Hesperia*, 15, 1946, 265, 290, pl. 38, 40; Burkert, *G.R.B.S.* 7, 99, pl. 3–4. Add another *A.S.M.G.* 8, 1967.

177 Cambridge, *C.V.* 2, R. and S., pl. 3, 3.

178 Heidelberg 279. *C.V.* 1, pl. 42, 7–8.

178a Louvre G 68. *C.V.* pl. 58 and 9; *A.R.V.*² 21; Roos, 85, fig. 21.

179 E.g. Munich 570. *C.V.* 6, pl. 301; R. M. Cook, *B.S.A.* 47, 1952, 123, A 1.

180 *Hesperia*, 35, 1966, 83, pl. 27 f.

181 *Delos*, 21, pl. 57; *A.R.V.*² 261 (Syriskos painter); Crowhurst, no. 180.

182 Kahil, *A.K.* 1965, pl. 7, 3; 8, 1–3, and pl. 10, 6–7 (Athens, N.M. 548, Beldam painter, *A.B.L.* 269, 66, pl. 54, 1).

183 Locri: Picard, *Manuel*, 374, fig. 105. Foce da Sele: Lullies and Hirmer, *Greek Sculpture*, 78; Crowhurst, no. 127; Richter, *Korai*, fig. 548.

184 Kahil, *A.K.* 1965, pl. 8, 5; 8, 7.

185 Louvre CA 2925. *A.B.V.* 587; Von Bothmer, *Amazons*, 110, no. 200; Kahil, *A.K.* 1965, pl. 10, 3–5. Cf. also Berlin, inv. 3766, Latte, *Salt.*, 40. Conceivably a pre-dramatic chorus, cf. interest of later comedy in dances of Lydian girls in honour of Artemis at Ephesos (Ar. *Nub.* 600; Autokrates, 1K).

186 Louvre MNB 910. *A.B.L.* 98, pl. 32, 2.

187 London B 346. *C.V.* 5, p. 12, fig. a. Frankfurt, K.H., WM016. *C.V.* 1, pl. 29, 1.

188 Copenhagen N.M. 8757. *C.V.* 8, pl. 316, 2.

189 Gotha, ZV 2476. *C.V.* 1, pl. 38; *A.B.V.* 384 (Acheloos painter). Perhaps, cf. above, n. 156.

190 Paris, Rodin 644. *C.V.* pl. 13; *A.B.V.* 620 (CHC group); Crowhurst, no. 146.

191 Athens, N.M. 1110. Ure, *J.H.S.* 75, 1955, 92, pl. 8, 1 (Sub-Krokotos group).

192 Oxford 305. *A.R.V.*² 416 (painter of Louvre G 265); *C.V.* 1, pl. 7; Trendall–Webster.

193 New York 27.74. *A.R.V.*² 407. *B.H.T.*² fig. 60; *M.T.S.* AV 5; Trendall–Webster. Cf. also Altenburg 229, *C.V.* pl. 70, 1, boy alone between herm and altar.

194 Cf. above, n. 160.

195 British Museum, E 287. *A.R.V.*² 214 (Manner of Berlin painter). *C.V.* pl. 47, 2.

196 British Museum B 188. *A.B.L.* 219 (Edinburgh painter), *C.V.* pl. 45, 10; Davison, *J.H.S.* 78, 1958, 11. Cf. also the boy at the music lesson by Phintias, Munich 2421, *C.V.* 5, pl. 222, 1; *A.R.V.*² 23–4.

197 E.g. Bonn 307, *A.B.L.* pl. 44/3 (Theseus painter). Stavanger 4305, *C.V.* Norway, pl. 28, 3–4. Oslo, Gulseth, *C.V.* Norway, pl. 32, 3; 33, 1–2 (Beldam painter). Baltimore 48.226, *A.B.V.* 523 (Athena painter).

198 British Museum B 649. *A.B.L.* 268 (Beldam painter).

199 Adolfseck 13. *C.V.* pl. 14.

200 E.g. (*a*) Berkeley 8/4582. *C.V.* pl. 43, 1; *A.R.V.*² 581 (Perseus painter). (*b*) Oxford 1924.2. *C.V.* 1, pl. 9, 1–2; *A.R.V.*² 865 (painter of Athens 1237).

(*c*) Oxford 1920.57. *C.V.* 1, pl. 9, 3–4; *A.R.V.*² 883 (Penthesilea painter).

(*d*) Fogg. *C.V.* Robinson, 2, pl. 39; *A.R.V.*² 899 (Splanchnopt painter).

(*e*) Winged maenads. Copenhagen, N.M. 1943. *C.V.* pl. 159, 1; *A.R.V.*² 976 (Zephyros painter).

(*f*) Winged maenads. Copenhagen, N.M. 150. *C.V.* pl. 152, 2. *A.R.V.*² 957 (Comacchio painter).

201   (*a*) Louvre G 369. *C.V.* 3, pl. 9; *A.R.V.*² 577 (Agrigento painter).

      (*b*) Berlin 3219. *C.V.* 3, pl. 142, 1.

202   Cf. above, n. 149.

203   (*a*) Oxford 523. *C.V.* 1, pl. 28; *A.R.V.*² 621; *P.C.F.*² fig. 18.

      (*b*) Louvre G 408. *C.V.* pl. 15, 2 and 7; Nilsson, *Gesch.* I, pl. 37, 1.

      (*c*) Würzburg 520. Langlotz, pl. 189.

      (*d*) Villa Giulia 983. *C.V.* pl. 13 and 14; *P.C.F.*² fig. 19.

      (*e*) Boston 90.155.

      (*f*) London E 451. *C.V.* pl. 23, 2.

      (*g*) Florence 4005. *C.V.* pl. 53, 3–4; 48, 3.

204   (*a*) Louvre G 409. *C.V.* pl. 15, 3 and 8; *A.R.V.*² 628 (Chicago painter).

      (*b*) Chicago 89.22 (Chicago painter).

205   Cf. above, n. 146, n. 148.

206   (*a*) Warsaw 142351. *C.V.* pl. 27; *A.R.V.*² 499 (Deepdene painter).

      (*b*) Milan. *A.R.V.*² 569 (Leningrad painter).

      (*c*) Cracow 1252. *C.V.* pl. 10, 2; *A.R.V.*² 672 (manner of painter of London E 342).

      (*d*) Campanian imitation. Castle Ashby 145. Trendall, *L.C.S.* 670, no. 50.

207   Beazley, *Attic red-figure vase-paintings in Boston*, ii, 58, nos. 17, 20–25. Note particularly no. 20. Rhodes 13129. *C.V.* pl. 3; *A.R.V.*² 563 (Pig painter). No. 21. Cleveland 26.549. *B.H.T.*² fig. 213–4; *A.R.V.*² 563 (Pig painter). No. 24. Bologna 234. *J.D.A.I.* 38–9, 130; *A.R.V.*² 524 (Orchard painter).

208   Lost. *A.R.V.*² 121 (Apollodoros); *M.T.S.* AV 7; Brommer, *S-S*², fig. 9.

209   Munich 2657. *A.R.V.*² 475 (Makron); *P.C.D.*² pl. 14a; *P.C.F.*² fig. 38; *M.T.S.* AV 6.

210   Boston 03.788. *A.R.V.*² 571 (Leningrad painter). *B.H.T.*² fig. 15; *P.C.F.*² fig. 40; *M.T.S.* AV 14.

211   Vienna 985. *A.R.V.*² 591 (Altamura painter); *P.C.F.*² fig. 41; *M.T.S.* AV 16.

212   Cf. above, p. 20.

213   British Museum E 467. *A.R.V.*² 601 (Niobid painter); *B.H.T.*² fig. 16; *P.C.F.*² fig. 42; *P.C.D.*² pl. 15a; *M.T.S.* AV 17.

214   Ferrara T 479. *A.R.V.*² 612 (painter of Bologna 279); *C.V.* Ferrara, 1, pl. 9–10; *P.C.F.*² fig. 43; *M.T.S.* AV 18; Trendall–Webster.

215   Boston 03.841. *A.R.V.*² 763 (Sotades painter); *P.C.F.*² fig. 44; *M.T.S.* AV 19.

216   Agora P 11810. *A.R.V.*² 495, 1656 (painter of Munich 2413); *P.C.F.*² fig. 32; *B.H.T.*² fig. 74; *M.T.S.* AV 9.

217   Ferrara, Valle Pega, Tomb 173c. *P.C.F.*² fig. 33; *M.T.S.* AV 10, pl. 1.

218 Cf. above, n. 102.

219 Berlin 3223. *A.R.V.*² 586 (Early Mannerist); Beazley, *Hesperia*, 24, 1955, pl. 80; *P.C.F.* fig. 35; *M.T.S.* AV 15.

220 See above, n. 213.

221 British Museum E 302. *C.V.* pl. 53, 2; *A.R.V.*² 652 (Nikon painter); *M.T.S.* 144; Trendall–Webster.

222 Corinth T 1144. *A.R.V.*² 571 (Leningrad painter); *Corinth*, XIII, pl. 98; *P.C.F.*² fig. 36. For the man cowering, cf. perhaps the satyr in the Perseus scene below, n. 285a.

223 Cambridge 12.17. *A.R.V.*² 623 (Villa Giulia painter); *C.V.* pl. 40, 8. Probably two Peliads and Medeia on Cambridge 2.1935, *A.R.V.*² 499 (Deepdene painter); Philippaki, *Stamnos*, pl. 40.

224 Villa Giulia 909. *A.R.V.*² 618; Lawler, fig. 38; *B.H.T.*² fig. 13.

225 Florence 3950. *C.V.* pl. 109; *A.R.V.*² 914 (Penthesilea workshop).

226 Leningrad. *C.R.* 1869, pl. 4, 14; Crowhurst, no. 169.

227 British Museum E 804. *C.V.* pl. 26–7; *A.R.V.*² 765.

228 British Museum E 306. *C.V.* pl. 54, 3. *A.R.V.*² 529 (Alkimachos painter).

229 Oxford 1919.23. *C.V.* 1, pl. 17, 8; *A.R.V.*² 529 (Alkimachos painter).

230 Another pyrrhicist. British Museum E 573. *A.B.L.* pl. 22/2. *A.R.V.*² 694 (near Bowdoin painter).

231 Cf. above, n. 200 (*f*).

232 Basel BS 415. M. Schmidt, *A.K.* 10, 1967, 70 ff.

233 Louvre G 488. *C.V.* pl. 33, 1–3 and 5; *Enc. Phot.* iii, 28a; *A.R.V.*² 1154. On Paris, Cab. Med. 357, the Achilles painter's pointed amphora, maenads play flute, tympanon, and kymbala, Shefton, *Wiss. Ztschr. Rostock*, 16, 1967, 529.

234 Cf. above, n. 227.

235 Berlin 2471. *A.R.V.*² 1247; Pfuhl, *M.u.Z.* fig. 560.

236 Providence 23.324. *A.R.V.*² 1188; *C.V.*, pl. 23, 1; Tillyard, pl. 23, 140; Lawler, *M.A.A.R.* 6, pl. 20, 2.

237 Boston 98.883. *A.R.V.*² 1017. *B.H.T.*² fig. 108; *P.C.F.*² fig. 34; *M.T.S.* AV 20.

238 Cracow 1225. *C.V.* pl. 12, 1. *A.R.V.*² 1121 (later mannerist); *M.T.S.*² 139; Trendall–Webster.

239 Woburn. *A.R.V.*² 1015; *B.S.A.* 30, 1928–30, pl. 18. Cf. a similar collocation by the Washing Painter, Laon 371043, *C.V.* pl. 33, 4 and 7; *A.R.V.*² 1130.

240 Cf. above, n. 153 (no. 1).

241 (*a*) Louvre G 407. *C.V.* pl. 15; *Enc. Phot.* iii, 25; *A.R.V.*² 1073 (Eupolis painter).
(*b*) London E 452 (Eupolis painter). *C.V.* pl. 23, 3; *P.C.F.*² fig. 23.
(*c*) Chicago. Frickenhaus, no. 25.
(*d*) New York 21.88.3. Philippaki, *Stamnos*, pl. 42, 4. *A.R.V.*² 1072 (Kensington Class).

The Archaeological Material

242 Warsaw 142465. *C.V.* pl. 26; *A.R.V.*[2] 1019; *P.C.F.*[2] fig. 20; Pfuhl, *M.u.Z.* fig. 571.

243 Naples 2419. *A.R.V.*[2] 1151; *P.C.F.*[2] fig. 22; *B.H.T.*[2] fig. 25; Pfuhl, *M.u.Z.* fig. 582. In literature tympana are implied for 'Lenaian' maenads by Ar. *Lys* 1 in 411 B.C., and as normal for maenads by Eur. *Cycl.*, 65, probably 408 B.C.

244 New York 25.78.66. *A.R.V.*[2] 1172 (Polion); *B.H.T.*[2] fig. 17; *P.C.D.*[2] no. 1, pl. 1a. Trendall–Webster. A lyre-playing satyr is named Dithyramphos on a fragment from the group of Polygnotos, *A.R.V.*[2] 1055, *P.C.D.*[2] 5, fig. 1.

245 Paris Market. *A.R.V.*[2] 1053 (Group of Polygnotos); Tillyard, no. 136; *M.T.S.* AV 21.

246 Cf. above, n. 213.

247 Paris, Cabinet des Medailles, 442. *L.C.S.* 36, no. 136, pl. 12 (Amykos painter); *M.T.S.*[2] 147; Trendall–Webster.

248 Cf. Beazley, *A.J.A.* 43, 1939, 618 ff.; 44, 1940, 212; *M.T.S.* 144; Trendall–Webster. Below only those vases are noted which have particularly interesting postures.

249 Oxford 1927.4. *A.R.V.*[2] 1046 (Lykaon painter); *A.J.A.* 43, 1939, 634, fig. 9; *M.T.S.* AV 22.

250 Oxford 1937.983. *A.R.V.*[2] 1153; *A.J.A.* loc. cit., fig. 1, etc.

251 Berlin 2578. *A.J.A.* loc. cit., pl. 15; *C.V.* 3, pl. 139, 1–4.

252 See above, n. 209.

253 Athens 1167. *A.R.V.*[2] 1104 (Orpheus painter); *A.J.A.* loc. cit., fig. 13; *P.C.F.*[2] fig. 47.

254 London 1923.10–16.10. *A.R.V.*[2] 1112 (Orestes painter). *M.T.S.* 140, pl. 7c. Trendall–Webster.

255 Boston 00.346. *A.R.V.*[2] 1045. *P.C.F.*[2] fig. 59. Trendall–Webster.

255a E.g. Vienna University 505. *A.R.V.*[2] 1030 (Polygnotos).

256 Rome, Vatican. *A.R.V.*[2] 1019 (Phiale painter); *M.T.S.* AV 58, pl. 7d. Trendall–Webster.

257 Oxford 530. *A.R.V.*[2] 1061 (Group of Polygnotos); *C.V.* pl. 32, 1; *B.H.T.*[2] fig. 105; *P.C.F.*[2] fig. 66; Trendall–Webster.

257a Boston 04.18. *A.R.V.*[2] 1177 (Aison).

258 Athens, Vlastos. *A.R.V.*[2] 1214 (Group of the Perseus dance); Trendall, *Phlyax vases*, 1; *B.H.T.*[2] fig. 202; *P.C.F.*[2] fig. 76; Trendall–Webster.

259 Copenhagen 13817. *C.V.* 8, pl. 347–9; K. Friis Johansen, *Eine Dithyrambos Aufführung; A.R.V.*[2] 1145; *P.C.D.*[2] pl. 1b; *P.C.F.*[2] fig. 15; Trendall–Webster.

260 Cf. above, n. 192–3.

261 London E 212. *C.V.* pl. 89, 4; *A.R.V.*[2] 1138 (Hasselmann painter).

262 E.g. Ferrara T 136. Arias, *R.I.N.A.S.* 1955, 129.

Karlsruhe 259. *A.R.V.*² 1315 (painter of the Carlsruhe Paris). *C.V.* pl. 22–4; Pfuhl, *M.u.Z.* fig. 595.

Ruvo, Jatta 1501. *A.R.V.*² 1338 (Talos painter); Sichtermann, *Bilderhefte des D.A.I.(R).* 3–4, pl. 34.

263 British Museum 1947.7–14.8. Trendall, *L.C.S.* 27, no. 85, pl. 8 (Cyclops painter); *M.T.S.* 157; Trendall–Webster.

264 Cf. above, n. 255.

265 Naples 3240. *A.R.V.*² 1335 (Pronomos painter); *B.H.T.*² fig. 20; *P.C.F.*² fig. 49; *M.T.S.* AV 25; Trendall–Webster.

266 British Museum E 790. *C.V.* pl. 37, 5; *B.H.T.*² fig. 26; *A.R.V.*² 1550 (Class W); *M.T.S.* AV 29.

267 Cf. above, n. 250.

268 Cf. above, n. 247.

269 Athens, N.M. 1302. *A.R.V.*² 1180 (painter of Athens Dinos); *B.H.T.*² fig. 27; *P.C.F.*² fig. 45; *M.T.S.* AV 23.

270 Cf. above, n. 245.

271 Cf. above, n. 213.

272 Agora, Pnyx T 139. D. B. Thompson, *Hesperia*, Supplt. 7, 1943, 147, fig. 61, no. 63.

273 Sydney 47.05. Cambitoglou and Trendall, *Plain Style*, 32; *M.T.S.* TV 18; Trendall–Webster.

274 Cf. above, n. 251.

275 Louvre CA 2938. Trendall, *Phlyax Vases*, no. 2; *P.C.F.*² fig. 79.

276 Louvre L 9. *A.R.V.*² 1335; Trendall, *Phlyax Vases*, no. 3; *P.C.F.*² fig. 77.

277 Heidelberg B 134. Trendall, *Phlyax Vases*, no. 7; *B.H.T.*² fig. 208; *P.C.F.*² fig. 85.

278 Cf. above, n. 259.

279 British Museum 98.2–27.1. Trendall, *Phlyax Vases*, no. 9; *P.C.F.*² fig. 87.

280 Agora P 23907. Trendall, *Phlyax Vases*, no. 12; *P.C.F.*² fig. 84; *B.H.T.*² fig. 209.

281 Agora P 23985. Trendall, *Phlyax Vases*, no. 13; *P.C.F.*² fig. 86.

282 (a) Agora S 1025, 1586. *M.M.C.* AS 2; *B.H.T.*² fig. 181; *P.C.F.*² fig. 103. (b) Agora S 2098. *M.M.C.* AS 3.

283 Milan, Moretti. Apulian, 400/375. Trendall, *Phlyax Vases*, no. 42; *B.H.T.*² fig. 43; Trendall–Webster.

284 Parma. Sommavilla painter, Etruscan but based on Attic original of about 420 B.C. Beazley, *E.V.P.* 37; *Mon.* 2, pl. 55a = Reinach I, 109.

285 E.g. (a) Taranto IG 8263. About 400 B.C. Trendall, *L.C.S.* 55, no. 280, pl. 24 (Karneia painter). Trendall–Webster.
(b) Taranto. Apulian fragment. Early fourth century. Trendall, *Arch. Reports*, 1966–7, fig. 12. Trendall–Webster.

286 Cf. above, n. 222.

287 Agora T 1546. D. B. Thompson, *Hesperia*, 23, 1954, 99, pl. 23.

288 (*a*) Athens, N.M. 3854. Poursat, *B.C.H.* 91, 1967, 102.
(*b*) Athens, Small Acropolis Museum, Walter 402, 402a; *I.G.* II², 3026.
(*c*) Athens, Acropolis Museum, 1338. S. Casson, Catalogue; *I.G.* II², 3025;
German Institute negative, AKR 1226.
I am much indebted to Professor A. E. Raubitschek for help with the
inscription.

289 Cf. above, n. 259.

II

Literary Sources

1·DOWN TO THE TIME OF HOMER

In the archaeological material a clear break can be made about the end of the eighth century B.C. and it seems therefore reasonable to take Homer, Hesiod, the earliest Homeric hymns, and Eumelos as a parallel first group in literature. We cannot tell how much memory Homer has enshrined of earlier choruses, nor how many choruses which we only hear of in classical times or even later are really very early: some of these will be quoted when the archaeological material makes this desirable.

We started the archaeological account with the fairly rare instances of mixed dances (nos. 8–11).[1] Homer has two on the shield of Achilles: in the vintage scene (*Iliad* 18, 567) 'girls and youths carried the grapes in baskets, in their midst a boy played the lyre and sang the Linos song, and they striking the ground in time with the song and lamentation went with him with flying feet'. This is certainly a processional. If the reference here is to the Linos song (which, apparently, though a dirge, could also be sung upon a cheerful occasion, cf. Euripides, *H.F.* 348), we may be able to reconstruct an early text in enoplian paroemiacs.[2]

The later chorus on the shield (*Iliad* 18, 590 f.) consists of boys with daggers and girls with wreaths, dancing with hands on each other's wrists. The parallel which the poet draws to the chorus which Daidalos arranged for (in honour of?) Ariadne in Knossos suggests knowledge of similar Cretan dances. In the seventh century a Euboean artist (no. 64a) and in the sixth century Klitias (no. 114) painted the dance which celebrated the victory of Theseus over the Minotaur as a dance of the

---

1. References so given are to vases, etc., listed in the numbered notes to Chapter I.
2. *P.M.G.* 880. Bergk's reconstruction needs the following emendations: 1. 1 ἰὼ Λίνε, 1. 4 λιγυραῖσιν, 1. 5 κότοισι (?), 1. 6 θρηνήσουσιν (?) For texts on the Linos song, cf. also Färber, *Die Lyrik in der Kunsttheorie der Antike*, 1936, II, 64.

Athenian ... iting with linked hands. Homer's
description ... ut he seems to have combined three
dances: ... ondly, a dance with ranks moving
towards ... y, a dance of two tumblers, whose
movem... g of the lyre-player. A mixed dance
with a l... the pretended marriage celebrations
towards ... , 146), but we are told nothing of the
movem...

The e... en, only rarely show the men and
women ... 64a); more usually the men are together a... r so that the change from the round
dance ... e easy. Lucian (*Salt.* 12) knows of a
Spartan ... h boys and girls alternate, and this
may of ... ric antithesis between the daggers of
the boy... girls has become for Lucian an antithesis b... of the boys and the feminine dances
of the g... trast appears in the strides of the boys
and the ... the early vases, and that part of the
dance ... of boys dancing towards a rank of
girls m... e fifth century Sophocles thinks of a
song o... l to the song of the girls to Artemis
when the news of Herakles' victory comes to Trachis (*Trach.* 207), and
at one moment in the victory songs at the end of Aristophanes'
Lysistrata (1275) husband is told to stand by wife and wife by husband
and dance in celebration.

One of the Attic vases (no. 9) has been connected with the Thargelia
by Mrs Karouzou. It is not quite clear why, unless the multiplicity of
lyre-players suggests Apollo, but a fifth-century Attic bell-krater in
Copenhagen[1] has also been connected with the Thargelia because the
action seems to take place in the precinct of Pythian Apollo, where the
prizes won at the Thargelia were dedicated: on this vase a man and a
woman dancer in decorated costume with feathers in their hair are
shown, so that it is possible that there were mixed dances at the
Thargelia.

As noted above, no obvious parallel suggests itself for the mixed
'rope' dance on the Tegean vase (no. 11), but it is perhaps worth

1. National Museum, Chr. VIII, 939. *C.V.* 4, pl. 147.

remembering the strange custom of the Hellotia[1] in Sparta and Corinth (Ath. 678a). A myrtle 'wreath', 30 ft long, containing Europe's bones, was carried in procession; possibly the 'rope' of the Tegean vase was something like this. The oracle reported by Herodotos (1, 66) attests Tegea as a place famous for dances.

We cannot usually tell from the literary sources which of the dances of women have linked hands and which have not, but Aristophanes in the *Thesmophoriazusae* (662 ff.) joins the archaeological record in testifying to circular linked dances in the fifth century. In the first book of the *Iliad* (603) Apollo plays his lyre while the Muses dance, answering with fair voice. In Hesiod's *Theogony* (2) the Muses are introduced dancing about the spring and the altar of Zeus. This is certainly a round dance. They make dances on the top of Helikon with flowing feet. Then they go by night singing beautifully, and later still (68) they go to Olympos, rejoicing in their fair voice, ambrosial song. He knows therefore processional song and dance as well as round dance. It seems to me possible that this combination explains the podium which occasionally appears on vases (no. 37): the painter shows that at a certain point the processional dance stops and the musician mounts a platform to play for the round dance. Processional in such contexts does not necessarily mean a slow dance but merely that the dancers move from place to place.

The vases with these linked dances of women come from many places (no. 13). Among them are the sanctuary of Artemis Orthia in Sparta, where Helen was dancing when Theseus carried her off (Plutarch, *Theseus*, 31), Argos, where there was a dance in which women carried flowers to Hera (Pollux, 4, 78)[2] and probably the sprays in the hands of the Argive women could be called flowers, and Delos, where the Delian women performed as described in the Homeric *Hymn to Apollo* (156). We shall have to return to the Delian women later; here it may be noted that Euripides thinks of them in the *Hecuba* (463) as singing songs of praise to Artemis and in the *Hercules Furens* (691) as singing a *paian* to Apollo 'circling about his temple', which would seem to be a round dance.

The women sometimes (no. 16) carry a wreath or the leader carries

1. Cf. Lawler, *T.A.P.A.* 77, 1946, 112 ff.
2. Cf. the Homeric *Hymn to Gaia*, XXX, 14.

a wreath. This must have been very common. Athenaeus (678a) speaks
of a wreath called a *pyleon* which the Lakonians put on the statue of
Hera, and the custom went back at least to the seventh century B.C.,
since Alkman twice speaks of it in maidens' songs: 'I pray to you,
bringing this *pyleon* of helichryse and lovely kypairos' (*P.M.G.* 60),
and 'Astymeloisa doesn't answer me, but, like a star speeding through
shining heaven, holding the *pyleon* or a golden bough or [. . .] she was
gone on slim feet' (3, 64). This is the perfect description of our dances.

The *Iliad* (6, 286 ff.) recalls a special processional. Hekabe and her
women take a robe to Athena's temple, and all raise their hands with a
cry of supplication (*ololyge*). This is a special occasion, but on many
vases with processionals the leader with the wreath raises her hand.

On one Attic hydria (no. 17) the chorus is led by a soloist. Nausikaa
in the *Odyssey* (6, 101) is the leader of her girls in the ball game and she
leads them in song; this was in fact a dance and was put on the stage by
Sophocles (see below). She is compared to Artemis sporting among her
nymphs, a beautiful chorus with a more beautiful leader, and it is possible that when Homer describes the wrinkled squinting prayers who
follow after the strong, firm-footed Ate (*Iliad* 9, 502), he is thinking of
ugly choruses with an uglier leader, in which the leader wore the
mask of a hideous goddess and the chorus wore masks of ugly old
women: we have such masks of the eighth century from Tiryns and of
the seventh from the temple of Artemis Orthia.[1]

The most elaborate dance with a women's chorus is in the *Hymn to
Apollo* (189): the Muses sing, the goddesses dance with linked hands,
among them Ares and Hermes 'sport', and Apollo plays his lyre among
them with 'fair and lofty step'. The connection of a male solo dancer
with a female chorus and a man, who is probably a lyre-player, is given
by a geometric vase in Argos (no. 44, fig. 1). Apollo's fair and lofty
step suggests the prancing lyre-players on vases from the sixth century
and later (nos. 107 and 159, fig. 6), and perhaps on one geometric
vase (no. 37).

The leader–chorus relationship is very clear in Homeric laments.
The mourners are sometimes men led by a man – Achilles leads the

1. Cf. *P.C.D.*[2] 163 ff., 167. Cf. also the rites of Demeter Kidaria in Arcadia. The priestess
wore the mask of the goddess and beat the *hypochthonioi* (Pausanias, VIII, 15). Athenaeus
(631d) compares these dances to the dances of tragedy.

Myrmidons in mourning for Patroklos (*Iliad* 18, 233, 315), or women led by men, as in the funeral of Hektor (*Iliad* 24, 720), or women led by the women of the family, as again in the funeral of Hektor and in the mourning for Patroklos at the beginning of *Iliad* 18 (51), where the Nereids are the chorus and Thetis the leader. The standard formula: 'X began the groaning' or 'X lamented' followed by 'the women groaned thereto' implies a considerable solo followed by short response by the chorus.

In men's dances again our literary sources do not usually tell us whether hands are linked or not. On the vases linked dances of men do not seem to survive into the sixth century. Homer gives a number of male dances. On the shield (*Iliad* 18, 492) there is a marriage: the bride is being brought through the town with a loud marriage song and young male dancers whirling round a flute-player and lyre-player.[1] This is clearly a processional dance and is the earliest mention of the new flute, which appears on a late Attic geometric vase (no. 41) as an accompaniment to young men in short chitons who dance with lowered clapping hands.

Then there are the *paians*: in the first book of the *Iliad* (472) they sang a fair *paian* all day to Apollo; this is a *paian* in its proper use, to avert evil;[2] we hear nothing of the form of the song. In the twenty-second book after the death of Hektor (391) Achilles says to the young soldiers, 'Come let us sing a *paian* and come to the hollow ships and bring the body of Hektor.' This is a thanksgiving for averted evil and a processional. Similarly, when Apollo in the Delphian part of the Homeric hymn moves from Itea to Delphi (516), he played the lyre 'with fair and lofty step' (as in the earlier dance on Olympos) and 'they striking the ground followed him [the same words were used of the vintagers on the shield] and sang, "Ie, Paieon"'. Again a processional *paian*, a prayer to Apollo to avert evil from the new settlement, and 'Ie, Paieon' is a quotation of the refrain (or part of the refrain), which cannot in that case have been in hexameters.

Another eighth-century processional sung by men is attested by Pausanias (*P.M.G.* 696), the *prosodion* to Delos in Doric dialect by the

1. Ancient Greek theory derived flute music from Phrygia. G. R. B. Huxley suggests a date about 700 B.C. for Olympos, who is founder of flute music in the theory of Glaukos of Rhegium (*G.R.B.S.* 9, 1968, 47). See also below, p. 56.
2. Färber, 31, 49; II, 31.

Corinthian poet Eumelos.[1] Unfortunately the text is uncertain. Bergk reconstructed the second line to make a hexameter parallel to the first but though the sense 'the Muse with a clean lyre and free sandals' is tolerable the jingle καθαρὰν κίθαριν is unlikely for an eighth-century poet. Nor is the text likely as it stands – 'the pure one with free sandals'; possibly ἃ κιθάραν should be substituted for ἁ καθαρὰ, 'who with her lyre and free sandals . . .' The point is important because without Bergk's insertion the line gives a dactylic pentameter following the hexameter, a slight variation of the epic metre for choral lyric.

Homer's Phaeacians are expert dancers (*Od.* 8, 262), and nine marshals (*aisymnetai*) smooth out a dancing place for them, which they beat with their feet while Demodokos sings to the lyre; later (370) two solo dancers dance a duet with a ball (a variant on Nausikaa's dance) and the other boys 'shout thereto'. We cannot say whether the choral dance which accompanies Demodokos' recital is a round dance or a dance in ranks or both. Essentially here we have solo singer–musician and an accompanying dance as in the vintage scene on the shield, with the difference that here the dancers are in a dancing-place; there they and the musician are moving in procession. Athenaeus (15d) interprets this relationship in the vintage scene as a *hyporcheme*, a word of many meanings.

In the description of the two soloists the phrasing of 'the other boys shout thereto' is parallel to the formula 'the women groan thereto' in laments, so that here the solo dancers are the leaders of the shouting chorus just as in laments the professional singers or the members of the family are the leaders of the groaning chorus. We have seen parallels for these trick dancers with a team of dancers forming the chorus on geometric vases (nos. 22–3 and 43). Whether the Phaeacian chorus, like those on three of the vases (no. 43), clapped as well as shouted we cannot say. One ancient term used for the soloist was 'dancing in front of' *prochoreuomenos*, which describes a boy jumping before a thigh-slapping chorus with a flute-player on an archaic Corinthian aryballos (no. 108), or *prochoreuon* used of Ares by Euripides (*Phoen.* 786 ff.) as leader of a komos with no sweet flute music. Similarly Lucian (*Salt.* 16) describes ancient dances in Delos with soloists and again uses the difficult term *hyporcheme*: 'choruses of boys danced to the flute and

1. Cf. C. M. Bowra, *C.Q.* 13, 1963, 150.

lyre: they performed in the chorus, and the best of them were chosen out (*pro*) to accompany them in dance (i.e. they were soloists). The songs written for these choruses were called *hyporchemes.*' One of the vases with a soloist and a clapping chorus (no. 43) comes from Delos. The geometric vases also show various armed dances which may be associated with pyrrhics. On no. 23 a man stands on his head between two men with linked hands. Tölle takes this as a pyrrhic – warriors with linked hands occur on no. 36. According to some ancient sources the pyrrhic was derived from Neoptolemos' leap off the altar at Delphi or from Neoptolemos' dance to celebrate the death of Eurypylos, in either case a solo, so that a soloist with a chorus in a pyrrhic is one of the possibilities.[1] On no. 32, a funerary vase, the male mourners stride with spears. The word used for male mourners in Homeric funerals is sometimes ἐρρώcαντο (e.g. *Od.* 24, 69), a dance word; and Aristotle (fr. 476 Rose) records that in Cyprus (usually emended wrongly to Crete) the army danced a pyrrhic at the funeral of kings: it is very likely that this was an old custom inherited from Mycenaean settlers. The old name for this particular kind of funeral pyrrhic was probably *prylis*. The pyrrhic at Athens was danced both at the Greater and the Lesser Panathenaia, and therefore is older than the introduction of the Greater Panathenaia in 566 B.C. It has recently been suggested that the athletic part of the Panathenaia, including the pyrrhic, originated at the tombs of the heroes in the Agora.

Tölle also claims that the two armed men on no. 14 are dancing a pyrrhic. I had explained them as a duel at funeral games, as in *Iliad* 23, 801 ff. But it must be conceded that in the entertainment offered to the Paphlagonians by Xenophon's troops (*Anab.* VI, 1, 5) the armed dance of the Thracian contingent included a mock duel, so that these may again be soloists but without representation of the chorus. The other two vases, nos. 15 and 35, show choral pyrrhics.

Homer provides no parallels for the dancers (nos. 39 and 47) who kick one leg forward with the other knee bent, a posture common later among the padded dancers, who are forerunners of comic and satyric choruses. These vases come from the sanctuary of Artemis Orthia, from

1. On all this, see Färber, II, 41; Latte, *De saltationibus armatis*, 1913; Lorimer, *C.Q.* 32, 130 f.; Leumann, *Hom. Wörter*, 286; Roos, *Tragische Orchestik* 226; Davies, *J.H.S.* 87, 1967, 33 ff.; Borthwick, *J.H.S.* 87, 1967, 18 ff.; *C.Q.* 18, 1968, 44 ff.; H. A. Thompson, *A.A.* 1961, 225 ff.; Poursat, *B.C.H.*, 92, 1968, 550 ff.

Argos and from Miletos; the Milesian dancers are padded. But this simply pre-echoes the situation as we know it in the early sixth century: independent sets of padded dancers in cities that we are accustomed to differentiate as Ionian–Athenian and Dorian. The eighth-century examples suggest that these dances could, if we had the evidence, be traced back to Mycenae.

Finally one probably Boeotian vase (no. 46) was interpreted as a picture of a maenad dance. Again the festival at which women danced as maenads at Athens, whether it was the Anthesteria or the Lenaia, is likely to have been very old and may well be Mycenaean in origin. Homer in the Lykourgos story (*Iliad* 6, 132) knows of the nurses of raging Dionysos (μαινομένοιο) and he compares Andromache to a maenad when she 'dashes through the hall throwing back her head', a typical maenad gesture (*Iliad* 22, 460). He may therefore have known of maenad dances in Ionian cities. In the next century the Laconian poet Alkman writes (56 *P.M.G.*): 'often in the mountains, when the gods are pleased by the glorious festival, holding a golden vessel, a great cup such as shepherds use, you milk a lion into it and make a great white-shining cheese'. Aristeides, referring to this poem, ascribes the power of milking lions to Dionysos, so that Alkman's woman must be a maenad, but the fragment does not show whether she is a maenad of legend or a Laconian girl who dances as a maenad (cf. *P.M.G.* 11). The latter is extremely possible if this is a description of the chorus-leader by the chorus, like the long description of Astymeloisa in *P.M.G.* 3.

A look at the vases shows that the dances are conducted in very different tempi. The women all move with a motion that we should describe as a walk, except the women who are possibly maenads. The men sometimes walk but they often do what I have called 'stride', although it clearly is a dance movement. Some of them, further, take more energetic attitudes, flexing their knees, kicking their legs forward or backwards, jumping, or standing on their heads. There must be some relation between those tempi and the rhythm of the dance, which was also the metre of the song sung by the dancers. It would probably be right to exclude the solo dancers, first because they do not sing (this, I think, is clear from the descriptions) and secondly, because it is perfectly possible for a solo dancer to keep the rhythm set either by the singing and dancing chorus or by a solo singer, but dance it twice or three times as fast by putting twice or three times as many steps to the beat.

For singing choruses I would suggest tentatively as a theory to be tested when the evidence becomes fuller that a chorus 'walks' when it has a long line to sing before it can pause in song and dance, that when a chorus 'strides' it is singing a shorter line, and that when it does kicks it sings a shorter line still. This suggestion clearly needs testing and refining in periods for which there is more evidence.

What, as far as I can see, can be said about eighth-century choral metric is this. First, in the Homeric *Hymn to Apollo* (137–76) when the poet says farewell to the Delian maidens and advertises their versatility on the assumption that they will advertise the virtues of his poetry, it is natural to think that they were the singers of this hymn in Delos, and therefore that hexameters were used for choral poetry. The hexameter is a long line with a well-marked Pause at the end,[1] and would be sung 'walking'. Secondly, the two lines of the choral *prosodion* of Eumelos[2] are either hexameters in Doric or a hexameter followed by a pentameter of the same kind; I am inclined to believe the latter. In either case each is followed by Pause, and I should not suppose that there was any change of tempo between the hexameter and the pentameter. We should perhaps add to these the song of the Messenian women after the victory of Aristomenes; Pausanias (4, 16, 6) dates it in 684 B.C. and says that it was still sung in his time. He quotes an elegiac couplet. The elegiac couplet consists of (*a*) normal hexameter followed by Pause and (*b*) 'pentameter' which consists of two hemiepe, in A. M. Dale's notation[3] dd'dd. As the halves are divided not only by the metrical cut (true long next to true long) but by word division, the pentameter could be regarded as two short lines and danced instead of 'walked' but this is perhaps unlikely.

Unfortunately I cannot prove that the two instances of shorter lines which I have quoted belong to the eighth century. The Linos song (*P.M.G.* 880) is in any case a reconstruction. In the Delphic part of the

---

1. Cf. A. M. Dale, *W.S.* 77, 1964, 16 f. = *Collected Papers*, 187 f. Further instances of hexameter lyric are quoted in the next chapter. Olen, Lycian or Hyperborean, who is quoted as author of very early hymns sung in Delos, is said to have written hexameters but he may be mythical: the hymns however existed.

2. Cf. above, p. 50.

3. *Lyric Metres of Greek Drama*[2], 176; *Collected Papers*, 62 f.

Literary Sources

Homeric *Hymn to Apollo* (514 ff.) Apollo was prancing as he played his lyre and his followers 'striking the ground with their feet sang "ῐ̄ē, pāĭē̆ŏn"'. This part of the hymn has been dated to the sixth century on political arguments, but I believe they are outweighed by the linguistic data which seem to me to put it very soon after the Delian hymn.[1] The cry 'ῐ̄ē, pāĭē̆ŏn' (of which we know many variants in later *paians*) could very well be the beginning of an enoplian paroemiac identical with those of the Linos song. The metre is xddx, a short line with Pause at the end, an admirable 'striding' line which could be used either for marching or dancing. In the Linos song and the *paian* it was marched; I suspect that it was also the enoplian traditionally associated with the pyrrhic dance.[2]

There is another reason for regarding the enoplian paroemiac as a very old metre. It is a segment of the dactylic hexameter: in fact the two commonest middle caesurae of the dactylic hexameter divide it into (*a*) blunt hemiepes + enoplian paroemiac with long first syllable and (*b*) pendant hemiepes + enoplian paroemiac with short first syllable. As 99 per cent of Homer's lines have one or other of these caesurae, both the two forms of hemiepes and the two forms of enoplian paroemiac were ready-made short lines when the natural movement of poetic language was still in double-short rather than, as later, in single-short.

Of more energetic rhythms we can say nothing except that the 'kicks' of the maenads and padded-dancers imply their existence. But there is one text which shows that there were more sung dance rhythms in existence in the eighth century than have survived. The poet of the *Hymn to Apollo* says of the Delian maidens that they know 'how to imitate the voices and the *krembaliastys* of all men'. 'Voices' means dialect, and Eumelos' *prosodion* is an instance of eighth-century choral lyric in dialect. *Krembaliastys* means playing the *krembala* or castanets, and the purpose of castanets is to emphasize rhythm. The rhythm 'of all men' is surely more varied than hexameters, pentameters, hemiepe, and enoplian paroemiacs.

1. Cf. *Greek Art and Literature, 700–530 B.C.*, 17, n. 15.
2. See p. 62

2 · SEVENTH CENTURY

Glaukos of Rhegion who lived in the latter part of the fifth and the beginning of the fourth century B.C. has left us a chronology of early lyric poets which is useful and interesting:[1] his order is Olympos, Terpander, Klonas (of Tegea or Thebes), Archilochos, Thaletas of Crete, Stesichoros. Archilochos and Stesichoros are reasonably fixed points about the middle of the seventh and the middle of the sixth century respectively. Alkman is omitted; he is coupled with Thaletas by Sosibios (Ath. 678b) and historical allusions seem to place him in Sparta in the late seventh century.[2] On the list Olympos is the inventor of flute-playing and a Phrygian. Professor Huxley's date of 700 B.C. seems too late for the reference to flute-playing in the *Iliad* and for the Attic geometric vase no. 41. But the tradition of an Eastern and more particularly Phrygian origin may be right. Terpander came from Lesbos and migrated to Sparta: the texts about him are obscure.[3] He is said to have sung his own poetry and Homer's in contests. He wrote a kind of lyric called a *nomos* which was certainly a solo later but may have been choral originally; he is said to have written in hexameters but also in trochaics. Nothing genuine survives. Klonas is said to have written hexameters and elegiacs; he invented *aulodia*, which seems to mean flute music composed by the flautist as the only music for a song written by the flautist, as distinct from *auletike*, which was either flute accompaniment to recitative or to a song written for the lyre or pure flute-playing. Alkman speaks of flute accompaniment (fr. 37) but also of someone 'fluting a Phrygian song' (126).

Alkman is the first choral lyric poet of whom we can form any idea. He was the earliest of the canon of nine lyric poets established by the Alexandrians, and this presumably accounts for the Souda's statement that he was the first to write lyric poetry which was not in hexameters: for the Souda or its source he came next after Homer and Hesiod. He was famous for his *partheneia*, songs for maidens. We can form most idea of the first (*P.M.G.* 1) because most of it is preserved. It raises many difficult problems which are perhaps incapable of solu-

1. *F.H.G.* 2, 23–4; Plutarch, *de Mus.*, 1133–4. Cf. Huxley, *G.R.B.S.* 9, 1968, 47. Campbell, *J.H.S.* 87, 1964, 67 on Klonas.
2. Cf. most recently West, *C.Q.* 15, 1965, 189; Harvey, *J.H.S.* 87, 1967, 69.
3. Cf. Färber, I, 33, 54; II, 37.

tion. The chorus consisted of ten girls (99), who were related (52); Hagesichora and Agido were their leaders. The aim was to make the gods accept their prayers (82) and thereby to achieve healing and peace (87 ff.). This much is certain, and the song could be called a *paian* in the sense of averting catastrophe. For the rest, the song seems to have been sung at sunrise (43, 61, 87, but no single one of these is conclusive). It seems to have been sung and danced in competition with another chorus. (One of the Corinthian female choruses (no. 51) walks away from a large mixing-bowl, which may be a prize.) I take the difficult ll. 60–3, 'they, like the Pleiads rising at dawn, fight with us as we carry the robe, like Seirios in the night,' to mean: the other chorus are a very weak light; we are a very strong light, because the robe we bring is so bright. Alkman remembers the robe which Hekabe dedicated to Athena to save Troy while her women sang (*Iliad* 6, 285 ff.): 'it shone out like a star'.[1] The next lines I take to mean 'the rival chorus are not strong enough to ward off our attack although they have elaborate clothing, ornaments, headbands, Nanno and other girls'. The sense carries on with archaic logic 'you will not go to Ainesimbrota's and say "Give me Astaphis, etc."', which means 'even if you have, you will not be able to defeat us'. It is, of course, possible that the choruses ran a race (hence the racehorse imagery) and only the winning chorus sang, but if the above interpretation of the robe is right, the robe was an essential part of the competition and therefore the song sung as the robe is brought is also part of the competition.

The poem is written in stanzas. Each stanza[2] consists of three sections: (*a*) has eight lines of alternating trochaic dimeters catalectic and enoplians. Pause is attested at the end of each line except the fifth, and can therefore be assumed also there. These are, then, alternating short lines sxs"xdsx"; (*b*) is all trochaic, 2 trimeters with Pause between, and 2 dimeters or perhaps rather 1 tetrameter acatalectic (sxsxsxsx); (*c*) is dactylic, a tetrameter B followed with no Pause by a catalectic tetrameter (ddddddd); it is very curious and perhaps a mark of early date[3] that in the preserved part of the poem, although stanzas 1, 2, 6 end like this, stanzas 3, 4, 5, instead of ending ddd, run out in ddsx. In dance

1. I follow Mr West, loc. cit., 197, but his emendation of φᾶρος to φάϜος is unnecessary.
2. Cf. A. M. Dale, *C.Q.* 1, 1951, 121 = *Collected Papers*, 84.
3. Cf. A. M. Dale, *W.S.* 77, 1964, 23 = *Collected Papers*, 194.

terms all the eight lines of (*a*) are short lines and danced. It is possible that the lines of (*b*) are long lines and are walked. The light dactyls of (*c*) are surely danced as an exciting end, even when as in stanzas 3, 4, 5 they end in single-short movement.

Another *partheneion* (*P.M.G.* 3) has the long description of Astymeloisa, 'gone like a falling star with wreath or golden bough or soft feather [?]', which may mean that it also comes from a processional chorus bringing some such offerings. The stanzas consist of (*a*) dactylic tetrameter B plus trochaic dimeter, (*b*) trochaic tetrameter catalectic,[1] (*c*) a doubtful line which starts with an enoplian with the single-short section extended, (*d*) dactylic tetrameter B + dactylic tetrameter B + encomiologus, ddxsx.[2] We shall see reason to suppose that the trochaic tetrameter (*b*) is a dancing or even running line, and that the encomiologus, which ends (*d*), is a 'walking' line in Pindar. I am inclined to think that the long lines (*a*) and (*d*) and possibly also (*c*) start in dancing tempo and slow up at the end – with the extended single-short in (*a*) and (*c*) and with the encomiologus in (*d*). In (*a*) and (*d*) although there is no metrical Pause after the dactylic tetrameters, there is diairesis (division between words), which perhaps allows the change of tempo.

In the description of the maenad (*P.M.G.* 56)[3] Alkman again uses dactylic tetrameters. Here the shape of the stanza is (*a*) dactylic tetrameter B plus dactylic tetrameter ending in 'spondee' (the A tetrameter), (*b*) the same, (*c*) dactylic tetrameter ending in 'spondee', (*d*) *either* dactylic tetrameter B plus trochaic metron with Welcker's emendation ἀργιφόνταν, *or* a dactylic hexameter A with Page's Ἀργεϊφόντᾳ (Hermes). Either is possible metrically, but it is difficult to see what Hermes is doing in this context. In either case each element is a dance line which slows up with a repeated long syllable (or its equivalent) at the end, but with Welcker the trochaic metron gives an extended slowing at the end.

Before considering the maenad fragment a little further, it may be useful to note some other metres. In 14 Alkman has a dactylic heptameter catalectic followed by an iambo-trochaic hendecasyllable;[4] this is surely a 'walking' metre (cf. also the full heptameters in 98). So

1. Cf. 55, 95a.
2. 83 is a longer line of the same type: dd⌣ss—.
3. Cf. A. M. Dale, loc. cit.
4. Cf. A. M. Dale, *C.Q.* 13, 1963, 47 = *Collected papers*, 178.

presumably are the various long lines most of which are preserved singly: the iambic tetrameter (three certainly and possibly four running are preserved in 2), the long aeolic line, xsd'dx, in 50,[1] and the cretic hexameter catalectic in 58. The seeming ionic tetrameter (46) is perhaps rather two dimeters, which could be danced.

The iambo-trochaic hendecasyllable in 14 belongs to a series of iambo-trochaic lines. In 5 fr. 2, 23, the same form, xssxsx, is used as an introductory line with Pause after it. A variation, xsxsx, is used in 19, 59a, 96, 30; in 19 three follow each other with Pause; these certainly could be danced. A decasyllable, sxssx, opens 59b (not demonstrably from the same poem as 59a) and is followed after Pause by an octo-syllable xsxs (the iambic dimeter), and that probably after Pause by a glyconic, three danced lines. An enneasyllable,[2] xsxsx, leads in 16, followed by a trochaic dimeter and a trochaic dimeter catalectic: after this Pause is certain. Then another enneasyllable is followed by a trochaic dimeter. Nothing compels us to assume Pause between the enneasyllable and the following trochaic dimeters (and the sense over-laps from l. 1 to l. 2) so that for dancing purposes it is possible that ll. 1–3 was one long line danced in slow time, and that ll. 4–5 began another similar triad.

In contrast to this 20 has four iambic dimeters. Pause is certain after the third, and it is natural to assume it after the first and second, and to take this as an excited song dance. Similarly the fragment of a *partheneion* (60) in which the chorus brings its wreath (*pyleon*) consists of a trochaic dimeter, a trochaic dimeter, a trochaic dimeter catalectic. Each dimeter is a complete sense unit. Nothing shows that there was not a Pause at the end of each line, and they could be danced energetically.

The maenad fragment (56) has no context. Page quotes on 11 a gloss of Hesychios explaining the Dysmainai as 'choral maenads in Sparta'. If these Dysmainai are the same as the Dymainai, for whom 5 fr. 2 col. 1, 23 was written, we have there the first iambo-trochaic line of a song written for maenads. A maenad song which is probably old[3] is the

---

1. Cf. A. M. Dale, *Lyric Metres of Greek Drama*[2], 128, 142.
2. Following the colometry of Diehl (13) and his text (with codd.) in l. 4.
3. The form Διόνυϲε does not necessarily make it later than the seventh century, *pace* Wilamowitz, *V.K.* 384 f. See Nilsson, *Gesch.* 538, 544. Sixteen women at Elis are responsible (1) for making a robe for Hera, (2) for these choruses, (3) for choruses in honour of Hippodameia (Plutarch, *Mor.* 251e, with Pausanias V, 16, 6).

prayer of the Elian women (*P.M.G.* 871) sung according to Pausanias at the festival of the Thyiae. When Dionysos appeared, empty bowls kept under seal in the temple filled with wine. The metre is probably best taken as anapaestic: paroemiac, hexamakron, hexamakron, dimeter (with Page's suggested text), monometer repeated. The first four lines are separated by Pause, and the two concluding monometers are separated by Pause, so that this is an excited dance and has nothing to do with regular marching anapaests.

Another song which may be old is the song of the sheaves (*ioulos*) quoted by Semos of Delos, which was sung to Demeter (*P.M.G.* 849), again an excited song with two short lines: sd; xd. Eratosthenes[1] speaks of a woman day-labourer singing sheave-songs while she is making cakes to put on a high wreath (*pyleon*), but this is presumably a rehearsal for the song which will be sung when the wreath with its cakes are offered to Demeter.

Semos also says (*P.M.G.* 847) that at the Thesmophoroi in Delos large cakes were offered at a festival called Megalartia and the bearers said, 'Eat an Achainas cake full of lard.' The line is an iambic trimeter. The bearers are masculine although one would expect this to be a women's festival. This ritual, or kindred ritual in Athens, may have been copied by the cake-bearers of comedy (see p. 31).[2]

The Rhodian swallow-collection song is also sung by men or rather boys (*P.M.G.* 848).[3] It falls into two parts. The first is in reiziana and pherecrateans; the second in iambics. The first describes the swallow and the demands of the collectors. The second is first a threat, and then a further demand that the doors will be open. The text is particularly uncertain in two lines. After the ten mixed reiziana (xdx) and phere-crateans (xxdx) follows a headless reizianum (dx). Then the first corrupt line: οὐκ ἀπωθεῖται· πότερ' ἀπίωμες ἢ λαβώμεθα. οὐκ ἀπωθεῖται completes the construction of the first part 'the swallow does not say "No" to cake'. I take it to be a dragged clausula, s͞s. Then the second part

---

1. Färber, II, 60; Powell, *Coll. Alex.*, fr. 10. For the connection of cakes with wreaths compare the 'Lenaian' vases, e.g. *P.C.D.*[2] pl. 2a.

2. Cf. Lawler, *T.A.P.A.* 74, 1943, 69 for other cake dances.

3. Morelli (*S.I.F.C.* 35, 1963, 121) rightly defends the age of the poem, but there is no reason to deny a seventh-century Rhodian poet the use of Attic–Ionic forms, particularly when he was using a metre invented by Archilochos. I am inclined to accept καὶ καλοὺς ἐνιαυτούς in 3, possibly κἀπὶ in 5, and πυρῶνα (on the assumption that it can mean wheat-cake) in 10.

perhaps opens with an iambic dimeter: ⟨πότερ'⟩ ἀπίωμες ἢ λαβώμεθα. Then four iambic trimeters. The second corrupt line perhaps conceals another iambic dimeter: ἂν δὴ φέρῃς, μέγα δὴ φέροις.[1] Then two iambic trimeters finish the poem. The whole of the first part consists of short lines with Pause between them: this is excited dance. And then in the iambic part they slow down to ordinary dancing tempo.

It is perhaps easiest to add here other work or play songs whether they are seventh-century or not. The *ioulos* naturally recalls the Eresos (*P.M.G.* 869) grinding song, which is very prettily constructed of Lesbian lines lengthening as the grinding becomes easier: ◡ d, − − d −, ◡◡d′d−. The memory of Pittakos' dictatorship which ended in 580 B.C. should be fairly recent. The flower song is a dialogue (*P.M.G.* 852), which if Athenaeus is to be trusted, was sung by men: 'Where are my roses, etc.? Here are my roses.' Perhaps this is a text which we can suppose sung by choreuts arranged in two lines. Each section consists of an iambic dimeter with metron-diairesis followed by an iambic dimeter catalectic. It is, however, also possible that there was a single questioner and a choral answer – the leader-form, which we have noticed so often before and which recurs in the games (*P.M.G.* 875–6): in the pot game first an iambic dimeter catelectic, then a full iambic dimeter is divided between the leader who runs round while the chorus hit at him or sits while the chorus run round. In blind man's buff the blindfold child and the chorus both chant spondaic paroemiacs. In Chelichelone the girl seated in the middle and the girls running round all chant iambic trimeters.

Alkman wrote songs for men as well as songs for women. His chorus to Zeus (*P.M.G.* 45) was surely sung by men, and he addresses Agesidamos as a young leader of a chorus (10b). He wrote for the Hyakinthia (10a). Athenaeus (139d) describes the Hyakinthia at a much later date: then there were choruses of boys singing to the flute and playing the lyre in anapaestic rhythm, and young men with dancers among them dancing the old dances. Two other passages of Athenaeus have a bearing on this. In one (678b) he quotes Sosibios for palm-branches carried in memory of the victory at Thyrea (547 B.C.) by the leaders of Spartan choruses when they performed the *gymnopaidiai*. There were three choruses, one of boys, one of men, and one of old

---

1. I assume that as later these resolutions of the anceps are possible.

men; they danced naked and sang the songs of Thaletas and Alkman and the *paians* of Dionysodotos the Lakonian. In the other (631c) he quotes Aristoxenos for the view that in early times they first practised *gymnopaidiai* and then went over to the pyrrhic before entering the theatre. The three choruses of different ages are given a text in iambic trimeters by Plutarch (*P.M.G.* 870): 'We were once brave youths'; 'We are now. Look at us'; 'But we shall be much better.' But this is only an incident in the songs. The mention of anapaestic rhythm and 'the old dances' in the account of the Hyakinthia (for which we know Alkman wrote) recalls the three preserved Spartan songs which may well be early (*P.M.G.* 856–8). The first two are military exhortations to young soldiers. The first is in anapaestic paroemiacs; the second has only two lines, an anapaestic dimeter followed by a paroemiac. The third is a *paian* to the river Euros to come and fertilize the Spartan fields: it is all in paroemiacs, including the last line which forces the *paian* formula into a paroemiac (ἰὲ Παιαν ἰήιε Παιάν). The second may be a marching song: the paroemiacs of the first and third song necessarily give a Pause after each line and therefore were probably danced, and this is the kind of anapaests to which Athenaeus refers, not the regular marching rhythm of the anapaestic dimeter.

The text of the first of these songs 'thrust your shield forward on the left arm, brandishing your spear courageously', if it is a dance, very much suggests a pyrrhic, which was traditionally danced in enoplian rhythm, of which the paroemiac is one variety.[1] And Aristoxenos is evidence for the connection between *gymnopaidiai* and pyrrhics. The Thyrea festival at which they sang the songs of Alkman and Thaletas was a sixth-century rearrangement of an older performance of *gymnopaidiai*, if Thaletas first organized the *gymnopaidiai* in Sparta. In making this statement Plutarch (*De Musica*, 1134b–d) adds the statement that according to Glaukos of Rhegion, Thaletas copied Archilochos in using paeonic and cretic rhythm in writing songs, but that in fact Archilochos did not use them but Thaletas got them from the flute music of Olympos. Again there is no word of Alkman, although two cretic hexameters catalectic by him are preserved (*P.M.G.* 58). This may be irrelevant if Thaletas' cretic lines were short lines and were meant for energetic dancing. A scholiast to Pindar (*Pythian* II, 69)

1. Schroeder, *Nomenclator*, 23. Cf *P. Oxy.* 2738 on Ar. *Nub*, 989.

speaks of Thaletas writing *hyporchemata* in Cretic rhythm, and the resolved cretic ($\cup\cup\cup\_$) was in fact called the hyporchematic foot. One meaning of the difficult word *hyporcheme* is certainly lively dance.[1] And to make matters more complicated the same scholiast to Pindar tells us that according to Sosibios the pyrrhic was a kind of *hyporcheme*. Probably for these Spartan dances, the naked dances and the armed dances, we should reckon three possible speeds, fast (of which cretics are an example), dance speed (enoplians and paroemiacs) and marching (anapaestic dimeters).

If this is right, Thaletas' cretics can be added to Alkman's wreath-bearers (*P.M.G.* 60) and to the more doubtful evidence of the popular songs, including the prayer of the women of Elis, as instances of seventh-century dancing faster and more energetic than the ordinary dance tempo, which is what is needed as a parallel to the dances of the padded dancers on Corinthian vases. Most of the evidence for identifying the padded dancers comes from the next period, but two key vases have already been mentioned: on no. 49 among the dancers is a large mixing bowl with a goat tied to it, and Payne naturally regarded this as evidence that the dancers danced in honour of Dionysos, but on no. 57 the dancers are so closely associated with a female chorus that it is natural to assume that they performed at the same festival, and the appearance of Artemis on one of the vases with a female chorus (no. 58) has suggested the Eukleia as the festival.[2] A possible solution is that Dionysos as well as Artemis was celebrated at the Eukleia in Corinth, but it is equally possible that the choruses of padded dancers belonged to both gods.

The padded dancers (see below) represent fertility spirits, and they dance at fertility festivals. It is likely that Archilochos[3] introduced a fertility cult of a phallic Dionysos in Paros, and that the dithyramb which he 'knew how to lead when his wits were fused with thunder-bolts of wine' (77D) was sung in this cult. We can only guess that he was the leader of a chorus of padded dancers, and the guess may be entirely wrong.

The vast majority of the fragments of Archilochos belong to his

1. Cf. A. M. Dale, *Eranos*, 48, 1950, 19 = *Collected Papers*, 38. Some texts in Färber, II, 41.

2. A. Seeberg, *J.H.S.* 85, 1965, 108; *S.O.* 41, 1966, 55; *Wiss. Zeitschr. Rostock*, 16, 1967, 525.

3. *Greek Art and Literature, 700–530 B.C.*, 31, 59.

solo poetry sung at symposia. But, as well as the dithyramb, he speaks of himself as 'leading a *paian* to the accompaniment of a Lesbian flute' (76D), and we have his hymn to Herakles (120D). This is preserved in the Scholia to Pindar, O, 9, 1, who had said there that after the actual victory Archilochos' triple ringing *kallinikos* was enough for the victor, but now at home he should have a more elaborate song. When Archilochos composed his hymn, according to Eratosthenes 'the flautist or the lyre-player was not there, and the leader therefore sang *tenella*, and the chorus of komasts added *kallinike*. The beginning of the song is ὦ καλλίνικε χαῖρ' ἄναξ Ἡράκλεης.' The suggestion that the musician was absent is presumably nonsense invented to account for the *tenella* which was not understood. It is clear that the leader sang *tenella* and the chorus answered *kallinike* 'victorious'. This is the leader/chorus pattern for which we have had literary and pictorial evidence before. It is not clear whether the iambic trimeters, ll. 2, 4, 6 in our text were sung by the chorus or the leader, nor is it clear whether *tenella kallinike* was repeated only between ll. 4 and 6, or also between ll. 2 and 3. Perhaps it is most likely that before each iambic trimeter sung by the leader he sang *tenella* and was answered by the chorus *kallinike*. Then the shape is (*a*) iambo-trochaic heptasyllable (= iambic dimeter catalectic) divided between leader and chorus, (*b*) after Pause iambic trimeter sung by the leader, and this shape is twice repeated. Two other early ritual chants have the same leader/chorus form (*P.M.G.* 879): according to a scholiast to Aristophanes at the Lenaia the torch-bearer said 'Call the god', and they shouted in answer 'Iakchos, son of Semele, giver of wealth'; the whole seems to make a long enoplian, xddddd. More simply in making libations an iambic dimeter is divided between the pourer and the bystanders. For Archilochos it may be right to remember the vases (nos. 66 and earlier 41–2) on which a chorus of men with clapping hands is led by a lyre-player or a flute-player.

The only other choral fragment in Archilochos consists of an iambic dimeter followed by lekythion (sss): the text (119D) is 'reverencing the festival of Demeter and Kore', and it is ascribed to the *Iobakchoi* of Archilochos. *Iobakchoi* is a song to Dionysos according to the ancient commentators,[1] in which the refrain ἰὼ βάκχε occurred. The words are not impossible if Archilochos, like the Attic poets, recognized a

1. Texts, Färber, II, 13, 26, 41.

connection between Dionysos and Demeter. The short lines would suit an excited song.[1]

The tradition preserved by Plutarch (*De Mus.* 1140 f.) that Archilochos invented both the iambic trimeter and the trochaic tetrameter catalectic may well be true.[2] We know of no earlier instances. This was a crystallization of iambo-trochaic verse into two great opposed forms. The earlier was the trochaic tetrameter catalectic which consists of a dimeter followed after diairesis by a catalectic dimeter; for the iambic trimeter Archilochos took from the tetrameter the prohibition against word-end after the last anceps if that anceps is long. The same prohibition holds for the first anceps in the tetrameter: in either case the heavy cut would break the dimeter, and obscure the essential cut between the two dimeters. This essential cut becomes the very common penthemimeral caesura in the iambic trimeter. Both metres have a great future for recitative (perhaps also sung) symposion poetry and in the spoken (iambic) and recitative (trochaic) dialogue of tragedy and comedy. But the iambic trimeters of the Hymn to Herakles were sung, and that tradition continued in the Cake song (847 *P.M.G.*), the Swallow song (848 *P.M.G.*), and the Spartan chorus (870 *P.M.G.*).[3] We have seen sung trochaic tetrameters catalectic in Alkman,[4] and this metre had a choral future, particularly in comedy.

In his solo poetry sung at the symposion Archilochos had a considerable range of metres besides elegiacs, trochaic tetrameters catalectic, and iambic trimeters. The trochaic tetrameter catalectic has been called a simple short stanza-form of two dimeters, one complete and one catalectic. These other metres are similar short stanzas mostly consisting of two lines, but in one case of three. The most like the trochaic tetrameter, because the two parts are metrically similar, is 89D (etc.): ia trim, ia dim. Each has Pause at the end. Others with Pause between the parts are iambic trimeter, hemiepes (79D); dactylic hexameter, ia dim (104D). Two others have diairesis (word-end) between the parts and Pause at the end of the whole: enoplian paroemiac, ithyphallic (107D); hemiepes, iambic dimeter (118D). In the three-part example

---

1. There is no reason for supposing that either the iambic prayer to Apollo (30D) or the trochaic prayer to Hephaistos (75D) is choral.
2. Cf. A. M. Dale, *C.Q.* 13, 1963, 46 f. = *Collected Papers*, 174 f.
3. See above, pp. 60 ff.
4. See above, p. 58.

(112D) the dactylic tetrameter is divided by diaeresis from the ithy-phallic which follows it, but the succeeding iambo-trochaic hendeca-syllable (iambic trimeter catalectic) is divided from it by Pause.

These experiments of Archilochos stand at a parting of ways: if they are regarded as single lines, they lead to the long line where the elements in double-short and single-short are linked together in over-lapping words. The enoplian paroemiac followed by ithyphallic (Archilochos, 107D Ἐρασμονίδη Χαρίλαε, χρῆμά τοι γελοῖον) has been called 'a form of ready-made dactylo-epitrite compound'[1] and later poets so use it: thus in Bacchylides 19(18) the antistrophe (21 f.) has the same cut between the parts as Archilochos, μεγιστοάνασσα κέλευσε χρυσοπεπλος Ἥρα, but in the strophe (3 f.) they are tied together, ὃς ἂν παρὰ Πιερίδων λάχηςι δῶρα Μουςᾶν. It is very interest-ing that Alkman has already advanced to this sort of compound in the encomiologus (*P.M.G.* 3, 9), dd-s-, ἄχι μάλιστα κόμαν ξανθὰν τινάξω, which has exactly the same word divisions as Pindar O., 11, 13 κόσμον ἐπὶ στεφάνῳ χρυσέας ἐλαίας, and in the longer line (*P.M.G.* 83) τῷ δὲ γυνὰ ταμία σφεᾶς ἔειξε χώρας, ddxss-, which is the same as Archilochos 107D without the opening anceps. But Alkman ties the two parts together with the overlapping σφεᾶς, x̆-, just as Euripides uses φάμα, x̄-, in *Medea* 415 οὐκέτι δυσκέλαδος φάμα γυναῖκας ἕξει. Perhaps in essence this development is an extension of the principle of slowing up a fast dactylic line at the end by a spondee (or by the very curious substitution of s- for d in the last lines of the *partheneion* stanzas) and what we regard as the essentially 'aeolic' combination of ds in the enoplians of *P.M.G.* 1 and 3 and the glyconic at the end of 59b is another manifestation.

But Archilochos himself always divides the parts of his compounds by Pause or at least diaeresis, and they may therefore be regarded as little stanzas like the trochaic tetrameter. Viewed in this way, they are the ancestors of the polymetric stanzas of Alkman's *partheneion*. In fact Archilochos could very well have composed the four opening couplets of trochaic dimeters catalectic and enoplian (just as the opening couplet of *P.M.G.* 3 dactylic tetrameter and trochaic dimeter is extremely like Archilochos 112D, dactylic tetrameter followed by ithyphallic). But Alkman goes on and adds two further sections, one

1. A. M. Dale, *Lyric Metres of Greek Drama*, 181.

trochaic picking up the first lines of the couplets and the second dactylic picking up the dactyl in the second enoplian line of the couplets. Thus both the distinctive developments of later choral lyric, the long line uniting double- and single-short rhythm and the stanza composed of different metrical elements have their roots in the practice of Archilochos.

3 · ARCHAIC PERIOD, 600–530 B.C.

From literary sources we know something about the Peloponnese, a very little about Athens, much more about Sappho and Alkaios in Lesbos, about Stesichoros in Sicily and about Ibykos in Samos. Anakreon's main work belongs to the next period; but if the vases have been rightly interpreted (nos. 100–2), his private performances with his boon-companions were not only depicted on vases themselves but were parodied in comic dances before 530 B.C.

Among the Peloponnesian poets Sakadas, the Argive writer of songs and elegiacs, who was also a very successful flute-player, is a link back to the preceding period because Plutarch (*De Mus.* 1134c) equates him with Thaletas; he mentions, besides the *gymnopaidiai* in Sparta, the *endymatia* in Argos, which was presumably a festival at which the statue of Hera was clothed. At such a festival the songs would be sung by women, and therefore we can probably attribute *partheneia* to Sakadas. In 582 and the two succeeding Pythian festivals he won a prize for flute-playing. This does not tell us much, but it is some evidence of the continued use of the elegiac for serious poetry as distinct from symposion poetry and exhortations.[1]

The records about Arion, the lyre-singer from Methymna in Lesbos who settled in Periander's Corinth, and the 'tragic' choruses which Kleisthenes of Sikyon transferred from the Argive hero Adrastos to Dionysos are notoriously difficult to interpret, but these Peloponnesian choruses in the early sixth century must have some connection with the padded dancers.[2] Kleisthenes' choruses are only relevant if 'tragic' means sung by goats, and if goats are equated with satyrs and satyrs

1. See D. L. Page, *Greek Poetry and Life*, 206; A. E. Harvey, *C.Q.* 5, 1955, 170; Campbell, *J.H.S.* 84, 1964, 67; Rosenmeyer, *Calif Studies*, 1, 1968, 217.
2. Cf. Pickard-Cambridge, *D.T.C.*[2] 11 ff., 97 ff., 171 ff.

with padded dancers. There is much to be said for both equations, and we have noticed already both the connection of the padded dancers with Dionysos, as well as with Artemis,[1] and the representation of a man dressed as a hairy satyr (no. 79), who may have been their leader. If this is valid, the padded dancers sometimes sang serious songs, since Kleisthenes' choruses dealt with the sufferings of Adrastos.

The same equations, if valid for Kleisthenes, are valid for Arion. He also is said to have written tragedy, 'goat song', and to have introduced satyrs and to have written dithyramb, one variety of which in Athens was certainly performed by men dressed as satyrs.[2] But whether the equation is valid or not, Arion has further interest. He is said to have given names to his dithyrambs which implies that he gave them narrative heroic subjects, and we know that the padded dancers sang of the Return of Hephaistos (no. 77). The only other hint of subjects for Corinthian choral poetry in Arion's time is the occurrence of Nereid names unknown to Homer or Hesiod on a Corinthian hydria,[3] and of a woman called Hipponika, a name which could not scan in hexameters, on a Corinthian picture of the Sack of Troy;[4] but it seems unlikely that either of these subjects occurred in dithyrambs. (Corinthian vases show us a processional chorus of men (no. 117) as well as the padded dancers and the choruses of women.)

Arion is also said to have 'taught' the dithyramb: the word is used in official Athenian drama records of the poet as the trainer of the chorus, and implies that Arion was not the leader of the dithyramb, like Archilochos, but that his dithyramb was completely choral. The Souda evidently refers to the same thing when it says that Arion first established a chorus, but this probably carries the additional implication that Arion's chorus sang in one place and was not processional. In itself there was nothing new in this. We have seen from the beginning both processional choruses and choruses which sang in one place, what we have called round dances, but it may have been new for the dithyramb, and the later dithyramb was known as a 'circular chorus' to distinguish it from the 'rectangular chorus' of drama.

1. Cf. above, p. 9.   2. Cf. below, p. 93.
3. Paris, Louvre E 643. Payne, *N.C.* no. 1446; Buschor, *Griechische Vasen*, fig. 79.
4. Delphi. Payne, *N.C.* no. 1453.

The artists certainly thought of the padded dancers as dancing in one place rather than processing, or at least 'running'[1] was only one of their lively postures and they are never represented as running in a body. Their energetic steps suggest songs written in a metre with short lines. The one clue that we have is the names inscribed against the dancers on no. 76 (fig. 2). These names, Komios, Lordios, Loxios, Paichnios, Whadesios, are not the names of the dancers but the names of the fertility spirits whom the dancers represent. They must have been quoted in the song that the padded dancers sang. An obvious analogy is the string of girls' names in Alkman's *partheneion* (I, 70 ff.) and the string of satyr-names in Sophocles *Ichneutai* (177 ff.). It seems to be a rule in satyr-play and comedy, that when the chorus name one another in the vocative, four is the maximum of names used together, and if the names are put together they are connected by 'and'.[2] Therefore Komios and his fellows were probably not addressed, but their names were strung together in the nominative, which would give short iambo-trochaic lines, either trochaic like the Alkman list or iambic with preceding definite articles like the Sophoclean satyrs. This seems more likely than a string of vocatives connected by 'and', which would give choriambs. In any case these names would very easily provide the kind of short excited lines which would suit the dance of the padded dancers.

For Sikyon, in addition to the choruses in honour of Adrastos, we have the phallophoroi (*P.M.G.* 851b).[3] They entered singing iambic trimeters, ending with a dimeter catalectic. This is the kind of use of iambic trimeters chorally that we have seen in the Rhodian swallow song.[4] They wore garlands and flowers and *kaunakai*. *Kaunakai* were thick woollen cloaks, often said to be Persian, and several times mentioned in comedy. It is possible that they are the curious cloaks worn by the attendants of Dionysos on a sixth-century Attic amphora (no. 106). When they had entered 'they ran forward and quizzed anyone they liked, and then danced in the orchestra, but the phallophoros walked straight on, plastered with soot'. In this form the performance may not be old, but elements of it certainly are. The chorus may or

1. Cf. above, p. 11.
2. Ar. *Equ.* 242, *Vesp.* 230, *Lys.* 254, 321, *Eccl.* 293.
3. Pickard-Cambridge, *D.T.C.*[2] 141 f. Perhaps the pompe (procession) of secret statues with torches and hymns mentioned by Pausanias II, 7, 5 is relevant.
4. See above, p. 60.

may not have been padded dancers; *kaunakai* could have been worn over the dancers' tights; the performance was certainly in honour of Dionysos, and was divided into a processional, a quizzing, and a dance (presumably with song). How the phallophoros performed is not clear, nor is it clear whether he carried a phallos-pole or whether he wore an artificial phallos, like the figure who walks with a 'greeting' gesture on a Corinthian aryballos (no. 80).

In Athens itself we have seen padded dancers (84), padded dancers dancing with men dressed up as nymphs (82) and choruses which anticipate later comedy, Titans (104), Anacreontes (101–2), lyre-players (107). These performances must have been in honour of Dionysos. Official comedy was not introduced at the City Dionysia until 486, but the Lenaia was an old festival and these pre-comic performances may have been part of the Lenaia.[1] The pictures of the padded dancers show them dancing in positions and with steps that are identical with or akin to Corinthian padded dancers, so that here too we should expect short excited metres. The Anacreontes (102) combine an entrance chorus and a dance on the spot; one would expect them to sing anacreontics or ionics. The lyre-players combine a walking entrance with a prancing entrance; both would be possible to anapaests. The Titans on stilts, if Kratinos later repeated their entrance in his *Ploutoi*, entered to anapaests. The assumption of pre-comedy at the Lenaia or at another Dionysiac festival accounts for these special choruses and for the normal komasts who prefigure the choruses of men in later comedy, but some of the special komast vases (86–8) show that there were Dionysiac dances more formal than the revels of the symposion and the komos through the streets which succeeded them, and which we cannot now identify.

The other major problem which the vases raise is whether the very numerous and exciting dances of satyrs and maenads had any basis in actual performance or whether they represent a sort of translation of the padded dancers into the mythical attendants of Dionysos whom they represent; this is rather suggested by the various kinds of equation that have been noted identifying padded dancers with satyrs,[2] but the

1. Cf. Pickard-Cambridge, *Dithyramb, etc.*[2], 144 f., 154. It is also true that when Aristotle (*Poetics* 1449b 1) refers to 'volunteers' before the archon gave a chorus, he may be referring to comedy before 486 at the City Dionysia.
2. Cf. Pickard-Cambridge, *Dithyramb*[2], 80 f., 100, 115.

existence of satyr masks in Athens and elsewhere[1] (as well as the possibility that some dithyrambs were already performed by men dressed as satyrs) means that at some festivals of Dionysos men did perform satyr dances, and the maenad dances of Athenian women are undoubtedly old but they cannot be positively identified until the next period.

The ithyphalloi are another chorus who sang to Dionysos in Athens. Various texts make[2] it clear that they performed in the orchestra and that they followed the phallos, which was presumably carried. This performance probably accompanied the offering of the phallos to Dionysos at the City Dionysia but they also performed on the third day of the Anthesteria (Ath. 129c). The text preserved by Semos (*P.M.G.* 851) is a standard text and they could sing special variations for special occasions (cf. below, p. 198). It is in iambo-trochaic metre: trochaic dimeter catalectic (lekythion), ithyphallic (which gets its name from this chorus), iambic trimeter, ithyphallic. Pause is certain between the second and third lines and probable between the others, an excited dance with perhaps a slowing on the long third line. They wore a long transparent robe, a chiton with a white stripe and sleeves over it, and masks. No satisfactory identification of them on vases has been made. The City Dionysia was probably instituted in the second quarter of the sixth century and the song may go back to that time.

In the sixth century also the Athenians had musical contests at the Panathenaia, including contests for singers to the lyre and singers to the flute.[3] These were, of course, solos, but we have no reason to suppose either that original poetry was always sung (Terpander is said to have sung Homer in the preceding century), or that the repertoire was restricted to solo poetry since there is no clear metrical division between solo and choral poetry. Such public performance would account for the very considerable knowledge of, for instance, Stesichoros, which Attic vases attest already in the sixth century. Fifth-century comedy shows the continuation of this knowledge of old lyric poetry in the next century: parodies and allusions in comedy are expected to

---

1. Cf. Pickard-Cambridge, *Dithyramb²*, 80; Webster, *Greek Theatre Production*, 157.
2. See Färber, II, 66; Pickard-Cambridge, *Dithyramb²*, 140 f.
3. J. A. Davison, *J.H.S.* 78, 1968, 37. One of the relevant vases is quoted under no. 196.

be understood, and the older men demand that their sons should sing the old songs in the symposion (*P.M.G.* 276b).

The division between solo and choral poetry was not hard and fast, and we cannot therefore omit Sappho and Alkaios: some of their poetry was certainly choral, and metrical units first found in them were used later in choral poetry. In the symposion itself, for which most of the solo-poetry was designed,[1] the guests, according to Plutarch (*mor.* 615b), first sang a *paian* to the god in unison, and presumably special songs were sometimes composed for this: Alkaios' Hymn to the Dioskouroi (34 L-P), which is in sapphics, might very well end with a prayer for the aversion of some present disaster and be so sung. Alkaios' hymns[2] which related the god's life in some detail or enlarged upon some particular exploit in it were surely designed for performance at a festival of the god, like the Homeric hymns, and sung by a chorus. They are the hymn to Apollo in alcaics (307), the hymn to Hermes in sapphics (308b), the hymn to Hephaistos in major asclepiads (349), the hymn to Artemis written in a kind of aeolic enoplian, xxddds (304). The hymn to Athena Itonia in alcaics (325) seems to be a cult hymn for a particular temple in Boeotia. As alcaics are established as a metre for choral hymns, it is not necessary to insist on the alcaic poem (129) in which Alkaios invokes Hera, Dionysos, and Zeus to punish Pittakos, but it is remarkable that he refers to '*this* precinct' and '*this* third god', which would suggest that the song was sung by him and his friends in the sanctuary.

It was probably in this sanctuary that the Lesbian beauty contests were held as well as choral dances of women in honour of Hera.[3] Sappho speaks of the same sanctuary (17), when she prays for a personal epiphany of Hera. The clear allusion to the particular sanctuary makes it likely that this is a choral hymn and not a private prayer of Sappho's like the first poem to Aphrodite and the fifth poem to Aphrodite and the Nereids. Similarly the prayer to Aphrodite (2) to come to *this* temple and pour nectar for her companions and Sappho's

---

1. Cf. *Greek Art and Literature, 700–530 B.C.*, 35 f., for the circles for which Alkaios and Sappho's songs were designed. For the symposion practice, cf. A. E. Harvey, *C.Q.* 5, 1955, 162.

2. On all these hymns, see D. L. Page, *Sappho and Alcaeus*, 244 ff. References to Alkaios as to Sappho, are given by the running numbers in Lobel–Page.

3. The evidence in Page, op. cit., 168.

(the sense is certainly this, but Athenaeus, who alone preserves the line, has changed the gender for his own purposes) is probably a choral prayer. That Sappho wrote for choruses of girls is known from her own poems (94, 154, 160) and from others. These two poems (2, 17) are in sapphics.

The Adonis fragment (140a) is a dialogue in major asclepiads catalectic. One line is sung by the girls: 'Fair Adonis is dead, Kythereia, what should we do?' The answer is 'Beat your breasts, girls, and tear your chitons.' Perhaps a priestess sings Aphrodite or perhaps the chorus is divided into halves taking the different parts (like the chorus in Bacchylides 18). This is a lament and the long halting lines, xxd'd'dx, would be 'walked' like the laments on contemporary plaques (nos. 133-4).

A different and varied choral group is formed by Sappho's marriage-songs.[1] Songs were sung first in the bride's house at the banquet, as in the feigned marriage feast in the *Odyssey* (23, 135), then while the bride was being brought to the house of the bridegroom, as on the shield of Achilles and on the Hesiodic shield of Herakles (274) and at the end of the *Peace* and the *Birds* of Aristophanes; then songs were sung outside the marriage-chamber at night, and finally again in the morning.[2] In the Hesiodic shield, which is probably to be dated in the sixth century, there are three kinds of music during the procession, pipes accompanying singing men, lyres accompanying dancing women, and flutes accompanying revelling boys. The pipes are paralleled on two roughly contemporary pictures[3] of the Marriage of Thetis, where they are played by a Muse on one and by a Nymph on the other. In Sappho's own description of the marriage of Hektor and Andromache (44), in the final stage which corresponds to the procession to the bridegroom's house, there is a flute, probably a lyre, certainly clappers, a holy song of girls, a supplication (*ololyge*) of older women and a *paian* to Apollo by the men.

1. Cf. Page, op. cit., 63, 119 ff.; R. Muth, *W.S.* 67, 1954, 23 ff., especially 38 f.
2. On the date of the Hesiodic shield, see R. M. Cook, *C.Q.* 31, 1937, 204. The *Phaethon* has a special instance of a processional, cf. my *Tragedies of Euripides*, 227 f. In Aeschylus fr. 43N² (*Danaides*) someone announces their intention of singing the song on the morning after.
3. Sophilos, Acr. 587; Pfuhl, *M.u.Z.* fig. 202. Kleitias, Florence 4209. Pfuhl, *M.u.Z.* figs. 215, 217.

Without clear internal evidence it is not easy to assign the surviving songs to the various stages. Page inclines to giving the Hektor and Andromache (44) and the very pretty hexameter fragments about Hesperos, the sweet apple, and the hyacinth (104–5) to the banquet, because Catullus in Poem 62, which imitates Sappho 104–5, says at the beginning 'it is time to rise and leave the rich board'; Muth on the same grounds assigns them to the procession because Catullus goes on to say that the bride is coming out. This is surely right, and the Hektor and Andromache was sung at a point in the actual ceremony which corresponded to the mythical description in the song, the escorting of the bride to her new home. The hexameters of the other fragments suit a walking chorus, and the Hektor and Andromache has a line which is not much shorter with its xxddds, 14 syllables with Pause at the end.

Page and Muth differ again over the division of poems between the procession and the song sung at the marriage-chamber. Both agree that the little poem to the doorkeeper (110a) belongs to the marriage-chamber; it is in dance tempo, short lines with Pause at the end, xxddx. Two poems in sapphics clearly belong to the procession: in 27 the girls sing that they are going to the marriage, and in 30 they call to the bridegroom to wake up and come so that they can sing all night. The excited little poem (111) telling the builders to raise the roof because the bridegroom will be so potent (the metre is xxdx″xs″xddx) is for Page rightly processional, but for Muth sung outside the marriage-chamber. Muth also gives 112 and 115 to the marriage-chamber. The case for 112 is the phrase 'your marriage is fulfilled', but this need not be taken in the literal sense that consummation has now happened, and the praise of the beauty of the bride belongs rather with the 'sweet apple' fragment. So too the comparison of the bridegroom to a slender sapling in 115. Both are in fairly long metres: 112 is dsxdsx, 14 syllables in each line, and 115 is xxdddx, 13 syllables in each line. This again brings them near the Hektor and Andromache. Finally, the dialogue (114) sung by the chorus – 'Maidenhood, where are you gone?' 'I will never come back to you anymore' – which is a long line, d′d′dsx, followed, after Pause, by what is probably a sapphic hendecasyllable, sxdsx, was either sung at the marriage-chamber or the next morning; there is no way of telling which.

The Amasis painter's lekythos in New York with a wedding scene (no. 123, fig. 5) shows the procession on the body of the vase and nine girls dancing on the shoulder. The music is provided by a seated flute-player and by a seated lyre-player. The fact that the musicians are seated must mean that the dances have nothing to do with the procession. They must take place in a house, but there is no way of deciding whether they are the dances at the banquet in the bride's home or the dances outside the marriage-chamber or both. What is interesting is the change of tempo between the walking girls who approach the lyre-player from the left and the running girls who approach him from the right. The same change of tempo can be seen on another lekythos by the Amasis painter (no. 122, fig. 6), where four women walk and four women run towards a seated goddess holding a wreath; again the main scene on the body may be connected; girls are weaving a peplos, and the shoulder may represent the dances at the Panathenaia when the peplos was given to Athena. In both cases the painter thinks of dances in different metres on the same occasion, perhaps change of metres between songs rather than change of metre within a song, but there is no other way that he could represent change of metre within a song if he wanted to show this.

The procession on the body of the wedding lekythos has, in addition to the two mule-cars and the leading pair, who have been identified as the bride's mother and the best man, two other men walking on the right of the cars and three other women on the left of the cars; these may be the singers of the processional song, which is evidently at this moment in a long metre like Sappho's Hektor and Andromache.

Thus the Amasis painter shows us three different speeds in marriage dances, walking, dancing and running. In the poems it seems likely that the lines of fourteen syllables and more are 'walking' lines, but it is impossible to draw a distinction between the 13-syllable Sappho 115 and the 14-syllable Sappho 44, especially as the shorter line is simply a catalectic form of the longer line. At the other end of the scale the song about the potent bridegroom (Sappho 111) was obviously danced fast with its opening short lines of five and four syllables; the succeeding enneasyllable may be danced at the same pace or may mark a slowing up. It seems possible to see an essential difference in tempo between this enneasyllable, which comes as a climax to two short lines, and the three repeated decasyllables of the doorkeeper song (110): it is the repetition more than the additional syllable at the beginning which gives this the slower dance tempo.

Finally there are the two stanzas which take the names of Sappho and Alkaios. The sapphic stanza consists of three lines: the first and second are hendecasyllables, sxdsx, followed by Pause; in the third the hendecasyllable is extended by dx so that it becomes a 16-syllable line, sxdsxdx. Similarly the alcaic stanza has two identical hendecasyllables followed by Pause, xsxds, and a third line xsxsxddsx making 19 syllables; each half of this long third line is nearly a duplication of the corresponding portion of the hendecasyllable,[1] so that the pattern is ab, ab, 2a2b. In the sapphic stanza the pattern is ab, ab, abb. In both the sapphic and the alcaic the hendecasyllables are well within the range of dance tempo and the long last line could be danced as a single climactic unity when necessary, but in the vast majority of cases there was the slighter pause of word-division before the final dx in the sapphic and before the final ddsx in the alcaic.

We pass to choral lyric on quite a different scale with their younger contemporary, Stesichoros of Himera in Sicily, who has become a considerably clearer figure with the publication of considerable papyrus fragments in *P.Oxy.* 32.[2] We knew before that his *Oresteia* had at least two books but we now know that the *Geryoneis* exceeded 1,300 lines because the number appears in the margin of a fragment of the new papyrus; unfortunately we cannot say how near the end of the story this fragment came. But if the Alexandrians divided the *Oresteia* into two books each book is unlikely to have been less than 1,000 lines long. Against this we have to set the colometry of our papyrus: the line-numbers are based on a triad of 26 lines, but as we shall see, we should probably now reckon it as 13 lines, so that for our purposes it is more meaningful to say that the *Geryoneis* was more than 650 lines long than to say that it was more than 1,300 lines long.

It is in addition the first time that we have been able to see the shape and size of a Stesichorean triad. All that we knew before was that Stesichoros was credited with the invention of the triad form. A triad consists of a pair of strophe and antistrophe which are identical in form

1. See A. M. Dale, *C.Q.* 1, 1951, 128 = *Collected Papers*, 95; Page, op. cit., 318, 323.
2. The best of the new fragments of the *Geryoneis* (*P.Oxy.* 2617) are presented with introduction and commentary in Page, *Lyra Graeca Selecta*, pp. 263 ff. See also Snell, *Gnomon*, 40, 1968, 116; Webster, *Agon*, 1968, 1; Robertson, *C.Q.*, forthcoming.

and an epode which has a different metrical form. After Stesichoros the form is found again in Ibykos, in most of Pindar and Bacchylides, and sometimes in tragedy. Stesichoros' triads (and those of many of his successors) were written for performance in the orchestra; they were stationary songs as distinct from processionals. The ancient view, which may be old,[1] was that the chorus circled the central altar in one direction for the strophe and in the other for the antistrophe, but were stationary for the epode: 'stationary' in this sense excludes circular movement but does not exclude movement sideways, forwards or backwards. In processionals there can have been no such distinction between the parts of the triad.

Stesichoros, then, was a considerable innovator, who wrote long choral odes on mythical subjects in a new form, which became standard. Unfortunately we know nothing of the occasions when these songs were sung. The only indication are the lines preserved by the scholiast to Aristophanes' *Peace* (*P.M.G.* 210–12) from what are probably the first strophe and antistrophe of the *Oresteia*. The strophe starts 'Muse, having thrust aside wars and singing with me the marriages of the gods, etc.', and the antistrophe starts 'such public performances [*damomata*] of the Graces we should sing at the beginning of spring, having discovered a rich Phrygian song'. Nothing certain can be extracted from this except that the *Oresteia* was sung in the spring; possibly we can add that it was a thanksgiving for the aversion of war, and this would fit with the fact that Aristophanes chose to quote it in the *Peace*; it may be therefore justifiable to think of it as a spring *paian*.[2]

The *Geryoneis* traced the story from the preliminary council of the gods to Herakles' slaughter of the three bodies of Geryon and perhaps beyond to his return journey and entertainment by the Centaur Pholos.[3] The new papyrus fragments fix the metrical shape of the strophe and antistrophe. The metre is dactylo-anapaest, which is distinguished from ordinary anapaests because the anapaests 'do not move in metra but merely in a continuous single-long double-short series, wherein the longs may not resolve'.[4] They are therefore counted in ones like dactyls and not in pairs like normal anapaests. The metre of

1. Cf. Färber, op. cit., I, 21; II, 15 ff.
2. In general, cf. A. Delatte, *A.C.* 7, 1938, 23–9; Bowra, *Greek Lyric Poetry*[2], 115.
3. Cf. above, p. 76, note 2.
4. A. M. Dale, *Lyric Metres of Greek Drama*[2], 67.

strophe and antistrophe is (*a*) tetrameter catalectic (paroemiac), (*b*) octameter catalectic, (*c*) hexameter catalectic, (*d*) hexameter, (*e*) octameter. The epode is not nearly so well attested in the papyrus and different schemes have been proposed; it is only safe to say that it began with a tetrameter catalectic and ended with a heptameter; the centre section may possibly have been one long line. It is immediately clear that Stesichoros operated with very long lines. In the strophe and antistrophe the syllable count is 10, 22, 16, 18, 24. This is borne out by fragments of other poems, which give a 20-syllable line in *P.M.G.* 187 and a 19-syllable line in *P.M.G.* 219.

The *Geryoneis* is in pure dactylo-anapaest with no admixture of single-short. In other poems Stesichoros admits single-short on two different principles. In the *Nostoi* (*P.M.G.* 209) a complete line of single-short, sxsxsx (12), precedes two purely dactylic lines: ddxddx (16), ddxdd (15). Similarly in *P.M.G.* 223 sxsxs (11) is sandwiched between xddxddx (17) and xddxdd (16).[1] But in the fragment already quoted from the *Oresteia* (*P.M.G.* 210, 212) he changes from double- to single-short within the second line and produces a regular dactylo-epitrite compound: xddxsx. *P.M.G.* 232 has an encomiologus, ddxsx, followed by a dactylic line dddd. Finally, *P.M.G.* 187 starts with a dactylo-epitrite line of 20 syllables, sxddxddx, which recurs without the final anceps in Pindar, *Nemean* 10, 2; this is followed by a 15-syllable line, ddxdd; unfortunately we cannot say whether the succeeding xddx was a complete line or not.

Except for the *Geryoneis* we cannot say how Stesichoros composed his stanzas, and in the shorter quotations we cannot be certain whether some of the lines that appear complete to us did not run on. The suggestion[2] that where he seems to us to be writing dactylo-epitrite he nevertheless has a higher proportion of double-short than most later verse of this kind is surely right. In these long stately poems he is essentially transposing epic into choral lyric.

With Ibykos we are back in dancing tempo again. He came from Rhegion in South Italy and was at the court of Polykrates in Samos from about 560 to 535. His poem to the younger Polykrates (*P.M.G.* 282), which like Theokritos' poem to Hiero (xvi) is an appeal for

1. Reading ἐτίθει for τίθησι with M. L. West, *Philol*, 1966, 151.
2. A. M. Dale, *C.Q.* 1950, 147 = *Collected Papers*, 57.

patronage,[1] is in triadic form. The strophe has two dactylic tetrameters in synaphaea followed by a longer line ending in single-short, ddddsx, also in synaphaea. This is the climaxing technique, and it is obviously possible to sing and dance the short strophe in spite of its close interconnection. The epode has three anapaestic paroemiacs followed by a 13-syllable line starting in single-short, sdddx, and a final clausula with a juxtaposition of two longs which halts the movement before the end, d′ds.[2] The well-known fragment (*P.M.G.* 286) about the Cretan quinces is perhaps antistrophe followed by an epode. The strophe has three ibyceans, dds; then three dactylic tetrameters followed by an alcaic decasyllable, ddsx, all in synaphaea but with diairesis. The epode probably has first an ibycean; then another ibycean followed by dactylic tetrameter and trimeter ending in a spondee), all in synaphaea, and finally an alcaic decasyllable again.[3] Here again the climaxing technique is clear. He has also a variety of lines beginning with single-short; in 298 two sapphic hendecasyllables going on in enoplian, and in 317 a dactylo-epitrite line, sxddx, between an enoplian and a prosodiac. One fragment is in pure single-short, 310, an iambic dimeter followed by a trochaic trimeter. Two fragments are in pure double-short; 287 and 288, and with their long lines read more like Stesichoros.

We are told that Ibykos wrote a dithyramb about the Sack of Troy (296), but dithyramb here probably only means a narrative poem. Otherwise we know nothing about performance. We cannot even say for certain that any fragment must have been sung solo or must have been sung chorally. All that we can say is that metrically he sometimes seems to have been nearer to Alkman and sometimes nearer to Stesichoros, and that for the first time the whole artillery of the high lyric style is used for the praise of contemporary men, Polykrates (282), Euryalos (288) and Gorgias (289).[4] This seems to be a step towards the fully developed victor–ode of the next period.

Pindar (*O.* 9, 1) proves that Archilochos' hymn to Herakles was still sung at Olympia in the fifth century to celebrate an athletic victory. It does not suggest that it was the only song ever sung after the victory,

1. Cf. J. Barron, *C.Q.* 14, 1964, 223.
2. Cf. A. M. Dale, *W.S.* 59, 1964, 29 = *Collected Papers*, 201. In l. 25 θνατὸς is a gloss on διερὸς and has replaced a word beginning with a vowel, perhaps ἄμων δ'.
3. Cf. A. M. Dale, op. cit., 24 = *Collected Papers*, 195.
4. C. M. Bowra, *Greek Lyric Poetry*[2], 251.

and it does not say anything at all about the songs sung when the victor came home. The excited youths beside the victor on a black-figure amphora (no. 112) could indeed be shouting *kallinike*, but the carefully draped men with libation saucers and drinking horns on an earlier cup (no. 111) are moving slowly and must be singing something composed in a long metre. The same is true of the singers at the end of the period (nos. 131–2) who, because of their ivy-crowns, may be singing the dithyramb. Who wrote these stately songs in Athens we do not know, but we have now got examples of them in Stesichoros, however different his subject matter was from victor-ode or Athenian dithyramb, and we know also that he was popular in Athens by the middle of the sixth century,[1] so that presumably Athenian and other mainland poets caught his manner.

4 · RIPE ARCHAIC PERIOD, 530–480 B.C.

The chief lyric poets of this period are Simonides of Keos, who was born in 556 and came to Athens at the invitation of Hipparchos probably at the beginning of the last quarter of the century, Anakreon of Teos, who was born some fifteen years earlier and came to Athens from Samos about the same time, Lasos of Hermione, who was born in 548 and was also in Athens in the last quarter of the century, and finally Pindar, born in 518, and his contemporary Bacchylides, whose earliest works were produced before 480.[2]

First, we have a number of problems connected with songs sung in honour of Dionysos, maenad songs of various kinds, dithyrambs, comedy, symposion songs. For the first time the maenad dances on vases give some indication which suggests an actual performance. Twice (nos. 138 and 139) they show a mountain, and the reference probably is to the mountain dances[3] on Mount Parnassos to which the Athenians sent a contingent every year: they not only joined the Delphian women at Delphi in the rites of Dionysos but also performed dances at various places along the road between Athens and Delphi. What they sang we have no means of knowing but the vases show that

1. C. M. Bowra, *Greek Lyric Poetry*[2], 119.
2. For dates, cf. C. M. Bowra, *Greek Lyric Poetry*, 269, 309; *Pindar*, 406. For Lasos, *P.C.D.*[2] 13. For Bacchylides, the Teubner text by B. Snell, 38 f.
3. Pausanias X, 4, 3. Cf. Nilsson, *Gesch.* 537.

g tempo and excited dance tempo, and it is a reasonable
the Briseis Painter's cup (no. 139) that they invoked
dance with them and that they thought of him coming
rs. It is this picture that Anakreon brings to mind when he
velling as wildly as Dionysos' (*P.M.G.* 442).
festival nor literary text can be quoted for the dances round
phallos (no. 142) or the dances round a satyr-mask (no. 144).
dances of maenads round a Dionysos mask (nos. 145–9) three
xplanations have been put forward: a private festival, the
teria, the Lenaia. The private festival was suggested by Dr
paki,[1] and the same explanation is given by the scholiast on
ophanes' *Lysistrata* 1 ff., a text which is certainly relevant to the
. Lysistrata, angry because none of her fellow-conspirators has
eared, says 'if anyone summoned them to a Bakcheion there
ould be so many tambourines that you could not get through'; in
11, the date of the *Lysistrata*, tambourines were part of a maenad's
quipment (cf. no. 233). The explanation is possible, but one wonders
whether a performance in a private house would either be mentioned
by Aristophanes or be responsible for the considerable number of
'Lenaian' vases; the surviving fifty or so can be only a small fraction of
those actually made. Such a large number, with a high preponderance
of a single shape, suggests that they were made for a particular festival
like the Panathenaic amphorae or the Anthesteria choes. The vases
show that these maenads were Athenian ladies dressed as maenads
and not mythical maenads, but they do not show that the festival was
private rather than public. Wilamowitz rejected the scholiast's explanation and says in his commentary that a Bakcheion is a place where there
are Bakchai, women dressed as maenads, and so equates it with
Lenaion.

Lenaion[2] has been derived from Lenai, maenads, rather than Lenos,
wine-press, and this is the chief reason for associating the vases with the
Lenaia; the only texts which name songs other than comedy and
tragedy at the Lenaia mention men as performers: one is the invocation
already quoted,[3] and the other a rather muddled scholiast on Clement,

1. Cf. above, p. 19.
2. See *P.C.F.*[2] 25 ff. For the equation, cf. his no. 20 (Herakleitos). Texts on songs, his
nos. 9 and 19.
3. Cf. above, p. 64.

who speaks of men with ivy-wreaths singing drunk songs – this
may possibly account for some of the ivy-wreathed rather formal
komasts that we have noted (e.g. no. 86). The case for the Anthesteria is
rather more complicated: the maenads dance before a mask of Dionysos, and a similar mask of Dionysos, lying in a winnowing fan with
two maenads making offerings of wine and fruit to it, appears on a
chous,[1] a kind of wine jug associated especially but not exclusively with
the Anthesteria. It is likely that the mask is to be used in a further rite,
and at the Anthesteria it is probable that the King Archon wore the
mask to impersonate Dionysos when he was carried in the Ship-car.
It is possible but not certain that the dances of the maenads before the
mask were a stage between the preparation of the mask and its wearing
by the archon *basileus*. The other argument is that the 'Lenaian' vases
commonly show the maenads with cups of wine and very often with a
mixing bowl, and this is equated with the *pithoigia* on the first day of the
Anthesteria when the new wine was brought from the storage jars and
mixed in honour of Dionysos. 'Being pleased with the mixture they
sang of Dionysos in songs, dancing and invoking him as Euas and
Dithyrambos and Bakcheutas and Bromios' (Athenaeus 465a). But
again here there are two difficulties: the 'Lenaian' vases never show the
filling of the mixing bowl, and the pictures do not differ from Pentheus' description in the *Bacchae* (221 ff.) of full mixing bowls standing
in the middle of bands of maenads as part of their normal rites.
Secondly, the description of the singers is in the masculine, and the
titles in the songs sound like a dithyramb; similarly Kallimachos (fr.
305 Pf), evidently contrasting the City Dionysia with the Anthesteria,
speaks of 'festivals with "stationary" choruses' at the Anthesteria without specifying that the dancers were women. In both cases the subject
could probably be a common 'the Athenians', but it is curious not to
specify the feminine gender, if they were in fact women, and, as we
shall see, there is a case for thinking that there were dithyrambs at the
Anthesteria. One last possible argument is the likeness of the fourteen
gerarai or priestesses, who supervised the Dionysiac rites at the Anthesteria, to the sixteen women who were responsible for the maenad

1. *P.C.F.*[2] 1 ff., fig. 24, *A.R.V.*[2] 1249 (Eretria painter), with discussion of the case made
by Nilsson. For a discussion of the timetable of the Anthesteria which reduces the pro-
gramme drastically, see A. Rumpf, *B.J.* 161, 1961, 208. The text for the *pithoigia*, *P.C.F.*
no. 20; Ath, 465a. Note that Kerenyi, *S.O.* 36, 1960, 9, refers it to the Lenaia.

chorus at Elis (see above, p. 59). But it remains unclear where and on what occasion the Athenian maenads performed in Athens. The vases show that they did perform, and that their dance was sometimes in dancing tempo and sometimes in walking tempo.

Nothing more can be said about the chorus of young men who might possibly be a very early chorus of maenads in tragedy (no. 152); but there is a real possibility that Anakreon and his boon-companions are pretending to be maenads. Anakreon himself in his considerable number of symposion songs has only one possible allusion to the practice of wearing women's clothes – 'I will be a Bassarid again' (*P.M.G.* 356), and Bassarid is his word for maenad (*P.M.G.* 411b). He describes them there as the 'high-stepping Bassarids of Dionysos'; high-stepping is not a bad description of posture C, which recurs often on the Anakreon vases, and the word is used of satyrs by Euripides (*Cycl.* 37). In another song (*P.M.G.* 410) Anakreon says, 'Let us put wreaths of parsley on our brows and celebrate a joyous festival in honour of Dionysos.' On the vases these revellers sometimes have wreaths; as far as I can see, some of them are not ivy-wreaths but might be parsley. If the texts do not forbid this identification, the vases rather point towards it. It is interesting that on the inside of a Brygos satyr-cup (no. 140) Dionysos plays the lyre in the same dreamy backward-leaning posture as Anakreon, and on a cup by Douris satyrs and maenads outside are paired with an Anakreon dancing with another man inside. But a stronger argument is the likeness of the dance steps of the Anacreontes to the dance steps of maenads. Many parallels could be quoted. The two most striking are the likeness of the welcoming Anacreontes on the Heidelberg painter's cup (no. 102) and the red-figure stage maenad in Ferrara (no. 217) and the likeness of the Psiax Anakreon (no. 153/1) to a maenad by the Phiale painter (no. 239).

The dance represented on the main body of Anakreon vases was accompanied by choral song, because on two at least (nos. 153/2 and 207/21) the little circles coming out of Anakreon's mouth show that he is giving them the note before he starts playing the lyre and singing.[1] The later pictures are so alike that it is tempting to suppose that there

1. Cf. *P.C.F.*[2] 262. (On a red-figure pelike in London E 354, *J.D.A.I.* 76, 1961, 69, fig. 25, a solo singer seems to be giving the note to his flute-player.)

was some well-known picture of Anakreon and his boon-companions painted perhaps about 490 to which they all go back. The three poems quoted above are all in ionic metre: *P.M.G.* 356 in anaclastic ionic dimeters (anacreontic), 411b is a catalectic ionic trimeter, and 410 in anaclastic ionic trimeters. In view of the possible identification of these dancers with maenads it is not irrelevant that all the earlier choruses of the *Bacchae*, our one preserved maenad play, are in ionics. Certainly, ionics, normal or anaclastic, up to trimeter-length (twelve syllables) would suit very well the fluid dance of the Anacreontes.

The Anacreontes would seem to be a very special kind of symposion performance. The ordinary songs sung in the symposion do not for the most part concern us since they were not choral. But Anakreon's salute to Artemis, who guards the city of Magnesia (*P.M.G.* 348), might well be a choral *paian* sung early in the symposion; it has two glyconics followed by a pherecratean, then four glyconics followed by a pherecratean, and this sequence is on the border between fast and excited dancing tempo. The first two of the collection of anonymous Attic drinking songs (*P.M.G.* 884–5) are a prayer to Athena and Demeter to look after *this* city, and they also may very well be the *paians* sung at the beginning of the symposion by all the guests. The first two lines are hendecasyllables (phalaecean), sdssx; the third line is an enneasyllable, ∧ds′d, and the fourth a dodecasyllable, ds′ds, so that the whole is in normal dance tempo.

The four preserved symposion songs of Simonides, Bacchylides, and Pindar which belong to this period raise rather the same question as Ibykos' poem to Polykrates: nothing in the words suggests that they are choral but they are in fully developed choral metre. It is true that both Bacchylides 20B and Pindar 124a, and probably Pindar fr. 120–1, were not sung by the poet but were sent to their recipients, Alexander of Macedonia (Bacchylides and Pindar) and Thrasyboulos of Akragas (Pindar), and therefore the poet may have arranged for a choir to sing them rather than a soloist. All three are in simple dactylo-epitrites. Bacchylides' quatrains[1] run xddxsx, ddxsx, ddxsx, sxsxs, which in general shape is almost like a sapphic stanza with three similar lines and a fourth which extends the second element of the other three. Pindar in fr. 124a has three-line stanzas, ddxsx, sxddxsx, sxd′sxsx (how

1. Cf. A. M. Dale, *C.Q.* 1950, 147 = *Collected Papers*, 58.

the periods worked in frs. 120–1 is unclear). If they were choral, Bacchylides could be danced, Pindar's lines are perhaps too long; their syllable count is 12, 16, 16, as against Bacchylides' 13, 12, 12, 11. Pindar's three lines seem to slow down deliberately as the proportion of single-short and long anceps increases.

Simonides' symposion song to Skopas was probably written some ten years earlier, shortly before 500 B.C.[1] The reconstruction is not entirely certain because it has had to be rescued from the prose of Plato's *Protagoras*, but the metrical pattern as given in *P.M.G.* 542 seems to be (*a*) ddxsx (12), (*b*) ∧dxsds'sdsxs (24), (*c*) ∧ds'sds'sds (21), (*d*) ∧ds'sdxs'sd (21), (*e*) ∧s'sxsdxssx (19). The first three lines are virtually certain; the articulation of the fourth is not guaranteed by word-overlap but the end is fixed by hiatus; in the fifth the final sdxssx is guaranteed as a unit. These are much longer units than are used in the other two songs, and they are much more complicated than the long lines of Stesichoros. This is the new periodic style in 'aeolic', of which the two songs of Pindar and Bacchylides are much simpler versions in dactylo-epitrite. Here, after the opening encomiologus, what characterizes the long periods are the headless beginnings, the repetition of aeolic elements (particularly sds) within the periods, and the frequent blunt junctions (true long next true long) between the parts, blunt junctions which are usually bridged by overlapping words, so that there is no doubt that the period continues. Again the last period slows up with only one double-short.

It may be that the new style in this developed form was first used in solo songs; unfortunately we have no evidence but the Simonides *skolion* is presumably a solo. By 498 when he wrote the tenth *Pythian* Pindar could trust his chorus to sing it. We have only fragments of the victor-odes of Simonides, and they seem to be simpler. They are, of course, in the high lyric style, and in that sense continue for athletic victors the line of elaborate choral eulogies of which Ibykos' praise of Polykrates is our first example. *P.M.G.* 506 (probably written in 480) is rather in the Stesichorean manner: the three preserved lines are xdddsx, ddds'', dddd. The three reconstructed lines of *P.M.G.* 509 (probably written in 520) are in simple dactylo-epitrite: s'ss, sxddx,

---

1. Cf. C. M. Bowra, *Greek Lyric Poetry*[2], 326 ff.; Finley in Rowell, *The Poetic Tradition*, 10 f., for the connection between Simonides' *skolion* and Pindar *P. x.*

ddxs. But *Pythian* X in 498 is in the elaborate style of the Simonides song to Skopas.

Pindar's victory odes can be divided into those which were sung immediately after the victory wherever it was won, and those which were sung when the victor had returned home. *Pythian* X is a song of four triads, each eighteen lines long, sung for Hippokles of Thessaly when he had returned. It has the normal Pindaric elements, praise of the victor and his family, moral, and myth of Perseus among the Hyperboreans. Metrically[1] it has the same chracteristics as the Simonides song: headless beginnings appear in strophe and antistrophe, but in the epode Pindar substitutes initial anceps; this change would be very noticeable if, as has been suggested, the headless beginning was actually preceded by a step corresponding to the lost syllable. Easily recognizable elements are the opening pherecratean, the enoplian paroemiac followed by adonean in the third line, the headless alcaic decasyllable at the beginning of the last line of strophe (and antistrophe), and in the epode glyconics and an extended hipponactean. There are six blunt junctions (true long next to true long within the period) in the strophe and five in the epode; every one of these is bridged over by a word in at least one of its occurrences.

The importance of this phenomenon, which is repeated in all the five victor—odes written in this style during this period, lies in something more than its convenience to us when we need to decide where to end the period when we have nothing else to guide us. It is rather that it shows a sort of tension between the dance rhythm and the sung words. The sung words must go on, and they hold the whole period together as a unity; but the dance rhythm must pause, however briefly, at the blunt junction – the sort of pause that there is in a series of cretics with their s's'... or of pure choriambics or asclepiads with their d'd'... There is some justification for using names like glyconic and choriambic dimeter for describing the parts of these periods because they probably do have the same steps as any other glyconic, but although the steps may be the same the time is probably slower, just because each recognizable element is combined into the larger whole of the period. The syllable count of *Pythian* X is 7, 16, 15, 22, 13, 14 in the strophe, and 13, 5, 14, 10, 10, 14 in the epode. Probably the very long 22-syllable line justifies

1. Analysed by A. M. Dale, C.Q. 1, 1951, 24 = *Collected Papers*, 69.

us in regarding the whole as in 'walking' time rather than in dancing time.

Pythian VI consists of six seven-line strophes, not triads. It was written in 490 for Xenokrates of Akragas, who had won a victory with a chariot race. The first line is 21 syllables long and probably fixes the pace; the other lines range between 14 and 11 syllables. The first line is xs'sds'ssd. This can be called iambic metron, glyconic, choriambic dimeter B, and this no doubt represents the steps used to dance it, but each of the two blunt junctions between these parts is bridged over by a word so that the period is bound into an indissoluble whole. The glyconic element recurs in ll. 2 and 5 and its catalectic form (pherecratean) in l. 6; the choriambic dimeter B recurs in ll. 3 and 4. Every line has at least one blunt junction and in every line a word bridges it over. Pindar speaks of himself as going to Delphi, so this was a festival song.

Olympian XIV only has two twelve-line strophes. It summons the Graces of Orchomenos, the home of the victor Asopichos, to see 'these dancers moving lightly', and Pindar says that he is singing in the Lydian manner, which refers to the musical scale that he is using. One would expect that 'moving lightly' implied dance tempo rather than walking tempo, but the syllable count is against this: two lines of 18, one of 16, two of 15, and only three under 12. Probably 'moving lightly' can be applied to any chorus, and it may be pressing its significance too far to note the very smooth movement of the first four lines, which not only have no blunt junctions within the periods but have the smoothest possible transition from period to period[1] because at each transition the final long of the first line is separated from the first long of the second by a single anceps, whether at the end of the first line or at the beginning of the second. The first four lines run xsd (7), xsxdssx (14, an alcaic hendecasyllable prolonged by an extra sx), dsxdx (12), sdssdss (18, which plays further with the ds theme). From here on all the lines except 7, 11 and 12 have blunt junctions within them (but they are all bridged by words) and the transitions between lines are only smooth after 7, 9 and 11. Pindar continues to play on the ds theme, and finally ends with two lines (which may, in fact, be one long line) reminding us again of the long last line of the alcaic stanza: xsxs, dsxdssx.

1. Cf. A. M. Dale, *C.Q.* 1950, 147 = *Collected Papers*, 58, on Bacchylides, fr. 20b.

Pythian VII has a single triad sung at the festival for the Athenian Megakles in 486. It is a tiny ode of twenty-one lines, and the shape and metre are much conditioned by the number of proper names that Pindar thought desirable to include in this compass. It does not show any new principles. *Nemean* VII, sung in 485 for Sogenes of Aegina, has five triads each twenty-one lines long. The poem ends with a prayer to Herakles, and this perhaps implies that the ode was sung at his shrine; the myth as so often in Aeginetan odes is about the Aeakids. Every period has blunt junctions within it, and only the last four periods of the strophe (and antistrophe) have smooth transitions between them. The elements within the periods are all variations on the ds theme and mostly very recognizable variations such as glyconics, telesilleans, and choriambic dimeters A and B.[1] The same is true of *Nemean* II, probably belonging to the same year. It is a short poem of five stanzas each of five periods: the longest period is the fourth sds'sds'sdx, 23 syllables with both the blunt junctions bridged. All the transitions between the periods are smooth. It ends with an instruction to the 'citizens' of Acharnai to praise Zeus in honour of Timodemos. The ode starts with Zeus, who was the god of the Nemean games. We need not necessarily suppose that this was sung at a shrine of Zeus in Acharnai, but the reference to citizens makes it a public occasion, like the reference to 'all the people' in Bacchylides XIII, 230.

For us, to turn from these odes to the dactylo-epitrite odes is to turn from the extremely complex to the comparatively simple. It probably is true that the elements in the periods of the so-called aeolic odes which we have been considering were much more recognizable and therefore much easier to dance than they seem to us, but the elements are much more numerous than in dactylo-epitrite and have many more variations and a much subtler variety of combinations. Dactylo-epitrite[2] is mostly limited to two units, s and dd; 'the varying combinations of these, with or without initial, link, and final anceps and in a variety of lengths, produce a supple, stately yet changeable rhythm, quite easy to grasp. Its flowing motion is due to the very frequent use of link anceps,

1. See A. M. Dale, *C.Q.* 1, 1951, 25 = *Collected Papers*, 71, for second period of strophe as dsss'ds'ss and fourth period as xs'ssdsx. The treatment of Neoptolemos in this ode looks back to the account in *Paian* VI which will be discussed with the other *paians* in the next chapter. Cf. Slater, *C.Q.*, 19, 1969, 91ff.
2. See A. M. Dale, *C.Q.* 1950, 145 = *Collected Papers*, 53 f., with analysis of *Pythian* XII.

so that the harder impact of blunt against blunt at a junction of units is not too often heard.'

Pythian XII was written for Midas, a flute-player of Akragas, in 490, and appropriately tells a myth of the invention of the flute. It was sung for him on his return home and consists of four strophes, each eight lines long. The pattern is (*a*) xddxdd (16), (*b*) ddxdd (15), (*c*) xddxsxs (16), (*d*) ddxdd (15), (*e*), and (*f*) repeat (*c*), (*g*) ddxs (11) (*h*) sxsxsx (12). Within these periods there is not a single blunt junction; the transitions between them are blunt except between (*b*) and (*c*), (*d*) and (*e*), and (*e*) and (*f*). The general pattern is a gradual invasion of double-short by single-short, which dominates in the last period.

Nemean V was written in 483 for Pytheas of Aegina and sung at the Aiakeion in Aegina (53), like the later Eighth *Nemean* (13). The myth tells of the Marriage of Peleus and Thetis. The three dactylo-epitrite triads have six-line strophes, antistrophes, and epodes. All the transitions between the periods are smooth except the transition between the first and second period of the strophe and between the fifth and sixth period of the epode. In both cases the blunt transition sets off a longer line from a shorter line, the initial 27-syllable period at the beginning of the strophe and the final 19-syllable period at the end of the epode. Within the periods themselves there are only two blunt junctions, in the first period of the strophe and the fourth period of the epode. These and the last period of the epode are worth examining because they are the only periods which are at all outside the normal range of dactylo-epitrite. The first period of the strophe has 27 syllables; xsxs is prefixed to a normal line, sxsxddxs, and the blunt junction is covered by word-overlap. The fourth line of the epode has the form xsxd'ddxs and again the blunt junction is covered. The last line of the epode has 19 syllables, and runs through, but here the double-short element is increased giving sxdddxsx. Strophe and antistrophe start and end with single-short; epode starts and ends with double-short.

Bacchylides celebrated the same victory in a very long dactylo-epitrite song (XIII): he says at the end that his sweet songs will proclaim the victor to the whole people, which perhaps implies performance in a more public place than the Aiakeion. In Victor-Ode XI for Alexidamos of Metaponton, Bacchylides says that 'because of the victory the town which the gods honour is full of the songs (*komoi*) and rejoicings of fair-limbed young men, and they sing of the wondrous Pythian victor'. Again this sounds like a public rejoicing. The long song is in very regular dactylo-epitrites like XIII; the majority of the periods start with the quick-running dactylic element and slow up on the epitrites. For this reason Snell dates it with XIII.

The last victor-ode of this time, *Isthmian* VI, has a very similar line to the last line of the epode of *Nemean* V as third line of the strophe but it is prefixed by an additional sx so that the syllable count comes to 23. The only other unusual line is the 21-syllable final line of the epode which runs sxdd's' sxs; again word-overlap bridges the two blunt junctions, but they serve to slow up the movement before the end. This ode was written in 480 for Phylakidas of Aegina and was sung in Aegina (21). It has three triads of twenty-five lines each.

The periodic style in its two main kinds of 'aeolic' and dactylo-epitrite and with variants between them is also used for other kinds of choral lyric. Simonides is interesting in this respect.[1] *P.M.G.* 581, which may very well be a fragment of a *threnos* or dirge, is very nearly regular dactylo-epitrite but one line ends up with a clear aeolic element with a dragged close, l. 4, sxsxsds̄. The praise of those who were killed at Thermopylai in 480, which was written to be sung in Sparta,[2] has nine periods of which the second, third and sixth are pure dactylo-epitrite, but the rest may all be called aeolic, and include extended glyconics and enoplia with many echoes between periods. *P.M.G.* 521, however, is pure aeolic with two lines like headless asclepiads, then a long enoplian with dragged single-short close, and finally a line in single-short. These solemn slow-moving songs seem to have been typical of the Greek *threnos*, which, as Mr Harvey[3] has pointed out, seems to have been consolatory and philosophical and is to be firmly distinguished from the wild lamentation with tearing of hair and cheeks and beating of breasts which we associate with funerals. The *threnos* would suit the men who walk with hands raised in greeting on the plaques and vases of Exekias and Sakonides (no. 134).

Simonides' dithyrambs are lost except for a single title, *Memnon*, which may have been wrongly assigned when any narrative choral

1. See A. M. Dale, *C.Q.* 1, 1951, 119 f. = *Collected Papers*, 80 f.
2. Text in A. M. Dale, loc. cit., rather than *P.M.G.* 531, except in l. 6 ὅδε rather than ᾧ δὲ. On the occasion, A. N. Podlecki, *Historia*, 1968, 255, 275.
3. *C.Q.* 15, 1955, 168.

poem could be called a dithyramb,[1] but he claimed to have won fifty-six victories with dithyrambs (79D). Lasos of Hermione[2] was a younger contemporary, born 548–545 B.C. He seems to have been in Athens well before the restoration of the democracy in 510, and is variously credited with introducing dithyrambic contests, being the first to compose stationary songs for circular (dithyrambic) choruses, altering the rhythms so as to achieve the dithyrambic tempo and adjusting it to the polyphony of flutes. Clearly, ancient critics saw Lasos as a first step on the road which led to mid-fifth-century dithyramb, and the changes which he introduced were metrical, i.e. dance, as well as purely musical (the enlargement of the range of flute music). We must also remember that 'first' means 'first on the record', whether the Athenian official records or any other available source. The one fragment that survives of Lasos is a hymn to Demeter (*P.M.G.* 702); the text is not entirely clear but the three surviving lines seem to be in the kind of aeolic periodic style which we have seen in Simonides. They run xs's'dd, s'ds, dxdd. It is therefore possible that the metrical change accredited to Lasos was the introduction of what we call the periodic style into dithyramb. The hymn to Demeter was known as the 'hymn without sigma' because Lasos disliked sibilants. Pindar has a clear reference to this dislike which takes us a little further (fr. 70b): 'Of old the rope-stretched song of the dithyramb and the debased sigma issued from the mouths of men, but now the gates are open for holy circles' (circular choruses). The reference to Lasos is clear, and Pindar evidently means that there was a stage in the history of the dithyramb before Lasos, and then Lasos inaugurated changes which have now born fruit in Pindar's own art. The early dithyramb in contrast to Lasos' dithyramb was 'rope-stretched'. Considering the later distinction drawn between the strung-along (*eiromene*) style and the periodic style in prose, this is a perfectly intelligible description if the early dithyramb was monostrophic, i.e. consisted of a string or rope of identical stanzas, until Lasos introduced the triadic form for dithyramb. If his dithyrambs were the earliest known with triadic structure and periodic style, he may well have seemed to be 'the first to compose stationary songs for circular choruses'.

1. Cf. Harvey, op. cit., 172 f.
2. Cf. Pickard-Cambridge, *Dithyramb, etc.*[2], 13 ff.

Pindar himself wrote a dithyramb in 497,[1] and won a victory in Athens with it. Another (frs. 76–8) refers to Artemision and the Persian wars and must have been written very soon after 480. In yet another (fr. 75) he refers to himself as coming to Athens a *second* time, so that it presumably comes between the other two. Nothing is left of the first and the fragments of the other two do not show whether they were triadic or not, but they clearly show the leisurely periodic style. In the absence of responsion the details are difficult to determine, but fr. 75 certainly has lines of 22, 19, and 16 syllables, blunt junctions within the line average more than one per line but are mostly bridged by word-overlap, and the majority of the lines have smooth transitions between them. Single-short with a good deal of resolution predominates over double-short, and there are not so many recognizable aeolic elements as in the victor-odes. The fragments of the post-Persian dithyramb (76–8) are too short to analyse, but it looks as if Pindar was using here rather long dactylic sequences.

In the second Athenian dithyramb (fr. 75) Pindar appeals to the Olympian gods and the gods of the Agora to come *here* and receive his spring song. Comparison with, for instance, *Olympian* XIV, where he appeals to the Graces of Orchomenos to come and see *these* dancers, suggests that this dithyramb must have been sung at the altar of the Twelve Gods in the Agora in the spring, and the early spring since he speaks later of the chambers of the seasons being opened. We know of dithyramb in Athens at the City Dionysia, the Lesser Panathenaia, and the Thargelia. The Thargelia was a festival of Apollo but Pindar here expressly speaks of Dionysos, 'the ivy-giving god, whom we call Bromios and Eriboas'. The Panathenaia took place in July. The difficulty about the City Dionysia is partly that late March is very late for the beginning of an Athenian spring and still more that, as far as we know, its dithyrambs were performed in the theatre. Friis-Johansen[2] has argued for the Anthesteria, which took place in February. The evidence for dithyramb at the Anthesteria is otherwise very slight and only consists of the two texts already quoted,[3] Kallimachos' festivals with 'stationary' choruses in honour of Dionysos Limnaios (the god of the Anthesteria) and the songs invoking Dionysos as Dithyrambos and Bromios at the Pithoigia, the first day of the Anthesteria. If Dionysos

---

1. *P.Oxy.* 2438, 9; Snell fr. 74a.   2. Cited on no. 259.   3. Cf. above, p. 82.

was invoked as Dithyrambos, the song should be a dithyramb, and he is called Bromios in the Pindar dithyramb.

Whether the occasion was the Anthesteria or not (and it is always possible that the songs sung in the great procession[1] which escorted the statue of Dionysos Eleuthereus from the Academy to the theatre to take part in the City Dionysia were dithyrambs), Pindar's dithyramb would seem to have been sung in the Agora, and we should imagine his chorus like the walking muffled boys (nos. 192–3, fig. 7) who perform beside the Stoa of Herms, which is not very far from the Altar of the Twelve Gods.

The Stoa of Herms (or possibly the Hermes Agoraios in the Agora before the Stoa was built)[2] was also the place where the prancing and walking satyrs performed (nos. 159–61, fig. 6). Here it is impossible to reject the association with the later fifth-century lyre-playing satyrs (no. 244, fig. 9), and they are entitled 'singers (victorious at) the Panathenaia', so that the whole sequence of lyre-playing satyrs can be accepted as men dressed up as satyrs and singing dithyramb at the Lesser Panathenaia. The combination of walking and prancing, as with the lyre-players of pre-comedy (no. 107), would be compatible with anapaests. Possibly Anakreon refers to them (*P.M.G.* 386): 'I saw Simalos' (a satyr-name like Simos) 'in a chorus holding a fair lyre'.

Comedy or pre-comedy is well represented in this period. The Oltos dolphin-riders (no. 163) are fixed as entering to anapaests by the words issuing from their mouths, and this is the natural entry metre for all the mounted choruses, the other dolphin-riders, the knights, and the ostrich-riders. The dolphin-riders belong to two different performances, an earlier one where they carry shields (Oltos) and a later one where they have cloaks or nothing except helmets and spears.

To be distinguished from these are the running entries, the London cocks (no. 169), the Thebes torch-bearers (no. 167), the running soldiers (no. 165), and, if they belong, the Minotaurs (no. 170), the soldiers carrying helmeted heads (no. 171), and the Amazons (no. 185). Here it is reasonable to think of trochaics: we have seen this running posture on the vases with padded dancers, who may have danced to short trochaic metres, and the word trochaic means running. It was

1. Cf. *P.C.F.*[2] 61.
2. Cf. Wycherley, *Athenian Agora*, III, 30, 102, and no. 296; *B.C.H.* 86, 1962, 640.

already a technical term in the fifth century[1] and Aristotle associated it particularly with comedy. Here the natural parallels are the trochaic tetrameters with which the Acharnians enter chasing Amphitheos in Aristophanes' play (204 ff.).[2]

Thirdly, the Berlin birds (166) walk muffled in their cloaks like the boy dithyramb singers. Unlike all the other choruses which move either towards their flute-players or past their flute-players, the Berlin birds are preceded by their flute-player.[3] This probably means that the other choruses are entering the orchestra where the flute-player has already taken up his position, but the Berlin birds are walking off at the end of the play. It is not impossible that they walk off to a parody of a Pindaric victor-ode, which would account for their solemn gait.

As before some of the choruses anticipate later choruses of comedy – the *Knights* of Aristophanes, of course; and *Birds* were written by Magnes and Krates as well as by Aristophanes. The dolphin-riders had a successor in a comedy in which the chorus rode fish and perhaps used the long oars to manoeuvre them into the orchestra (no. 279). The running warriors remind us of the *Soldiers* of Hermippos and perhaps the *Deserters* of Pherekrates. It is possible that the two vases with running Amazons belong here too since *Amazons* are found as a title in later comedy (Kephisodoros and Epikrates); Kallimachos speaks of them dancing round the statue of Artemis in Ephesos (*Hymn* iii, 241 f.), and in the fifth century both Aristophanes (*Nub.* 600) and Autokrates speak of the daughters of the Lydians dancing in honour of Artemis of Ephesos, and they may be recalling an earlier comic or pre-comic chorus. All these choruses are entry choruses or exit choruses, in later terms *parodoi* and *exodoi*, and they have some interest as showing that not only were kinds of chorus already established but also the normal entry to anapaests or trochaics. The only picture of a dance in the orchestra is the curious picture (no. 172) of the men with grotesque ears. Here again we can suggest names: Kratinos speaks of a Myllos

---

1. Plato, *Rep.* 400b (ascribing it to Damon). If Terpander's *trochaios nomos* is genuine, it may be older. Aristotle, *Rhet.* 1409a1, etc.

2. Note that early in the next period Epicharmos' metres were (besides the iambic trimeter) trochaic tetrameters and anapaestic tetrameters and dimeters, cf. Pickard-Cambridge, *Dithyramb, etc.*[2], 279–80.

3. The scholiast to Aristophanes, *Vesp.* 582, attests this custom for tragedy.

who hears everything (89K), and two names of noted dunces were titles of later comedy, Boutalion and Mammakythos.

The two earliest vases (nos. 208–9) which show satyrs wearing the canonical costume of the satyr-play belong in the earliest decades of the fifth century and fit chronologically with Pratinas, but there is nothing to connect them with a particular play.[1]

5 · EARLY CLASSICAL PERIOD, 480–450 B.C.

The bulk of the material for this period is formed of the victor-odes of Pindar and Bacchylides and the tragedies of Aeschylus, but we have also considerable remains of other kinds of choral song which may be considered first.

Hyporcheme we have seen already is a difficult word with various ancient interpretations. For this period we have several fragments of Pindar and Bacchylides which we know were classed as *hyporchemes* by the Alexandrians. It is not clear how valid the classification is. One criterion is the use of cretic metre, and this has brought in the three examples from Bacchylides (frs. 14–16): the first has no clear reference, the second is a hymn sung by men at the temple of Athena Itonia in Boeotia, and the third may very well be a drinking song. Cretics inevitably have a certain liveliness since all the transitions within the periods are blunt, but the hexameters of 15 and the pentameter of 16 cannot have been danced very fast. In 14, however, which mixes cretics with double-short as well as single-short, the syllable count for the three preserved lines is 7, 14, 6, and it may be that rapid change of tempo is characteristic of the *hyporcheme* in the sense of lively dance. On this criterion it is tempting to add Bacchylides' invitation to the Dioskouroi to attend a simple symposion (fr. 21), which seems to consist of three-line trochaic strophes counting 12, 8, 7 syllables.

It is difficult to see anything except variation of tempo that connects Pindar's *hyporchemes*: fr. 105 has both 6-syllable lines and 13-syllable lines, 106 varies from 8 to 19 syllables, 107a, b from 8 to 23, 108 from 3 to 10 (but the short line may be incomplete), 110 from 10 to 21; it is also true that in each of them cretics can be seen, never in series as in Bacchylides, but identifiable at the end or beginning of periods in

1. Pickard-Cambridge, *Dithyramb, etc.*[2], 65 ff.

other metres. Pindar himself speaks of 'Cretic manner and Molossian flute' in 107b. Here he tells his chorus to 'imitate Pelasgian horse or Amyklaian hound, whirling with competitive foot, pursuing the twists of the song' and then says that he knows how to blend lightly dancing feet with the flute. As he also thinks of the hound (in the simile) as chasing over the plain in pursuit of a deer, there can be no doubt that this is a swift dance, we must suppose that the long lines are danced as a climax. The metre is two lines, xsxs (and conceivably the cretic would be heard at the end); then two long lines, ∧ddddxssx, dddddddx; then sxd; then sxs's'sx (here the blunt junction would make the cretic clear); then after a gap sxd's (with the cretic very clear), sxd'xssx. So also in 108 the cretics are clear in three of the five lines, but again the fragment only speaks of the power of god, and we know nothing of its purpose. In 109–10, which is a prayer that the Thebans may continue in peace, the metre is 'aeolic' but again it would be possible to perceive the concealed cretics. In 105 the cretic at the beginning of the first line and in 106 the cretics at the beginning of the last two lines could perhaps be felt in their 'aeolic' surroundings, but there is much to be said for regarding them both as normal victor-odes to Sicilians.[1] The *hyporcheme* remains an unsatisfactory class, and the best that we can say is that there seems to have been a lively type of chorus with at least a cretic flavour which the Alexandrians thought they could identify.

Partheneia we know from vases (nos. 224–7) and they are described by both Bacchylides and Pindar. Bacchylides (xi, 40, 110) describes the women's choruses which the daughters of Proitos instituted after they recovered from madness, and in xiii, 83, choruses in Aegina in honour of Zeus, Aegina, and Endais, the mother of Peleus and Telamon: the dancers wear wreaths of red and purple flowers, and leap as lightly as fawns. Pindar describes the swift dance of the maidens of Delphi singing to Apollo both on the lofty rocks of Parnassos (*Paian* ii, 97) and beside the omphalos (*Paian* vi, 15).

The fragment of Telesilla (*P.M.G.* 717)[2] is certainly fast, as it is

1. Cf. R. W. Burton, *Pythian Odes of Pindar*, 122.
2. Telesilla wrote in Argos in the early fifth century. The story of *P.M.G.* 717 is given in Paus. VI, 22. Artemis escaped Alpheios by disguising herself and her nymphs so that she was unrecognizable. The hymn to the Mother of the Gods in telesilleans (*P.M.G.* 935) has been ascribed to Telesilla but may be much later.

written in the 7-syllable metre named after her, xds; it is a dialogue or a feigned dialogue like Sappho's Adonis song (140): 'But Artemis, maidens, running from Alpheios.' But Praxilla's[1] hymn to Adonis (*P.M.G.* 747) is in epic hexameters, and must have been sung by walking maidens. The Boeotian poetess Korinna, who may have been writing at the end of this period,[2] speaks of herself leading the maidens of Tanagra in songs in which she adorns old stories in a new way, giving great joy to her city (*P.M.G.* 655). She writes in monostrophic stanzas of five or six lines in ionic or choriambic dimeters. The ionic stanzas end with a 10-syllable line, a dimeter ending with short anceps and prolonged by two long syllables, which give an anaclastic effect like an anacreontic but should perhaps be regarded as a contracted catalectic metron (*P.M.G.* 654, i). Overlap is common but not universal between the second and third line and fifth and sixth line and occasional elsewhere. This does not necessarily take the predominantly 8-syllable lines out of dancing tempo. Overlap, however, only occurs five times in the sixty or so lines of two choriambic poems. The text of the second (655) has no *paragraphoi* and we cannot tell how it was divided. At first sight it looks as if the strophes had ten lines and began with a glyconic but l. 21 certainly began with four long syllables so that we have to assume that in both poems, as sometimes in the choruses of tragedy, glyconics can be substituted for choriambic dimeter B. The first poem (654, iii), which has 5-line stanzas ending with a pherecratean, has this substitution at least four times in eight stanzas.

Pindar's two surviving *partheneia* (fr. 94) are both written for the same Theban family of Aioladas; both are in triads with 'aeolic' lines of considerable length. In the first the syllable count is 15, 10, 21 for the strophe and 23, 22 for the antistrophe; in the second 24, 15, 6 for the strophe and 22, 14 for the antistrophe. Both are in walking tempo, and the second is a processional in which the family carried sprays of laurel to the temple of Apollo Ismenios. The procession is described in the song, which Pindar, like Alkman before him, puts in the mouth of the chorus. The chorus themselves carry sprays of laurel, and wear wreaths; they are led by a granddaughter of Aioladas, and in front of her walks the grandson of Aioladas. According to the description of

1. Praxilla wrote in Sikyon about the middle of the fifth century.
2. Cf. A. E. Harvey, *C.Q.* 5, 1955, 176.

this ceremony in Proclus this boy, who must have both parents alive, wears a golden wreath and a long chiton stretching to his ankles. He carries a laurel spray, and he in his turn follows a near relative (not mentioned at any rate in the preserved portion of the Pindaric poem) who carries a yellow staff to which are attached wreaths of flowers and two bronze balls one larger and one smaller.

Here for once we really see something of the ceremony for which a Pindaric processional ode was written.[1] Other processional songs were classified by the Alexandrians as *prosodia*. Only scanty fragments remain but enough to show that both Pindar and Bacchylides wrote in long lines[2] which would admirably suit what we have called the processional choruses on vases.

Bacchylides has left nothing that has been classified as a *partheneion*, but among his so-called dithyrambs (under which title the Alexandrians collected narrative poetry which they could not otherwise classify) is a description of the marriage of Idas and Marpessa in Sparta (20), which starts 'Once in Sparta fair-haired Lacedaemonian girls sang a song like this', and this beginning very much suggests that it was sung by girls at a contemporary marriage. The marriage of Idas and Marpessa is a mythological parallel, like the marriage of Hektor and Andromache in Sappho's marriage-song (44). Unfortunately the ends of all the eleven surviving lines are lost, but the sense suggests that the lines were quite short enoplians of 8–10 syllables in dancing tempo.

A *paian*, as we have seen, is both a song to avert an evil and a song of thanksgiving when the evil has been averted. After Salamis in 480 the young Sophocles, 'naked and anointed, led the victory songs with a lyre for those who were singing the *paian*'. The story is told in the ancient *Life* (3) and by Athenaeus (I, 20 f.). It is surely not fanciful to remember Theseus with his lyre leading the dance of Athenian boys and girls after their escape from the Minotaur (no. 114). We do not know what they sang, and the fragments of a hymn which may have been sung after Marathon in 490 (*P.M.G.* 932) only show that Datis and his proud Achaemenids learnt by their sufferings, a good Aeschylean sentiment;

1. See text in Färber II, 55. Pindar himself wrote a similar song for his own family (94c).
2. Pindar frs. 89, 91–4; Bacchylides frs. 11–13. All dactylo-epitrite except Bacchylides frs. 11–12.

the metre seems to have been largely dactylic but occasionally the lines ended in single-short.

Fragments survive of more than twenty-two songs by Pindar which the Alexandrians classed as *paians*. The external marks are the occurrence of the word *paian* in some form, the use of the cult cry *iê* or *iêie*, and perhaps also use of or allusion to the rhythm which was named paeon after the *paian*. This was in fact the cretic with the first or second long resolved, so that further confusion with the *hyporcheme* was possible.[1] Only the end of Pindar's First *Paian* survives, saying that the time has come for the festival of Apollo (Ismenios) and praying that Thebes may flourish in discipline and good order. The last epode is introduced by *iê*, *iê*, and the paeonic rhythm can be heard six times in ten periods. Too little is left to make the periodization clear, but the metre is predominantly single-short with an outburst of double-short at the end of the epode.

In the Second *Paian* Pindar writes in the person of the Abderitan chorus which prays to Apollo for success in impending war. In the first strophe the song is called a *paian*, and the refrain is repeated at the end of each epode. The metrical form of the 18-syllable final period is xd'sd'sdx, but the repeated refrain *iê*, *ie Paian* divides this into three segments, each xdx, which is repeated as part of the metrical pattern again and again all through the triad. The paeonic rhythm itself occurs at the beginning of the third line in the strophe and antistrophe and of the sixth line in the epode. The whole is in Pindaric aeolic with recognizable aeolic elements and longish periods, 16 syllables once in the strophe and 18 syllables twice in the epode.

The Fourth *Paian* for the Keians to Apollo of Delos tells the story of Euxantios, who renounced a Cretan kingdom in fear of war with the gods. Too much is lost to see how this fitted in with a prayer for peace or a thanksgiving for averted war. The refrain recurs as the last period of the epode in the metrical form xs'dx, but this does not repeat elsewhere in the metrical pattern. The paeonic rhythm is alluded to three times in the strophe–antistrophe and three times in the epode. In general there is more enoplian–prosodiac than glyconic in this poem. The strophe–antistrophe ends with a 36-syllable period and the epode begins with a 21-syllable period. The other Delian *Paian* (V), perhaps

1. Cf. above, p. 95

written for the Athenians, is completely different. It is monostrophic and written in the simplest dactylo-epitrite, predominantly in double-short. The four short lines climax in a 15-syllable last line so that it could surely be danced. It ends with a prayer to Apollo and Artemis to receive the singer and his *paian*, and the refrain occupies the first line of each stanza. Its form is xddx, and so is echoed by the dd in each line of the dactylo-epitrite stanza.

The Sixth *Paian* is a much more elaborate affair with three 37-line triads in 'aeolic'. Pindar wrote it for the Aeginetans in 490 B.C. to be sung at the Panhellenic theoxenia which the Delphians offered to Apollo to avert a famine (61). The refrain comes at the end of the second epode and separates the story of Neoptolemos' punishment from Pindar's praise of Aegina (121). At the very end he prays to Apollo as *Paian* to accept a banquet of lawful food from a wise poet. The refrain, '*iê*, sing *iê* now, in the measure of *paians* sing *iê*, young men', is the end of the 30-syllable last period of the epode, which runs sd′sd′sxsd′ssd. The blunt transitions are all bridged by word-overlap, and the refrain itself starts within a metrical unit with xsd. If it has an element of pattern which is recognizable through the ode, it is probably xdx, which recurs three times in the last period and constantly earlier, though generally slightly disguised as being part of a longer unit. The paeonic rhythm itself never occurs isolated, but is recognizable as an element in other rhythms particularly where Pindar resolves a long syllable unexpectedly or even abnormally as in the beginning of the last period of the epode where sd is abnormally —⌣◠⌣⌣—.[1] Most of the elements within the periods are of the normal aeolic type as is indicated by the frequency of xdx which expands either way into sdx or xds, but once in the strophe–antistrophe and once in the epode Pindar bursts into a long run of dactylic prosodiacs. In the epode (8) this produces the unremarkable period ddddds (18 syllables), but in the strophe–antistrophe (8) an enormous nearly symmetrical period of 47 syllables starting and ending in single-short ss′ddxddd′dddxdd′s′s. The blunt transitions are as usual bridged over by word-overlap. The last s but one has its first syllable resolved so that it could be felt as a further

---

1. Note also 149 which gives the paeonic effect in one instance at the end of the fourth period of the strophe, and more normally the beginning of the third period of the epode and the junction between dactyls and iambic close in the eighth period of the strophe.

dactyl followed by ʌs's, a transition which can be paralleled in Sophocles.[1] In fact, however, here the s's is clearly a balancing and slowing-up of the initial ss.

The last *paian* of which anything useful can be said, the Ninth, sung to beg Ismenian Apollo for prosperity after the eclipse of 463 B.C., has much more double-short than any of the others, and the prevailing rhythm in the strophe–antistrophe is prolonged glyconic (cf. Sappho, 110, 131.)

The only classified *paian* of Bacchylides of which it is possible to make anything is the Fourth written for Asine in honour of Apollo and telling the foundation legend of Asine. Nothing in the text shows that it was a *paian*, but we only have parts of three triads. They show, however, that the poem was written in dactylo-epitrites of the simplest and most regular kind. Much better preserved and much more interesting metrically is the story of Theseus and the ring of Minos (17). This is classified as a dithyramb, but the end makes it almost certain that it is a *paian*: when Theseus appeared again from the sea, the Athenian boys and girls 'sang a *paian* with lovely voices. Delian Apollo, be cheered by the chorus of Keians and grant them heaven-sent good fortune.' With this clue it is justifiable to interpret the paeonic rhythm which appears in almost every period right through the poem as an allusion to its purpose. If we ask what has 'Theseus and Minos' got to do with Apollo, the first answer would no doubt be that it was an Athenian story and Delos was now the centre of the Athenian empire, but it would also be fair to remember that after killing the Minotaur, for which the voyage to Crete recounted in this poem was a preparation, Theseus dedicated a statue of Aphrodite on Delos and danced the Geranos round Apollo's altar.

The colometry of the papyrus is not satisfactory, and we should probably recognize thirteen periods in the strophe–antistrophe and sixteen in the epode. With this colometry there are only four smooth transitions from period to period in the strophe–antistrophe and only one in the epode. Inside the periods there are a very large number of blunt junctions (true long juxtaposed to true long) because this poem is

---

1. Cf. A. M. Dale, *L.M.* 37 f. In Sophocles' *Electra* 190 the dactylic tetrameter runs out into a syncopated iambic clausula. Nearer still are the unique lines, *O.C.* 216 ff., cf. *L.M.*[2] 138.

a sort of symphony in cretic–paeonic and has only a single period of double-short, the seventh (l. 10) in the strophe–antistrophe, dssxddxss (22 syllables). Of the rest the 18-syllable first period may be taken as typical. It runs ss′ss′s′ss; the resolved first syllable gives a paeonic opening, and the rhythm recurs in the lone s, which has its second long resolved.

This elaborate and beautiful song is a *paian* and not a dithyramb. The little Idas and Marpessa (20) may very well have been a marriage song. For the *Antenoridai* (15), which is in simple dactylo-epitrite triads, the evidence, if any, is lost in the lacunae. The story of Herakles and Deianeira appears to have no relevance either to Dionysos or to Apollo (16), but the opening makes it clear that the poem was a dithyramb sung at Delphi during Apollo's winter absence. It consists of a single triad in 'aeolic'. The strophe–antistrophe opens with a telesillean, xds, and this rhythm is repeated in the sixth period of the epode but most of the rest is in dactyls or headless dactyls with an occasional single-short close (prosodiac-enoplian). It is interesting that in the third period of the strophe–antistrophe and the third period of the epode the juxtaposition of d and resolved s gives the same transition from dactyls to iambics as in the long period of Pindar's Sixth *Paian*. Here the periods run up to 21, 22 and 25 syllables so that probably this dithyramb is in walking tempo.

The arrival of Theseus in Athens (18) may be a dithyramb sung at the Thargelia in Athens because Theseus had a legendary connection with this festival, but the connection (through Androgeos, son of Minos) is extremely weak. Formally it is unique because the first and third stanzas consist of questions which are answered in the second and fourth stanzas. To give the answers the chorus take on the character of Aigeus (he is addressed at the beginning as 'King of holy Athens'). Kenyon suggested that the questioner was Medeia, and the Athenians would know full well why Medeia was interested in the arrival of Theseus and what she proposed to do about it. It may be relevant that marble reliefs of the second century B.C.,[1] which supported a bronze tripod, are decorated with Aigeus, Medeia and Theseus; they may have celebrated a Hellenistic choir's victory with a revival of this dithyramb. We do not know the ancestry of this dialogue form, but there is some

1. Athens Agora S7327. *The Athenian Agora*, XI, pl. 30.

analogy in the fragment of Telesilla quoted earlier in this chapter. Metrically this poem is beautifully simple. The first three periods of each strophe consist of two aeolic elements, a glyconic followed by an extended glyconic, then a short period of one glyconic, then longer periods again of the same kind, and finally two periods, each of an extended glyconic.[1]

Lastly, Dithyramb 19 is headed Io for the Athenians. In a single triad Bacchylides describes Io's persecution and flight ending with the birth of Epaphos, from whom Dionysos is descended. It is a simple and easy little poem, in which the poet evidently delights in his ingenuity in starting with Inachos of Argos and ending with Dionysos, 'the lord of wreathed choruses'. There is no reason why it should not have been written for the City Dionysia and it probably gives us a better idea than any other surviving poem what the poems in this festival, at which ten choruses of men and ten choruses of boys competed, were like. Metrically,[2] the song combines normal aeolic elements, such as dss and sdss, and dactylo-epitrite elements like ddx. The periods range from a shortest of 8 syllables to a longest of 23 syllables, and are woven together into a very pretty and easily appreciated whole; it is noticeable that there is only a single blunt junction in all the ten periods, and that is in the long fourth period (l. 8) which runs xdd'dssxssx.

Pindar's Athenian dithyrambs were discussed in the last section. The Theban dithyramb, which starts with an allusion to Lasos of Hermione (fr. 70),[3] is by our standards a strange poem: the new dithyramb is compared to a concert of the gods which is a wild bacchic rite; then Pindar claims to be sent by the Muse to pray for Thebes where Dionysos was born. What is not clear is how Pindar got from here to Herakles' descent to Hades which gave the poem its title. We have two stanzas, each of fifteen longish dactylo-epitrite periods, but we cannot say whether the poem was triadic or not. The dactylo-epitrites are fairly regular, but it should perhaps be noted that the third and tenth periods begin with headless dactyls and that only just under half the periods are joined by a smooth transition.

Another poem about Herakles has no classification, and nothing in

1. For details see A. M. Dale, C.Q. 1, 1951, 25, 26 = *Collected Papers*, 71, 72.
2. Analysed by A. M. Dale, C.Q. 1, 1951, 120 = *Collected Papers*, 82.
3. Cf. above, p. 91. On a possibility that *P.Oxy.* 2622 belongs see H. Lloyd-Jones, *Maia*, 19, 1967, 217.

the surviving text of parts of two triads suggests a classification; this is the famous account of the labours of Herakles as an example of *Nomos* (fr. 169). Here Pindar emphasized the violence of Herakles' treatment of Diomedes and Geryon, who were fighting in defence of their own possessions, and nevertheless found some justification; the text breaks off with Herakles going on his twelfth labour alone, while Iolaos buries Amphitryon in Thebes. It seems to me a possible conjecture that, whether the twelfth labour was the quest of the golden apples or the fetching of Kerberos from Hades, the poem went on with the translation of Herakles to heaven, so that belief in the immortality of Herakles is the *nomos* which justifies his whole violent life. It seems possible on the analogy of the Theban dithyramb already discussed that this story of Herakles could also have occurred in a Theban dithyramb.[1] But it might also be argued that the reference to Amphitryon's grave is an indication that it was sung there, or that the opening paeon and the other instances of this scansion prove that it was a *paian*. We can only say that we do not know the occasion of this very interesting poem. Metrically the ode is aeolic of the kind that comprises both aeolo-choriambic and prolonged double-short elements; much is uncertain in the unsatisfactory state of the text, particularly in the epode, but the strophe-antistrophe after opening in short periods has two longer periods from l. 5, xsxs'ds, ddddx, and ends with two long periods xs'dd'sx (here again the first long of the last s is resolved so that it can sound like dactyls fading into iambics), s'dddxsx; these last two periods are 16 and 18 syllables long so that the whole probably is, as one would expect from its character, in walking rather than dancing tempo.

Among other types of song the *threnoi* or dirges of Pindar are all in normal slow-moving dactylo-epitrite with long lines; one of them was written for an Athenian, Hippokrates (fr. 137). Praises of men other than victor-odes were classed by the Alexandrians as *enkomia*. As we have seen already, they were generally meant to be sung at symposia, and it is generally impossible to say whether they were designed for a chorus or not. Two of Pindar's are in short dancing aeolics and are certainly symposion songs (frs. 127-8). The rest are in dactylo-epitrite with lines of moderate length, 15-19 syllables; one is certainly triadic

1. Cf. on this fragment particularly W. Theiler, *Mus. Helv.* 22, 69-80; M. Ostwald, *H.S.C.P.* 69, 1965, 109.

(fr. 123) and one certainly monostrophic (fr. 124a, b). The songs to Hiero of Syracuse and Thero of Akragas were probably to be sung at a symposion after an athletic victory (frs. 118–19, 124d–6). The song for Xenophon of Corinth (fr. 122), who won a prize at Olympia in 464, does not belong here at all. Although Pindar himself calls it a *skolion*, the text makes it quite clear that it was sung in Aphrodite's precinct at Corinth when Xenophon dedicated the hundred prostitutes which he had vowed to the goddess if he was successful.

Bacchylides fr. 20c was sent to Hiero after the foundation of Aitna in 475, and after a victory in a horse-race at Olympia, possibly in 472. Here the intention is entirely clear. Bacchylides is 'sending' his song to Aitna, and it is meant for fellow-drinkers. How it was to be performed we, of course, do not know. It is monostrophic. It is in simple dactylo-epitrite stanzas with six periods, the first 21 and the second 16 syllables long.

It is impossible to discuss all the victor-odes, and what follows is a selection chosen chiefly because they tell us something about the details of performance, and particularly when we have more than one ode celebrating the same victory. The main distinction is between the song sung at the games immediately after the victory and the song sung when the victor has returned home. But the song sung at home may be sung at a shrine or at the victor's house or in some public place, and there is the further class of songs sent by the poet and performed without him.[1] In 476 Thero of Akragas won a chariot victory at Olympia which Pindar celebrated with the Second *Olympian*.[2] It is remarkable for being entirely in single-short except for the last line of the strophe–antistrophe, which runs xs'sxsd. Otherwise the dominant movement is s's's, with a great many blunt transitions between the elements. There are five triads of twenty periods. Pindar twice mentions the lyre (1, 47), and it may have been sung to a pure lyre accompaniment. The fragmentary song for Thero in dactylo-epitrite, which we have mentioned already (fr. 118), starts 'I wish to tell the children of the Greeks'; this would be a fitting beginning if Pindar were introducing the Sicilian at a Panhellenic assembly, and this may therefore be the remains of the song sung at Olympia immediately after the victory. Yet another song

1. Cf. above, pp. 84, 86.
2. Analysed A. M. Dale, *C.Q.* 1, 1951, 29 = *Collected Papers*, 78.

which certainly celebrates this victory is the Third *Olympian*, and this was written for a Theoxenia (cf. above, p. 100), since Herakles is prayed to come to this feast with the Dioskouroi (37). This ode has three triads fifteen lines long in regular dactylo-epitrites. The longer lines have 19, 20 and 24 syllables, so that this is certainly a stately song. *Olympian* II is also probably meant for 'walking' rather than dancing but its syllable count does not rise above 17. This is an interesting case where we probably have three songs for a single victory, the song at the festival itself in dactylo-epitrites, the song at the palace in a very remarkable version of 'aeolic', and the song at a shrine in Akragas in dactylo-epitrite, which Pindar curiously calls 'discovering a new manner of fitting to the Dorian sandal the joyous voice of the victory song' (4). He goes on to describe it as a mixture of 'bright-voiced lyre and cry of flutes and arrangement of words' suitable for Thero. In view of the emphasis on the lyre in *Olympian* II, is it perhaps the mixture of lyre and flute which constitutes the difference in this song? At any rate the Dorian sandal must mean that Pindar regarded dancing dactylo-epitrite rhythm as Dorian.

In 476 also Hiero of Syracuse won an Olympian victory with his racehorse. Pindar celebrated the victory with *Olympian* I.[1] He speaks of himself as coming to the hearth of Hiero, so that this is a palace song, and it is sung at a banquet (16). He takes his 'Dorian lyre' (17) and 'crowns the victor with Aeolian song' (100). Aeolian in Pindar seems to be a musical rather than a metrical term, since in fr. 191 he speaks of the 'Aeolian flute entering the Dorian path of hymns', which would naturally mean that he proposed to sing in dactylo-epitrite rhythm (the metre of the fragment) and in the Aeolian mode. So here too the mode was presumably Aeolian, but he speaks of his Dorian lyre, although the metre is 'aeolic'. There are two possible explanations: either Hiero and his audience would take a reference to a dactylo-epitrite song sung immediately after the victory at Olympia, or Pindar regards himself as naturally writing in Dorian dactylo-epitrite as being a pupil of Lasos of Hermione. But the First *Olympian* is in 'aeolic' and a kind of aeolic that we know well, largely made up of glyconic and extended glyconic elements with one period with a run of dactyls and the last four periods of the strophe–antistrophe in single-

1. Analysed A. M. Dale, *C.Q.* 1, 1951, 22 = *Collected Papers*, 64.

1. Geometric fragment from Argos (p. 7, no. 44)

2. Corinthian skyphos (p. 11, no. 76)

3. Attic black-figure kylix by the Heidelberg painter (p. 14, no. 102)

4. Shoulder-picture of Attic black-figure lekythos by the Amasis painter
(p. 16, no. 122)

5. Shoulder-picture of Attic black-figure lekythos by the Amasis painter
(p. 16, no. 123)

6. Attic black-figure neck-amphora (p. 20, no. 159)

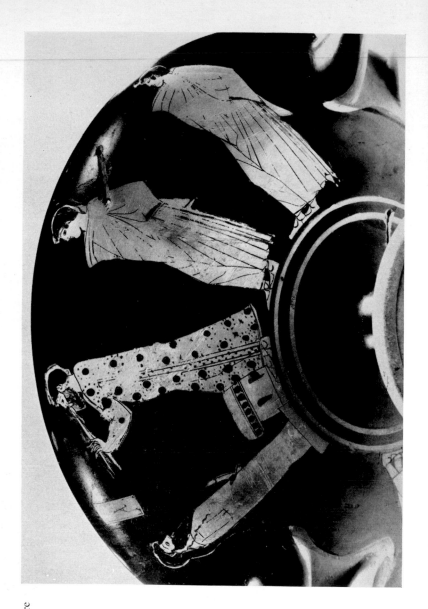

7. Attic red-figure
cup (p. 22,
no. 192)

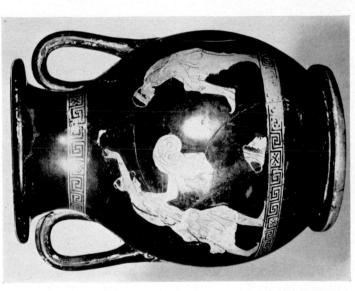

9. Attic red-figure bell-krater by Polion (p. 28, no. 244)

8. Attic red-figure pelike by Phiale painter
(p. 27, no. 237)

10. Attic red-figure kalyx-krater by the Dinos painter (p. 28, no. 250)

11. Attic marble relief (p. 32, no. 288c)

short. There are four triads, each thirty periods long and individual periods run up to 21 syllables in the strophe–antistrophe and 18 syllables in the epode. For the same victory Bacchylides *sent* his fifth Epinician Ode to Hiero (10, 197). Perhaps we cannot press the phrase 'send to your famous city' and say for certain that it was for public performance rather than for performance at the palace or at a shrine. It has five triads, each nineteen periods long, going up to 23 syllables in the strophe–antistrophe and 21 syllables in the epode. They are in regular dactylo-epitrite; the only variations are the blunt transitions from dd to s in the first period of the strophe–antistrophe (and in the sixth and seventh periods of all except the first pair) and from d to s in the first period and from dd to s in the fifth period of the epode; except in the last, these blunt junctions are generally bridged by word-overlap.

In the same year 476 another western Greek, Hagesidamos of Lokroi, won a victory in the boy's boxing match, and Pindar wrote the single triad of the Eleventh *Olympian* for immediate performance. This is in regular dactylo-epitrite (except for the single d instead of dd at the end of the third period of the strophe–antistrophe). 'There join the praises' in l. 16 is an appeal to the Muses to come to Olympia. This interpretation is confirmed by the much longer 'aeolic' song, *Olympian* X, which Pindar excuses himself for sending to Lokroi much later (1 ff.). At the end (99) Pindar looks back to the victory: 'I praise the lovely son of Archestratos, whom I saw winning by the strength of his arm beside the Olympian altar at that time, when he was lovely to look at in the bloom of youth.' The ode has five triads in a rather difficult 'aeolic' with a few recognizable 'glyconics', a good many resolutions, including resolutions of long anceps and of the frame of a choriamb, and a great many blunt junctions within the period. It would seem that Pindar repaid his debt by an unusually elaborate song. Again he stresses the mixture of lyre and flute (93). The song has come to light in Thebes, and it *will* resound to the flute (84), so that it is probably safe to suppose that Pindar sent it to Lokroi to be performed by the local chorus in his absence.

In 470 Hiero won a Pythian chariot race, and Bacchylides celebrated the victory at Delphi with a tiny song (IV) of two 'aeolic' stanzas. Most of the elements are familiar, but the second and third periods start with dactylic runs. The second period, which is 24 syllables long, should be taken as ddd's'sds's. Pindar wrote the song to be sung in Sicily, the First *Pythian*. That it is a palace song is clear from the description of Phalaris at the end: 'No lyres beneath his roof receive him in sweet harmony with the voices of boys' implies that the reverse is true of Hiero, and that this is a palace song. As the emphasis is on Aitna all the way through, Aitna is the probable place, the new palace of Hiero's son Deinomenes rather than the old palace of Hiero at Syracuse. The song starts with the splendid invocation to the lyre as the controller both of the steps of the chorus and of their voices, their steps because it gives the dance rhythm (the metre), their voices because it gives the melody. The five triads are in stately dactylo-epitrites with lines of 21, 23 and 30 syllables in the strophe–antistrophe. There are rather more blunt junctions within the period than usual, and the second period of the strophe–antistrophe shows at the end what can only be either a contracted d or a dragged s, presumably the latter; the whole period runs sxd'sxdds.

We have noticed already the charming fragment of the song written by Pindar for the dedication of the prostitutes vowed by Xenophon of Corinth if he won an Olympic victory in 464 (fr. 122). That song is monostrophic and in dactylo-epitrite. In the Thirteenth *Olympian* Pindar asks Zeus to continue Xenophon's good fortune and accept from him the customary praise of the crowns that he won (28). It looks therefore as if this song was sung in the precinct of Zeus in Corinth. It is unique in having a mixture of dactylo-epitrite and aeolic.[1] Bacchylides in 468 wrote his third Epinician in honour of Hiero's victory in the Olympic horse-race; in its six triads the strophe–antistrophe is in aeolic, and the epode in dactylo-epitrite. But in the Thirteenth *Olympian* Pindar 'melts into orthodox dactylo-epitrite in the middle of the sixth period of the strophe' after an 'aeolic' beginning. The sixth period runs xsdxsxdd's. The epode is in orthodox dactylo-epitrite throughout.

The Fourth and Fifth *Pythian* both celebrate the victory of Arkesilas of Cyrene in 462. The Fifth is sung in the garden of Aphrodite (24): it is therefore a shrine song. It is in 'aeolic' with recognizable aeolic elements and many of the characteristic blunt junctions. The strophe–antistrophe could well be in dance-time as only a single period has as

---

1. Analysed A. M. Dale, C.Q. 1, 1951, 21 = *Collected Papers*, 63 f.

many as 15 syllables, but the epode has one period of 18 syllables and a final period of 19. The immense Fourth *Pythian* of thirteen triads was sung at Arkesilas' palace (1–2) and contains Pindar's very special appeal to him. The dactylo-epitrites are very regular except for runs of three dactyls instead of two in the fourth and sixth periods of the strophe–antistrophe and the fifth period of the epode. The periods run to 23, 20 and 18 syllables in the strophe–antistrophe and 18, 19 and 20 syllables in the epode, so that there is no doubt that this song is in walking tempo.

For 456 and 452 we have two odes by Bacchylides, in each year one sung at the place of victory and one sung at home. Epinikian II is a tiny 'aeolic' poem for a boxer from Keos sung after the Isthmian games; the structure of the strophe–antistrophe is interesting. It opens with a catalectic iambo-choriambic trimeter, and then has two choriambic dimeters, a glyconic and a pherecratean, all linked together by word-overlap. Except for minor variations the four lines of the epode match these four lines of the strophe but have no word-overlap, so that one would naturally take them as four short periods in dance tempo. It is therefore tempting to suppose that the strophe and antistrophe were also danced and that the four lines are not one vast period in the normal sense but four lines linked together by a variety of the climaxing technique which we have seen before. The First Epinikian is a long poem with a local Keian myth sung at home for the same victory. It is in regular dactylo-epitrites with 15–16 syllable lines in the strophe–antistrophe going up to a 28-syllable period in the epode (157), which runs sxddxddxsxsx. In the little song sung at the festival Bacchylides writes 'all that we displayed in the company of seventy wreaths'. If the wreaths belong to the festival chorus, as presumably they must, this is our one indication of the size of a festival chorus.

Again for a Keian Olympic victor in 452 we have two songs, VI and VII, both of only two stanzas, the first 'aeolic' and the second dactylo-epitrite. The second is very badly preserved but enough remains to show that the dactylo-epitrites are perfectly regular, and the last period but one runs to 25 syllables. The poet addresses the sixteenth day of the Olympian month, the day on which the wreaths of victory were given. This very particular reference rather suggests that this was the song sung at the festival itself. The 'aeolic' song speaks of the victory and its celebration in the past, and says that 'a hymn now honours you with a song before the house for your victory'. This, then, is the song sung in Keos at the victor's house. The periodization is not entirely clear but this seems to be a gay song, which one would expect to be danced. The first two lines cannot be run together into a single period without spoiling the effect of the pun on Lachon's name. Probably we should recognize five short lines, climaxing in a 23-syllable close, sds′sds′dsx, with all its blunt junctions bridged by word-overlap.

Finally in the very late Eighth *Pythian*[1] of 446, Pindar refers back to the ode sung in Delphi after the victory: 'Apollo received him crowned with Parnassian laurel and a Dorian song of Praise' (18), and as Pindar speaks of himself setting out for Delphi (58) he probably composed it himself. 'Dorian' implies, as we have seen, dactylo-epitrite in contrast to the 'aeolic' of the song sung at home in Aegina. Perhaps the final prayer for freedom for Aegina 'with the goodwill of Zeus, Aiakos, Peleus, Telamon, and Achilles' (99) implies that the song was sung, like the fifth and eighth *Nemean*, at the Aiakeion. Metrically this song contains the normal elements of 'aeolic': sd and ds prolonged on either side by further s elements, a certain amount of resolution (once in the frame of a choriamb), blunt junctions often bridged by word-overlap. What is remarkable, however, is the number of times that the short syllable of an s is dragged in one or more of its appearances in the five triads. In the seven periods of the strophe–antistrophe there are three such permissive drags and in the six periods of the epode six, one of which occurs all through the ode. Probably by this time the periodic style was so familiar that such licences were readily accepted by the chorus. The period-lengths vary from 7 to 14 syllables in the strophe–antistrophe, and from 13 to 16 in the epode; but this is a long and complicated song and probably we should be justified in thinking that it, like the vast majority of the victor-odes, was performed in walking time rather than in dancing time.

To turn from the victor-odes of Pindar to the choruses of the *Persae*, the earliest surviving play of Aeschylus, is to move into a completely different world. This is the more surprising when we consider how pervasive the periodic style was. Victor-odes, *paians, threnoi, partheneia*, and dithyrambs, as far as we can see, were written in the same musical,

1. Analysed A. M. Dale, *C.Q.* I, 1951, 25 = *Collected Papers*, 71.

metrical, and dance style. On our evidence in Athens itself dithyrambs were written in periodic style for the City Dionysia, the festival at which tragedies were produced. How the actual periods of tragic lyric differ from the periods of Pindar must be considered in more detail later, but first a more obvious distinction stands out. All the non-dramatic lyric of Early Classical date is either monostrophic (i.e. repeated stanzas of identical metrical shape) or triadic, consisting of repeated identical triads of strophe, antistrophe, and epode. Dramatic lyric has pairs of strophe–antistrophe, and the pairs differ from each other in metrical shape (I omit for the moment recitative anapaests and trochaics, and lyric dialogues between actor and chorus, because they belong to a different tradition). It is, I suppose, arguable that the typical tragic *stasimon* with its three or more pairs of metrically different shape is the invention of Aeschylus because in fact we have no complete dramatic chorus earlier than Aeschylus. We should then, I think, have to suppose an original form of antistrophic *stasimon* modelled on the analogy of the leader–chorus performances[1] in which the leader sang, recited, or spoke, the chorus responded with strophe a, the leader continued and the chorus responded with antistrophe a, the leader continued and the chorus responded with strophe b, and so on. This form of lyric dialogue survives in tragedy and in comedy. The creation of the *stasimon* consisted of omitting the solos and putting the pairs of strophe–antistrophe together into a single system which then had metrically diverse pairs. This is only a possibility, and if it happened we cannot say whether it was Aeschylus who did it or Phrynichos or Thespis or whether it was a known form of choral song before the invention of tragedy. The other pointer backwards from the lyric of preserved tragedy is the curious convention that tragic choral lyric, as distinct from recitative and dialogue, is in Dorian dialect, or, to be more accurate, is faintly stylized as Dorian. This must mean that at some moment the Attic tragic poets felt that Dorian was the right dialect for choral song in the same sense that epic–ionic was always the right dialect for hexameters. It seems most unlikely that the choral lyric of tragedy was restyled in this way once tragedy was established, and so we are almost compelled to suppose that the moment was when Thespis started competing in 534. It is too early for Lasos of Hermione

---

1. Cf. above, p. 49.

who was only born 548–545. But Stesichoros, as we have seen,[1] was
known and was popular in Athens, and Arion was performing in
Corinth in the early sixth century. Metrically Stesichoros may be
relevant, but formally his repeating triads have nothing to do with
tragedy. Arion's 'stationary' dithyrambs[2] may have been monostrophic like Bacchylides' Aigeus (18), but it is always possible that they
were antistrophic with successive pairs in different metres like the
choruses of drama (but then the contrast with Lasos of Hermione's
triadic dithyramb is not so clear as it is if Arion's dithyramb was monostrophic). At least Stesichoros and Arion provide us with a possible
source for the Doric dialect of tragic choruses. One other possible
source for the form should be noticed. Aristophanes (see below, p. 189)
has a number of hymns in which the chorus call on different gods in
different metres. This may enshrine an old form of chorus, such as the
songs which were sung at the altar of the Twelve Gods at the Dionysia
(Xen. *Hipp*. iii, 2), and the origin of the form of the tragic chorus may
lie here. But we have in fact no evidence for the particular form of
tragic choruses before Aeschylus.

While the lyrics of tragedy are in Doric the recitative anapaests to
which the chorus enter in Aeschylus' *Persians* and *Agamemnon* are in
Attic. These anapaestic dimeters with inserted paroemiacs and monometers are an old marching metre, as we have seen.[3] Phrynichos'
Phoinissai takes us back four years before the *Persians*, and its female
chorus entered to anapaestic dimeters (9N). His *Alkestis* is not dated:
there the chorus described Herakles struggling with Death (2N), in
what may have been a choral exit (*exodos*), again anapaestic dimeters.
The vases give us evidence for anapaestic entrances in comedy or pre-
comedy.[4] The late references to the four-sided or rectangular dramatic
choruses with their ranks and files probably only refer to their entry
and exit and not to their dances in the orchestra.[5]

The three other quotations from choruses by Phrynichos are all in
different metres and are all undated. The fragment about the light of
love on red cheeks (13N) refers to Troilos and scans xddxsx, a dactylo-
epitrite verse found in Stesichoros but not until Sophocles' *Antigone* in

---

1. Cf. above, p. 80.   2. Cf. above, p. 68.
3. Cf. above, p. 62.   4. Cf. above, p. 93.
5. Texts in *P.C.F.*[2] 239. The words 'four-sided chorus' are used by Timaios (Ath. 181c)
of the Lakonistai; we know nothing about them but they may have sung marching songs.

preserved drama. The account of Meleager's death in the *Pleuroniai* (6N) is in greater asclepiads, sd'd'ds, found in Sappho (e.g. 140) and Alkaios, but again not in preserved plays until Sophocles. What seems to be an account of the Danaids murdering the sons of Aigyptos (14–15N) is in catalectic ionic tetrameters. Ionics we have seen already in the Lesbian poets and in Anakreon. In general ionic choruses in tragedy seem to be given to Orientals, like the councillors in the *Persae*, or to women like the chorus of the *Septem*, or to both like the daughter of Danaos in the *Suppliant Women* and the maenads of the *Bacchae*.[1] On our evidence the catalectic tetrameter is not found again until Sophocles (*O.T.* 487).

Aeschylus' *Persians* was produced in 472 with the *Phineus* and the *Glaukos Potnieus*. After sixty-four lines of marching anapaestic dimeters the chorus of Persian elders sing three pairs of strophe–antistrophe and a mesode (between the second and third pair, but transposed after the third pair in the Oxford text) in ionics and then two pairs in iambo-trochaics. The first two pairs confidently describe the army; the mesode gives the theory of Ate; the third pair applies the theory; the two iambo-trochaic pairs describe future disaster and present disillusion. Thus the content is beautifully adapted to the rhythmical structure. The ionic pairs differ from each other in length and arrangement (but it is not always clear where we should speak of two dimeters and where of one tetrameter), and each, including the mesode, has a different clausula: the first a syncopated pentameter (71–2), the second an ana-clastic tetrameter (85–6), the mesode a catalectic tetrameter (99–100 = 113–14), the third a catalectic anaclastic pentameter (105–7 = 97–9). The first iambo-trochaic pair (115) consists of two periods separated by an interjection; the first is sss'sss, and the second sss'sss's'sss. The second iambo-trochaic pair (126) is best taken as three periods: s's'sss, s's's'sss, ʌsxssxdd'ssx. The dominant element is the lekythion, sss, and the single-short rhythm is only broken by the hemiepes just before the end. All through the ode each pair has one or more long lines so that the whole is probably walking tempo rather than dancing tempo. It is all very simple and intelligible, and only the second iambo-trochaic pair has something of the complexity of the Pindaric periodic style, but on a very small scale.

1. Note also two fragments from Aeschylus, *Heliades* 69, 71N[2].

When the messenger with the news of Salamis arrives, there is a brief lyric dialogue between him and the chorus which takes the old Homeric form of lament.[1] Here it is stylized so that the messenger is given two iambic trimeters (254 f.) before each of three strophes and antistrophes by the chorus. Essentially each pair sung by the chorus is in iambo-trochaic (like the conclusion of the *parodos*) with a clausula containing double-short. The first strophe and antistrophe form each a single long period: xsxs′s′s′s′dsx, 24 syllables. Pause is certain between the third and fourth lines of the second pair, and it is natural to take the whole as four short lines: it opens with ss, which in this resolved form may be either dochmiac or hypodochmiac and it is interesting to see this isolated first appearance of what is to become one of the most distinctive metres of drama. The close is hipponactean followed by pherecratean. In the third pair Pause is certain between the second and third lines and probably all four should be regarded as separate. In the antistrophe the manuscripts give the last line as ddsx, and perhaps the strophe should be emended to correspond. Except for the first pair, everything is in dancing tempo, if not excited dancing tempo, and probably the single period of the first pair with its many blunt transitions was danced too.

After the messenger speeches the chorus lament the disaster by themselves (532). This is still a wild lament, not a calm dirge like Simonides' *threnoi*. After an introduction in recitative anapaestic dimeters the first pair of strophe–antistrophe is again in iambo-trochaic with double-short close of two pherecrateans. The general shape is six dimeters or syncopated dimeters, of which the first and fifth are preceded by a metron with double syncopation: ––. Then two linked syncopated dimeters, and then the two pherecrateans. The second pair is in double-short till the clausula, which is a syncopated iambic dimeter with a pendant extra syllable. The punctuation is made clear by the interjections between the lines. The first line is a pendent hemiepes; the second and third are the same but with the first double-short contracted so that they are indistinguishable from pherecrateans and so make the transition to the following glyconic, which is linked to an aristophanean (dsx). The same transition occurs in the third pair, which consists of four pendent hemiepe, two pherecrateans, and an aristophanean.

1. Cf. above, p. 49. On the text, cf. Coxon, C.Q. 8, 1958, 48, and Broadhead's edition.

Hiatus divides the third hemiepes from the second, and probably we should regard the four as two periods, each ddxddx. Word-overlap joins the final aristophanean to the preceding pherecratean, but the uncertainty of the text makes it impossible to say whether the first pherecratean was separated from the second or not. The general impression is of a wild lament which becomes calmer and slower towards the end.

In the next song (623) the chorus summon up the ghost of Dareios. The first pair starts slowly with a choriambic tetrameter followed by an iambic penthemimer with the first long resolved so that it picks up the choriambs; probably the whole is a pendent choriambo-iambic pentameter (21 syllables). Then two glyconics linked by word-overlap, followed by an iambic metron and a trochaic metron (Miss Cunningham suggested to me that they were probably, as in 581, separated by an interjection, which has been lost). The second pair begins with a pendent choriambic dimeter, picking up the first pair, and goes on in ionics, ending with an alcaic decasyllable (ddsx).[1] The third pair starts with two corrupt lines which are possibly dochmiacs but more probably syncopated iambics, then a pendent choriambic dimeter known from Anakreon, dssx, then ionics again, and finally an iambic dimeter. The epode returns to lamentation, the middle lines are corrupt, but it begins and ends dactylic, ddd at the beginning and at the end d̄d̄d̄d̄d̄x, ddx. When Dareios' ghost has appeared (694), the chorus greet him with two ionic dimeters followed by a clausula, which, though it scans ʌ dddx like a paroemiac, should perhaps here be regarded as an ionic trimeter syncopated and contracted. If the hydria in Corinth (no. 222) depicts the *Persians*, it is this moment of 'ancient fear' that it shows and there is no doubt that the figures are dancing, as the metre requires.

The next song (852 ff.) devotes three pairs of strophe–antistrophe and most of the epode to the glories of Dareios' empire and only returns to the present disaster at the very end. It is predominantly dactylic and has long lines. Although some of the divisions are uncertain, the first pair certainly has two periods of 29 and 22 syllables, and the third pair has a probable 21 followed by a certain 38. The long

---

1. Alternatively 647–8 is pendent choriambic–iambic tetrameter. Then syncopated ionic trimeter, then ionic metron + alcaic decasyllable.

dactylic runs remind us of Stesichoros and Alkman. Aeschylus has three ways of slowing up his dactylic runs. In the first line (852) the eight dactyls run out in single-short as in prosodiacs, and the period ends dss. In the second period (855) link anceps mediates between hexameter A and an ithyphallic, as in dactylo-epitrite, but here both the double- and the single-short elements are much longer than in normal dactylo-epitrite. The same method is used in both periods of the second and third pair, and in the last period of the epode.[1] But in the first and second periods of the epode the dactyls simply slow up with a final spondee like the epic hexameter.

After this magnificent stately song Xerxes' arrival returns the chorus to the present and lamentation. It was a stroke of genius to crown the mounting anxiety of the play with the arrival of the man who caused the disaster, and to make him lead the final, wild, extended lamentation. Xerxes enters to recitative anapaestic dimeters and the chorus answer in the same; but then they change to melic anapaests in Dorian dialect (922).[2] These also are dimeters but end (930) with a metron consisting of six shorts and a long, which can be taken either as an anapaest or as a dochmiac according as one regards the third and fourth syllables or the second and third and the fourth and fifth syllables as resolved long. It is anapaestic if it is ∪∪ ∪̃∪ ∪∪—, but dochmiac if it is ∪ ∪̃∪ ∪̃∪ ∪—.

After this introduction three pairs of strophe–antistrophe follow n which Xerxes sings the opening lines and the chorus the remainder, then four more pairs and finally an epode, in all of which Xerxes and the chorus sing alternate lines. The epode here, as in 672 and 897 and like the mesode in 93, belongs to the whole chorus and not to the pair of strophe–antistrophe which it follows.

In the first pair both Xerxes and the chorus sing anapaests, and the 'dochmiac anapaest' appears at the end of Xerxes' part and at the end of the chorus's part and is used as a pair in the chorus's second line (936). In the second pair Xerxes sings ionics, a dimeter, and two trimeters, and the chorus sing anapaests at the beginning and end but in the middle a choriambic dimeter followed by two lekythia (sxs); the last

---

1. The only real doubt here is the transition in 865: Roger's ποταμοῦ ποτ' for the un-metrical and nonsensical reading of the MSS. would restore sense and metre.

2. On text and metre, see A. M. Dale, *Collected Papers*, 25 ff.; *L.M.*[2] 54.

metron of the final anapaests is again a dochmiac anapaest (961). In the third pair Xerxes starts each of his three lines with an iambic penthemimer (xsx); the first continues with a paroemiac, the second with a dochmiac, the third with an anaclastic ionic dimeter. The chorus sing anapaests through to the last two lines. The last line but one (985) has a dochmiac anapaest and then four long syllables (contracted anapaestic metron), the last has an iambic penthemimer and a dochmiac anapaest. The likeness of this line to Xerxes' second line (976) makes it clear that we should reckon a dochmiac here too.

From this point on Xerxes and the chorus sing alternate lines except that twice the chorus has a rather longer clausula. The first pair is pure iambic till the clausula, which is d'ssx. The second pair starts iambic, then three iambo-choriambic trimeters, an iambic dimeter then three pherecrateans, and a syncopated iambic trimeter as clausula. The third pair is pure iambic except for the aristophanean clausula (dsx). The fourth pair is pure iambic. The epode is iambic except for three lines of Xerxes; 1073 is a dochmiac, 1075 is in the best manuscript four long syllables plus four long syllables, 1076 is four long syllables plus a dochmiac. As the chorus open 1077 with two long syllables which must represent an iambic metron with double syncopation, I think the four long syllables in 1075 and 1076 should here be regarded as iambic dimeters with double contraction.

If we look back at this long lament, it is first clear that the second part, in which Xerxes and the chorus sing line for line, is much poorer metrically than the first part where they are separated. In the second part iambics dominate, and very many of them are dimeters so that the whole may be in the tempo of excited dance. In the first half the longer anapaestic dimeters predominate and they are in dancing tempo. This kind of melic anapaest appears here for the first time, but there is no reason to suppose that Aeschylus invented them; it is more likely that he took them over from the grave lament and that they were originally processional, like marching anapaests, and sung while the body was being taken to the grave. The ionics may reasonably be thought of as picking up the ionics of earlier songs.

The loss of earlier wilder laments, for which there is some evidence on vases, makes it impossible to confirm the view that they were an important source of inspiration for the early writers of tragedy. So much of this play is lamentation that although we can quote parallels for nearly all the metrical elements and therefore say that the dance steps were traditional, the parallels are mostly from songs with quite a different flavour. Only in the ode which describes Dareios' empire (852 ff.) is the emotional as well as the metrical atmosphere familiar. This is the proud description that we know from the victor songs of Pindar or the *Geryoneis* of Stesichoros, and it is interesting that metrically the affinities are with Stesichoros rather than Pindar, although the *Persae* was written twenty-six years after the earliest preserved ode of Pindar. This is some evidence that the manner of tragedy was traditional and was formed before the crystallization of the periodic style, as we know it, in Pindar.

This is not to deny innovation to Aeschylus. Not only is the combination and arrangement of traditional metrical elements uniquely designed for the particular purpose of this play, but in the dochmiac as he used it later we have a new metrical element. In this play we can almost see him introducing it. All the four forms ∪⌣̃—∪— (268), ∪⌣̃∪⌣̃∪— (930, etc.), —⌣̃∪⌣̃∪— (976, 1076), ∪—⌣̃∪— (1073) are well attested elsewhere in Aeschylus, but generally occur in pairs whereas here they are slipped in singly, all except the second in iambo-trochaic or iambic contexts. It looks as if Aeschylus felt them and expected his dancers to feel them as a variant of syncopated iambics and had not yet felt them as a new rhythm to be used on its own. The second form ∪∪∪∪∪∪— comes in with anapaests. Possibly it should be regarded as anapaestic all through, but in 986 where it follows an iambic penthemimer, which is here itself a syncopated iambic ending in true long, it would naturally be taken as a dochmiac so that the rhythm echoes Xerxes' earlier line, 976, and the pair in 936 suggests dochmiacs rather than anapaests. This is not a purely academic problem as the dancing of ∪∪ ⌣̃ ∪∪ — (anapaest) would be quite different from the dancing of ∪ ⌣̃ ⌣̃ ∪ — (dochmiac).

Of the other plays produced by Aeschylus with the *Persians*, the *Phineus*, as we have seen (no. 221), probably had a running exit of the Harpies, perhaps in trochaics. A tattered fragment of the *Glaukos Potnieus* looks like iambo-trochaics with a dactylic refrain (36 Murray). Much more interesting is a fragmentary chorus from the satyr-play, *Prometheus Pyrkaeus*. We have pictures of the satyr-chorus receiving fire from Prometheus (nos. 248–53, fig. 10), and the papyrus fragment, in which the satyrs rejoice in the gift of fire and prophesy that the nymphs will dance in honour of Prometheus, must come very near this. There are many difficulties of detail, and while it is clear that we have two verses followed by an identical refrain, it is not clear that the two verses must be emended or explained as strophe and antistrophe: they may rather be antistrophe a and strophe b, or the song may not be anti-strophic in the normal sense. But there is no doubt that it contains iambics and dochmiacs. The very short stanzas and refrains probably allow more excited dancing than the period-lengths suggest. The uneven rhythm of the dochmiacs particularly but also the syncopated iambics would admirably suit the dance postures of the satyrs. The last period of the first stanza (4 f.) is a syncopated iambic trimeter to which two dochmiacs are linked. The first period of the second stanza (9 ff.) has two dochmiacs linked to an iambic trimeter and this is followed by a further lone dochmiac. The dochmiacs are of two very common forms: ᴗ——ᴗ—, and —᷎ᴗ—ᴗ—. Again they must be felt as belonging to the iambic context and here they are twice composed in pairs. Possibly the excited dances of the satyr-play are the birthplace of the dochmiac, and dochmiacs were transferred from there to tragedy.

Aeschylean satyr-plays are only represented in scanty fragments and no other certain dochmiacs appear in them. It is perhaps reasonable to say that short metres predominate and that where lines are run together by word-overlap, the result is not to create a stately period but a hurried patter. The *Diktyoulkoi* has one patch of choriambic dimeters (786 ff.) with apparently an enoplian–paroemiac clausula, and a long stretch of glyconics and pherecrateans with an occasional phalaecean hendecasyllable to break them. In the *Theoroi* the chorus sing or recite iambic trimeters but they are interspersed at intervals with (*a*) an iambic dimeter, (*b*) a curious group which is perhaps two bacchiacs and a dochmiac (8 ff.), (*c*) an ithyphallic, and (*d*) iambic dimeters fading into a final trimeter, after which the chorus move into trochaic tetrameters catalectic. Later on they break into a long iambic speech of Dionysos with a group of six short lines: xs's, d's, s's, dxs, three bacchiacs, and an ithyphallic. All these fragments are within the range of excited dancing. It is interesting that Dionysos (74) calls his dances 'double-row dances', meaning perhaps dances of satyrs and maenads.

In 467 B.C., five years after the *Persians*, Aeschylus produced his Theban trilogy, of which the third play, the *Septem*, is preserved. The opening chorus of the play is almost entirely in dochmiacs, which are now fully established as a metre in their own right. The frightened Theban women rush on to the Acropolis and pray various gods in turn to save Thebes from the invading forces led by Polyneikes, who are described as a barbarian army. The first seventy lines (78–148) are not divided into strophe and antistrophe, but are punctuated partly by Pause between the dochmiacs (ten of these are certain), partly by brief sections of other metre, spoken iambic trimeters (100, 103, and 106), three bacchiacs (104), and sung iambics (118 f., 123, 126, 131, 136 ff., 142 ff., and 147 f.). The first line of all is doubtful because the gender of *phobera* is uncertain; if neuter, then a syncopated iambic dimeter; if feminine, an anapaestic monometer followed by a cretic. This makes better sense, and seems metrically possible because of the affinity between anapaests and dochmiacs. It could then also carry an allusion to the marching anapaests of the ordinary *parodos*: this in contrast is a wild, undisciplined kind of entry. Each dochmiac is normally complete in itself, and they are probably rightly printed in pairs, but sometimes word-overlap shows that two (85, 99) or three (81, 91) are to be run together. After this long opening the first pair of strophe–antistrophe is pure dochmiac (151 ff.) and the second pair has short lines of syncopated iambic ending with three dochmiacs. The whole is excited dancing, in sense a prayer to the gods to avert evil and in so far a *paian*.

The mood of excited fear is carried on in a lyric dialogue with Eteokles (200 ff.). Between each short strophe and antistrophe of three pairs Eteokles speaks three iambic trimeters. The form is essentially the same as the dialogue between the messenger and the chorus in the *Persians*, and we should perhaps think that Aeschylus has transferred lament-technique to another purpose. Each lyric pair begins in dochmiacs; the first goes over into cretics and ends with an iambo-choriambic tetrameter, the second has an ibycean clausula (dds is, of course, a dochmiac with an extra d), the third ends with a resolved lekythion (sss).

The chorus continue their fears and prayers and describe the horrors of a sack in their next song (287 ff.). In the first two pairs they are calmer. The first is in dancing tempo in syncopated iambics with a long pherecratean insertion. The second plays on double-short metres all through until the clausula, which goes back to syncopated iambic. The first part seems to be ionic with a glyconic clausula, then ionic and choriambic with an anacreontic clausula, then aeolo-choriambic to the end. After the anacreontic (327) the long period sds'dss'sss (23 syllables) recalls the Pindaric periodic style and must almost have been in walking time. But in the third pair (345) the excitement flares up again with dochmiacs, but then after a transition passage of short lines in double-short ends in long periods of iambo-trochaics.

Dochmiacs continue all through the short responses which the chorus make to the accounts of the seven champions on either side, and on into the final lyric dialogue with Eteokles. When Eteokles has gone to fight his brother, the chorus comment on the history of the house of Laios in five pairs of strophe–antistrophe in dance time (720 ff.). The first is ionic introduced by an iambic penthemimer but ends with an alcaic decasyllable, ddsx. The second is syncopated iambic with a remarkable final run of 29 syllables tied together by word-overlap. The third opens with a syncopated iambic trimeter followed by an enoplian paroemiac, then three shorter periods each with a section in single-short and a section in double-short so arranged that the pattern of the whole four periods is ab, ba, ab, ba. The fourth pair is iambic but ends in a contracted hemiepes and an aristophanean (dsx). The fifth opens with an isolated dochmiac, then goes into iambic with two inserted hemiepe and an iambo-choriambic clausula.

After the news that the brothers have killed each other the chorus (822) sing strophe–antistrophe and a long epode in iambics, and the final lament (875) is shaped like the final lament of the *Persians* except that instead of the single Xerxes the solo parts are divided between Antigone and Ismene. The sisters sing iambics with occasional dochmiacs, the chorus have recitative anapaests for their response in the first pair, iambics with dochmiac clausula in the second, dochmiacs running into a remarkable long choriambic period in the third, iambics in the fourth, dochmiacs and iambics in 975 ff. when the sisters have started singing antiphonally. Metrically this *kommos* is more like the latter part of the *kommos* of the *Persians*; it lacks the metrical richness and variety of the earlier part, but then Xerxes' entry is a dramatic high point, whereas here the *kommos* is simply the natural end of the play, and

Aeschylus has no intention of creating the sisters into characters. In the earlier part of the play the domination of dochmiacs is obvious, and clearly characterizes the fears of the women in opposition to the strength of Eteokles. In their quieter songs it is perhaps legitimate to see more metrical difference between the stanzas and more metrical variety within the stanzas than in the earlier play.

The *Suppliant Women* must now be dated after the Theban Trilogy and possibly in 463. It is the first play of a connected trilogy, but of the other plays only a single lyric fragment of the second, the *Aigyptioi*, remains. In the *Suppliant Women* the daughters of Danaos enter at the beginning of the play to recitative anapaests, and then sing a long prayer to the gods to receive the suppliants. The shape is the same as the beginning of the *Persians*. Here too the long strophic song falls into two parts, a predominantly double-short part and a predominantly single-short part. The first four pairs are mostly dactylic, but the second pair is choriambic, and the third partly choriambic. This opening is much calmer than the opening song of the Theban women in the *Septem*, and the long lines of 19 and 20 syllables in the first pair, 22 in the second, 17 in the third and 23 in the fourth suggest that this section was in walking time. The fourth and fifth pairs make a sort of transition from the long slow double-short lines to the quicker-moving single-short lines: the fourth, which starts dactylic, ends with plenty of single-short, ssxsdsx, and the fifth, which starts in single-short, ends with plenty of double-short d'd, dxs, dss'dsx. The sixth, seventh, and eighth pairs are largely lamenting iambics, and each pair has its own refrain. The long song gives the exposition, the past history, and present plight of these strange women.

When the king arrives, the women tell their story and make their appeal in a long iambic dialogue, but for the essential moment of persuasion they go into lyric metre (348), and Aeschylus has formed this lyric dialogue so that the chorus sing three pairs of strophe–antistrophe and the king speaks five iambic trimeters between each verse; after the last verse he speaks eleven trimeters, and they sing two more pairs uninterrupted, and then he finally gives his decision. Here the women are almost as agitated as the chorus in the *Septem*, and paired dochmiacs dominate the first three pairs of strophe and antistrophe. In the first the dochmiacs climax in a long, rushing, tripartite

line, which runs ds′dss′dsx (ds is, of course, one of the common forms
of dochmiac). In the second the opening dochmiacs are followed by
three syncopated iambic trimeters, and the stanza ends d′ssx. The third
is pure dochmiac, and at the end two linked dochmiacs are linked to
dsx. After the king's longer speech the fourth pair consists of eleven
cretics, an agitated metre, as we have seen, and the fifth pair of three
cretics and five dochmiacs, of which only the last two are linked.

When the king takes Danaos off to get the approval of the Argive
assembly, the women, as instructed (521), call on the protection of
Zeus and tell the long story of their ancestor Io (524 ff.). This is an
elaborate song in five pairs of strophe and antistrophe, the first largely
enoplian and the second largely in prosodiac, the third and fourth in
iambic and aeolo-choriambic but with prosodiac conclusion, the fifth
in calm iambics. Probably the whole is in dancing time and slows up
for the long choriambic close of the second pair, d′d′d′dsx (19), and the
linked choriambic-prosodiac close of the third pair, dss′dss′dsx (23).

When Danaos returns with the news that the Argives have accepted
them, they pray for blessings on Argos (625 ff.). After an introduction
in anapaestic dimeters, the first three pairs of strophe and antistrophe
are largely dochmiac, particularly the dochmiac form ds, and exten-
sions of ds, such as dsx and ddsx. Each of the six verses has a refrain with
different words but the same metre, two pherecrateans followed by a
glyconic plus a pherecratean. We have seen such refrains on a very small
scale in cult hymns, in Archilochos' hymn to Herakles, and in the
Elian women's hymn to Dionysos and in *paians*, so that it probably is
right to look for their origin in cult hymns; what is curious here and in
some other refrains, is that the metre stays constant but the words
change with each repetition.[1] The last pair of this song is all in quiet
iambics with no refrain. The whole song is in dancing time.

The news of the ship's arrival produces an excited lyric dialogue
(736) between Danaos and the chorus, in which the chorus sing two
pairs of strophe–antistrophe largely in dochmiac. Danaos leaves them
to seek help, telling them not to forget the gods (773). They sing first
of their wish to escape, to the underworld, to the upper air, or if
necessary by death, and then in the fourth strophe pray to Zeus to
help his suppliants. The whole song is in iambics except for an

1. On refrains, cf. A. M. Dale, *L.M.*[2] 148. Cf. also above, pp. 59, 99.

iambo-choriambic trimeter as clausula to the first pair and what seem to be a galloping conclusion to the third pair (814 ff.) dss'dsxdsx.

The dialogue where the Egyptian herald tries to seize the women is too corrupt to expound. But the play ends with a final chorus (1018 ff.), in which the first strophe and antistrophe praises Argos but also prays for virginity. The attendants of the Danaids sing of the divine ordinance of marriage in the second pair; the third pair is shared between the Danaids and the critical attendants, and in the final pair the Danaids reiterate their view. The metre of the first three pairs is ionic: dimeters and trimeters in the first two pairs with an anacreontic clausula (the first has also a mid-stanza pause with an anacreontic with long fourth syllable); in the third pairs dimeters only and no variant clausula. As in the first song of the *Persians* the homogeneous ionic section is followed by a homogeneous iambo-trochaic section, here only a single pair of strophe–antistrophe, which consists entirely of lekythia, except for an aristophanean as second period and a cretic inserted between two lekythia to form the third. The first three pairs are the first considerable ionic passage in this play. Possibly at the end of the play Aeschylus is emphasizing that there is something un-Greek about this passion for virginity.

There is another problem about this last chorus. Who are the attendants and how was it sung? The singers must be the *opadoi* who are told to take up the song in l. 1022. It is curious that this word is usually masculine when it is used in a literal and not metaphorical sense, and Aeschylus has so used it of the bodyguard given to Danaos in l. 985. Argive men could be asked to 'take up the song', and Argive men could better than the women's own maids give the good advice of the second and third pair of strophe–antistrophe.

This leaves the production problem. If the singers are the handmaidens of the Danaids, either silent performers, who have been present all through the play but are first mentioned in l. 977, suddenly find a voice, or the chorus, which we have always thought of as Danaids, suddenly turns out to be half Danaids and half handmaidens, and this change is marked by the rearrangement in l. 977. This does not seem to me impossible. If the singers of the second and in the third pair are Argive men, these men have arrived with Danaos at l. 980, and the re-grouping of the Danaids and their handmaidens in l. 977 is to make room for them in the orchestra. There is a further possibility: the two surviving subsidiary choruses of the *Eumenides* and the *Hippolytos* sing very simple songs which are completely independent of the main chorus. Here and in the *Supplices* of Euripides the subsidiary chorus appears to sing in the strophic structure of the main chorus; it is possible that they only mimed and the actual song was sung for them by the main chorus which remained stationary during this part of the song. For the rest of the trilogy we only have a tiny fragment[2] of very characteristic lamentation from the *Aigyptioi*, in syncopated iambics with aeolo-choriambic insertions.

Only the *Oresteia*, produced in 458, shows Aeschylus' choral technique over a whole trilogy. The chorus of the *Agamemnon* are the elders of Argos, who come to the palace because they have seen the altar fires lit at Klytemnestra's command when she has been told of Agamemnon's beacon (83 ff.). The hope of news from Troy naturally sends them back to the beginning of the war (40 ff.). After the long anapaestic introduction they tell the story of Agamemnon's fatal decision to sacrifice Iphigeneia in the six pairs of strophe–antistrophe which form the *parodos* (104-257). The first pair, which has its own epode so that it makes a triad, describes the omen of the eagle and the hare and Kalchas' interpretation. This is mostly in very long, stately dactylic lines up to 20 syllables in the strophe–antistrophe and 26 in the epode. For the Zeus hymn in the next pair the chorus change to iambotrochaics with a penultimate run of ddddx picking up the earlier dactyls. The introductory double syncopation keeps the movement stately. The third pair, which in the antistrophe goes back to the story, is again iambo-trochaic. The fourth which leads up to Agamemnon's decision is iambic but then shifts through two aristophaneans (dsx) to a remarkable choriambic conclusion d'd'd'd'd'dsx (31 syllables). The fifth and sixth pairs take the story to its conclusion in syncopated iambics with in each case double-short in the conclusion.

The first *stasimon* gives the chorus's reactions to the beacon speech (355 ff.): Zeus' punishment of Paris, Helen's flight from Menelaos, Greek resentment to casualties in the war. After an anapaestic introduc-

---

1. Cf. my *Tragedies of Euripides*, 126 f.
2. *P.Oxy* 2251, interpreted by M. L. Cunningham, *Rh.Mus.* 96, 1953, 223; 105, 1962, 189.

tion they sing three pairs of strophe–antistrophe in stately iambics, each stanza has a dancing refrain in aeolo-choriambic, sdx, sdx, sds'sdx, with different words each time. Finally there is an epode in iambics, which is probably danced in spite of an 18-syllable line in the middle (481).

The second *stasimon* (681) has no anapaestic introduction and describes Helen in Troy. Again the long lines keep the metre stately. The first pair moves from iambo-trochaic through ionic to aeolo-choriambic, the second is aeolo-choriambic at beginning and end but dactylic and iambo-trochaic in the middle, the third repeats in different forms the rhythms of the first; the ionics introduced in the first strophe (689) for the puns on Helen's name come in here for the moment when Helen brings disaster (744). The fourth pair is iambic with aristophanean clausula, dsx.

The third *stasimon* (975) follows Agamemnon's return. The first pair is in stately iambo-trochaics with a dactylic run early, ddddx, which perhaps intentionally recalls the *parodos*. A much longer dactylic run forms the penultimate period of the second pair here (1014). This pair again is mainly iambo-trochaic. The beginning is corrupt, but, as Murray has seen, there must be an anticipation here of the binding song in the *Eumenides* (329); it is the antistrophe that is essential here, 'once lethal blood has fallen on the ground who can recall it?' The metre is probably two paeons, pherecratean (with paeonic opening), running into ʌdddddx.

When the chorus ask Kassandra to go into the palace (1073), she leads them in a long lyric dialogue, in which they respond with two spoken iambic trimeters for the first four pairs of strophe–antistrophe but for the last three pairs with lyric, mainly dochmiac. Her part all through is mainly dochmiac but interspersed with bacchiacs and iambics.

After the two murders there is another long lyric dialogue between the chorus and Klytemnestra, who stands on the *ekkyklema* over the two bodies. Here the chorus start with dochmiacs (1407) and Klytemnestra follows with an iambic speech, and this grouping is repeated. Then a new structure starts which continues for the next three pairs (1448–1577). In each pair the chorus sing strophe, then add a refrain, then Klytemnestra has recitative anapaests; the refrain is probably repeated in the same words after the antistrophe, and Klytemnestra again recites anapaests in the same pattern but with different words. The first strophe is largely dochmiac and iambic, and the refrain is similar after an anapaestic opening. The second strophe is prosodiac, aeolo-choriambic, and iambic, and the refrain again opens in anapaests. The third strophe is iambic and the refrain prosodiac and iambic after the anapaestic opening.

In the *Choephoroi* the chorus are Trojan captives sent to assist Elektra in pouring libations to avert the consequences of Klytemnestra's dream. Their entry is in theory at least processional but the marching anapaests are omitted. They come from the palace to the tomb of Agamemnon which is shown on the *ekkyklema* (during the chorus. 585 ff., the *ekkyklema* rolls back and the central doorway becomes the palace of Agamemnon for Orestes' entry in 652). The first pair is stately iambic except for a penultimate contracted dactylic pentameter. The second pair is also iambic except for an aeolo-choriambic clausula; the second period seems to be a monster of 26 syllables (43–7). The third pair is corrupt but seems to be iambic all through. While she pours the libations Elektra calls on the chorus to sing lamentations, which will also be a *paian* of the dead (150), a prayer to Agamemnon to avert her misery; they sing an astrophic stanza in resolved iambics changing into dochmiacs, probably in dance time in spite of one 16-syllable period (154–5).

After the recognition scene Orestes, Elektra, and the chorus sing a long and complicated lyric dialogue in which they summon Agamemnon to help Orestes (306 ff.). The technique is entirely different from the summoning of Dareios in the *Persians*. This song has eleven pairs of strophe and antistrophe. The earlier pairs contain varied metrical elements, prosodiac, aeolo-choriambic, iambic, dactylic, but from the seventh strophe (423), where the chorus describe their lamentation for Agamemnon, the metre is predominantly iambic until the last pair (466), which the chorus sing alone, ds, dsx, dsx, sdsx, sdsx. Strophes and antistrophes are interwoven, and the whole pattern is: choral anapaests, strophe a Orestes, b chorus, a′ Elektra, choral anapaests, c Orestes, b′ chorus, c′ Elektra, choral anapaests, d Orestes, e chorus, d′ Elektra, choral anapaests f Orestes, e′ chorus, f′ Elektra, g chorus, h Elektra, i Orestes, i′ chorus, g′ Elektra, h′ chorus, k, k′ Orestes, Elektra, chorus, l, l′ chorus, choral anapaests.

When Orestes has gone off and Elektra has entered what is now the palace, the chorus sing a generalizing chorus (575) on the crimes of women. The first pair is iambo-trochaic with penultimate ddddx. The second starts the same but after two long lines in the middle goes into aeolo-choriambic for the end. The third is syncopated iambics with one period of 18 syllables (624–5). The fourth is the same. In the next *stasimon* (783 ff.) the chorus pray for Orestes' success while they wait for Aigisthos. The text is desperately bad, but it looks as if the three pairs are in iambo-trochaic with a mesode between each pair in different metres, including ionic in the first and third. Aigisthos' final cry is a dochmiac, and the chorus answer with a dochmiac and three cretics. The last chorus of all after the death of Klytemnestra (935 ff.) is almost pure dochmiac with two iambic dimeters in the first pair. This is excited dancing.

In the *Eumenides* the chorus are the Furies. At least three are grouped on the *ekkyklema* which rolls out after the priestess has spoken the prologue (63). They wake each other, and followed by the rest stream into the orchestra, as the *ekkyklema* rolls back. They sing dochmiacs interspersed with iambic trimeters for three pairs of strophe–antistrophe (143). Apollo drives them from the temple (232) and they leave by one *parodos*. Orestes enters by the other *parodos*, and the scene has changed to Athens. After his nine iambic trimeters they enter. The leader speaks ten iambic trimeters as they come up the *parodos*, and then they search, find him, and threaten him in an astrophic song, again in dochmiacs interspersed with iambics (254 ff.).

After his appeal to Athena they say that he shall hear their 'Binding song'. The introduction is recitative anapaests. The first pair is iambo-trochaic in long lines. The refrain is the excited binding song, four paeonics, a pherecratean with resolved opening to pick up the paeonics, and then short iambo-trochaic. The second pair is dactylic with lekythion clausula; the refrain starts with a lekythion and ends with an aristophanean but has paeonics between them. The third pair is also dactylic with a refrain in paeonic and pherecratean. The fourth pair is iambic in long lines with a dactylic penultimate; it has no refrain.

The next song (490 ff.) comes when Athena has promised to set up the court to try Orestes, and the Furies sing of the consequences of his acquittal. The first three pairs are iambo-trochaic; the third has two long dactylic lines inserted (ddddddx and dddd'dx) and an aristophanean clausula. The fourth pair is iambic with dss, dsx at the end. This is probably all in dance time. The actual trial follows and Orestes is acquitted and gives thanks. There follows (778) a lyric dialogue in which the chorus vent their anger in two pairs of excited strophe–antistrophe (the antistrophes repeat the words of the strophes). After each stanza Athena reasons with them in an iambic speech and finally persuades them. The first pair is iambic and dochmiac, the second almost entirely dochmiac.

Finally, like the daughters of Danaos, they sing blessings on their new home (916). This again is a lyric dialogue with Athena reciting anapaests after the dancing stanzas up to and including the third strophe. The three pairs are all iambo-trochaic. The first has a pendant hemiepes as penultimate. The second has considerable dactylic inserts, and the third begins with a dactylic period, dddsx (praxillean). After the third strophe Athena says that she must go first to show them their dwelling by the light of 'these escorts', whom she then tells to lead. These are orders to form a procession, while the chorus sing the last antistrophe. Obvious and very suitable escorts are the jurors who have formed the first murder court to try Orestes: nothing was said to dismiss them at the end of the trial. The final iambic speech of Athena after the last antistrophe is unsatisfactory; she seems to be speaking about a much more elaborate procession, and she does not give the Furies their new name of Eumenides. Something is certainly wrong. Then the escorts lead the chorus off with two pairs of strophe–antistrophe in very simple dactylic lines with a paroemiac clausula to the second pair.

As one looks back over the immense structure of the trilogy, it appears that Aeschylus' staple metre is iambo-trochaic with the lekythion, sss, as the favourite line. Syncopated iambics probably come next, particularly the syncopated trimeter. Dochmiacs are used for agitated choruses, and dactyls for stately choruses. Other metres are comparatively rare and are used either for special effect or as a variation on the standard metres with which they have an affinity. The *Agamemnon* with its chorus of aged councillors has more stately songs than any other play (the Persian elders come next, but they are Orientals and perhaps for this reason are given dance time more readily), and the only excited song is the dialogue with Kassandra. In the *Choephoroe* only the *parodos* is stately; the other songs are in dance time except for the single excited *ololyge* near the end (935). So also the women of the *Septem* and *Supplices* and the Furies of the *Eumenides* have very little in slow time. The *parodoi* of the *Septem* and *Supplices* are entirely in excited time, and it is obviously right that excited time should be used for the Furies' search for Orestes, the refrain of the binding song, and the angry dialogue with Athena. The Danaids go into excited time at their moments of greatest agitation – the persuasion of Pelasgos, the news of the ship's arrival, and the attack of the Egyptian herald.

The technique of the iambic trimeter, the dramatic structure, possibly also the allusion to Naukratis,[1] place the *Prometheus Bound* in the last years of Aeschylus' life, and it has much less lyric than any of his other preserved plays. When Prometheus is left alone, in his first speech he moves up after five lines into recitative anapaests (93–100), and then again, when the chorus are approaching, he sings four bacchiacs,[2] an iambic trimeter, an iambic dimeter, two iambic trimeters, and then has another stretch of recitative anapaests before they enter (113–27). He also has recitative anapaests after their first strophe and antistrophe and their second strophe, so that the whole *parodos* is in the form of a lyric dialogue. The chorus of Oceanids are given mostly anaclastic ionics for the first pair: these are introduced by an iambic penthemimer in the first period and the last period but two (132), and the enoplian clausula (xddsx) is clearly akin to them. The two middle periods are a choriambic dimeter B and an alcaic decasyllable, ddsx, which has a similar pendant ending to the anaclastic ionics. The second pair starts iambic but ends with a blunt hemiepes (164), an ithyphallic, and a run of dactylo-anapaests leading into an alcaic decasyllable. The whole impression is light. There is, of course, no question of dancing except for arm movements, if the Oceanids are still on their winged chariot.

For the first *stasimon* they are in the orchestra (397), and again the first pair is in anaclastic ionics with the same opening period as the *parodos*; the second period is 20 syllables long and the last 16, so that this is presumably danced in slow time. The second pair is in trochaic

---

1. On the metre, cf. Yorke, *C.Q.* 30, 1936, 117. On the allusion to Naukratis, Braccesi, *R.I.F.C.* 96, 1968, 28.
2. Two similar bacchiac tetrameters occur in the *Bassarai* (23N²), a maenad play.

dimeters with an aeolic ending: sds'dsx. The third pair (or epode?) is corrupt, but seems to have a good deal of iambic with an ending something like dactylo-epitrite. The second *stasimon* (526 ff.) is a stately song with the first pair in regular Pindaric dactylo-epitrites and the second in a kind of inverted dactylo-epitrite in which pure anapaests run into iambics. The clausula is a normal dactylo-epitrite line, ddxsxsx. This is the earliest preserved dactylo-epitrite chorus in drama,[1] and the stately metre is probably chosen to contrast with the wild monody of Io which follows it.

Io starts in anapaests, then moves into catalectic iambics and dochmiacs before her strophe and antistrophe, which are largely dochmiac but include also cretics, bacchiacs, and iambo-trochaics. In all this it is difficult to be certain where the periods end, but ll. 577–8 (3 cretics plus 5 bacchiacs) runs to 24 syllables. This is probably taken fast but the whole impression is rather of dancing tempo than of excited dance. Strophe is divided from antistrophe by four lines of iambics from Prometheus. The first long interchange between Prometheus and Io is followed by a little iambo-dochmiac verse from the chorus (687 ff.), which includes a prosodiac. Io finally goes off to recitative anapaests and the chorus (887) wind up with a strophe–antistrophe of regular dactylo-epitrites and an epode which is iambic until the aristophanean close, a solemn commentary on the advantages of not marrying above one's station. The choruses of the *Prometheus Vinctus* differ in metre and in time from the other women's choruses in Aeschylus. The use of ionics in the first two songs is perhaps not surprising; these are exotic nymphs contrasted with the rugged defiance of Prometheus. It is more startling to find their two stately commentaries in dactylo-epitrite, but perhaps both of them should be felt primarily as contrasting with the wild emotion of Io, the first (526) with her arrival and the second with her departure, since her recitative anapaests are in dance tempo.

The only play of Sophocles with lyric fragments which can certainly be put in the early classical period is the *Thamyras*.[2] Two fragments in recitative anapaests describe the Muses coming to Athos equipped with stringed instruments (237–8P). There is no difficulty in the Muses

---

1. Note, however, A. *Herakl.* fr. 74N[2] and Phrynichus fr. 13N[2].
2. See my *Introduction to Sophocles*[2], p. 200.

having this variety of instruments: it is implied in the description of them in the *Rhesus* (922), and a slightly later vase shows a Muse playing a harp.[1] The obvious interpretation is that these fragments come from the entry of the chorus of Muses. But the three other lyric fragments come from an admirer or sympathizer with Thamyras. The vases (nos. 256–7) show that his mother, Argiope, had a part in the play. When she dances with raised knee to crown him, this would perhaps fit the resolved trochaics describing the new dances (240P) rather than the ionic tetrameter, following a line which runs ds'ddx, in which she describes the effect on her of Thamyras' music (245P). On the other vase (no. 257) she dances with torso bent forward, tearing her hair, and this would fit the aeolo-choriambic description of Thamyras in disaster, which runs sds, sd'ds (244P). On this vase the Muse walks muffled in her cloak, and it is reasonable to suppose that the song with which the Muses defeated Thamyras was a stately song, perhaps in dactylo-epitrites.

6 · CLASSICAL PERIOD, 450–425 B.C.

The main works of this period are the four earlier plays of Sophocles and the early group of Euripides' plays. Before considering them we have a little evidence for dithyramb. Melanippides of Melos[2] is regarded as beginning a trend of music which developed further with Timotheos and Philoxenos in the next period. The new trend was regarded as effeminate and more emotional, and involved a sub-division of the seven basic notes of the lyre. Melanippides also intro-duced *anabolai*; the word means preludes and is contrasted with the antistrophic form. Melanippides therefore introduced free preludes, like the opening of the *parodos* in Aeschylus' *Septem*, before beginning the triadic system; it is often said that they were solos but there is no evidence for this. He wrote a *Marsyas*. The story of Marsyas, the satyr who picked up the flute when Athena threw it away and challenged Apollo to a contest and when defeated was converted to lyre-playing, becomes extremely popular in Athenian art in this period, starting with the sculptured group by Myron, and it is a natural suggestion that

---

1. London E 371. Schefold, *Bildnisse*, 60; *A.R.V.*[2] 1039.
2. Pickard-Cambridge, *Dithyramb, etc.*[2], 39 ff; Lloyd-Jones, *Philol.*, 112, 1968, 119.

the inspiration was the *Marsyas* of Melanippides.[1] As several of the vases show a tripod, and a tripod was dedicated after the performance of a dithyramb, the *Marsyas* probably was a dithyramb. The surviving fragment (*P.M.G.* 758), describing how Athena threw away the flute, probably belongs near the beginning, and is in nearly regular dactylo-epitrite. The other long fragment of Melanippides, from the *Danaides* (757), is also in dactylo-epitrite, with a great deal of single-short and two very long periods, so that it would certainly suit the stately dithyrambic chorus on the bell-krater by the Kleophon painter (no. 259).

The story of Marsyas was probably a conscious allegory of the victory of the new lyre music over flute music. The same struggle is reflected in a song by Pratinas (*P.M.G.* 708), in which a satyr-chorus claims that the flute-player should take second place. This has long been connected with the lyre-playing satyrs by Polion, who are labelled 'singers at the Panathenaia' (no. 244, fig. 9). The chronological difficulty of the connection is removed by Professor Lloyd-Jones,[2] who suggests that the song does not belong to the earlier Pratinas, whose satyr-plays were being produced before the end of the sixth century and who was dead before 467, but to a later lyric poet, Pratinas; the metre would fit much better in the classical period. The poem is called a *hyporcheme* by Athenaeus, who quotes it, and he uses the same words almost about the undesirable prominence of the hired flute-player as Plutarch in speaking of Melanippides. *Hyporcheme* need only mean lively dance, but the use of the word as a description does at least imply that the song does not come from a satyr-play, so that it may very well have been a dithyramb sung by men dressed as satyrs at the Panathenaia as on the Polion vase. The metre[3] is anapaestic for the first four periods, but half the anapaests have the rare form with four short syllables (proceleusmatic). As anapaests they would be admirable for the prancing satyrs of the Polion vase. One must assume that the tradition is so well established that the double and triple proceleusmatics would cause no trouble in dancing; in the *Persae* Aeschylus used only one at a time. Pratinas goes on in trochaics, broken by two very long dactylo-epitrite lines (6 and 8), which would be in walking tempo; again walking as well as prancing

1. J. Boardman, *J.H.S.* 76, 1956, 18 f.; H. Metzger, *Représentations*, 159 ff.
2. H. Lloyd-Jones, *Cuaderno de la Fundación Pastor*, 13, 1966, 18.
3. I have followed A. M. Dale's text, *Collected Papers*, 167, and Pickard-Cambridge, *Dithyramb, etc.*[2], 292.

is traditional with the lyre-playing satyrs. The rest is dancing and perhaps excited dancing with two runs of cretics and two trochaic lines with all long syllables resolved. The cretic trimeter followed by lekythion (14) reads: 'See here I fling out right hand and foot.' This sounds like one of the old postures, B or C.

The satyr chorus dances its dithyramb quite differently from the beautifully draped men of the Kleophon painter's krater (no. 259), and it is interesting to compare Pratinas with preserved fragments of Sophoclean satyr-plays. *Pandora*, *Dionysiskos*, and *Inachos* were all produced early in this period or even just before it on the vase evidence.[1] The Pandora vase (no. 214) shows the traditional attitudes of the satyr-play, but unfortunately no useful fragments of the play itself are preserved. The *Dionysiskos* has a single fragment of linked glyconic and pherecratean (172P). The *Inachos* is much more interesting; the book fragments only produce normal aeolo-choriambics (277, 286P), and a paroemiac followed by a lekythion (278P). The old papyrus (Page, no. 6) has three runs of dochmiacs among trochaic tetrameters. The new papyrus also shows dochmiacs (*P.Oxy.* 2369), but there are not enough to show their quality. In the old papyrus the second and third runs are certainly dochmiacs; in the only two places where we can check they are separated by Pause, so that it looks as if they were not dimeters but single dochmiacs all through, and therefore danced excitingly. Like Aeschylus in the *Persae*, Sophocles seems to be playing here with the likeness of dochmiacs to anapaests. In the first run the dochmiacs are, all except one, of the anapaestic form, ⏑⏑⏑⏑⏑⏑—. The exception (l. 3) would more naturally be scanned as an anapaestic monometer, ⏑⏑—⏑⏑—, than as a dochmiac, ⏑⏑——⏑—. In the second run four of the six dochmiacs have the freak form which opens with an anapaest,[2] and in the third run of five two certainly and probably three are ⏑⏑⏑⏑⏑⏑—. In anapaestic terms, of course, they start with a proceleusmatic. But they are dochmiacs because the context is dochmiac.

The date of the *Ichneutai* is unknown. The first lyric (170 ff. P) is very badly preserved, but it clearly contains a number of proceleusmatics and here they seem to be anapaests rather than dochmiacs. The next

---

1. Cf. *M.T.S.*[2] 148, 150.

2. Regarded as a freak, *L.M.*[2] 105. Conomis, *Hermes*, 92, 1964, 49, quotes no other examples from satyr-play or comedy; in tragedy of the instances discussed by him on p. 36, E. *Hipp.* 670, 1276, *El.* 1152 seem tenable.

lyrics, 207 ff. are probably cretics, 237 ff. are syncopated iambics interspersed with cretics, 321 ff. are the same with a great many cretics, and we remember that we have seen cretics before as a lively metre.

Outside Sophocles the satyr-plays of Ion of Chios have left us one fragment with two iambic dimeters (20N, *Omphale*) and the satyr-plays of Achaios a fragment with an iambic dimeter followed by a pure dactylic tetrameter (12N, *Alkmaion*). These are dancing metres.

The obvious differences between the tragedies of Sophocles and the tragedies of Aeschylus, as far as the chorus are concerned, are first the reduction of the actual amount of choral lyric (the Oxford text gives 413 lines of lyric for Aeschylus' *Persae* and 299 for Sophocles' *Oedipus Tyrannus*), and secondly the reduction of the number of pairs of strophe–antistrophe in each song; in Sophocles the chorus sing a smaller number of longer pairs so that metrical variety occurs within the pair rather than from pair to pair. The *parodos* of the *Oedipus Tyrannus* is unique in having as many as three pairs. Sophocles' range of metres is much the same, but in this period he uses dactylo-epitrites and aeolo-choriambics (particularly asclepiads) much more than Aeschylus and iambo-trochaic and ionic much less.

The *Ajax*, which is probably the earliest surviving play, has an unorthodox *parodos* to fit the situation as Sophocles has shaped it. Ajax has been seen among the dead bodies of the cattle in the prologue. Everything now has to lead up to his next appearance when he will be sane. The chorus of his faithful sailors enter to a long anapaestic recitative as in the *Agamemnon*. They then sing a short triad (172–200), which starts in dactyls and moves into dactylo-epitrites with an aeolo-choriambic clausula.[1] The epode also starts dactylic but then moves into aeolo-choriambic; several of the lines close with three long syllables[2] as a result of syncopation, drag, or protraction, and this is an effect which Sophocles repeats later in this play; it is surely meant to be gloomy. After the triad Tekmessa enters and a lyric dialogue follows in recitative anapaests, then a sung strophe by the chorus, more anapaests from Tekmessa, the antistrophe by the chorus, and more anapaests from Tekmessa. The earlier triad is in dance time, but this pair (221 ff.)[3]

---

1. Analysed *L.M.*[2] 182.   2. Cf. *L.M.*[2] 85.
3. On the text, see *L.M.*[2] 155. In 372 accept Hermann's χερὶ μὲν and in 387 προπάτωρ, L.A.

is in slow time: the four periods have 23, 22, 15, 13, and 16 syllables. The first two periods and the last may be called free dactylo-epitrite; the third and fourth are like asclepiads with a lengthened close.

After a short scene with Tekmessa Ajax is heard shouting inside; the doors are opened, and he is again seen among the slaughtered beasts. He sings (348 ff.) three pairs of strophe–antistrophe separated, and the second pair also punctuated, by iambic trimeters from the chorus and Tekmessa; each pair starts in dochmiac and moves into something else, iambic and aristophanean in the first, a kind of dactylo-epitrite (372) in the second, and in the third a choriambic enoplian with, later, a strange run of hypodochmiacs, apparently each a separate tiny period (401 ff.). Here, unlike for instance, the lyric dialogue with Kassandra, all the development is in the soloist's part.

The first *stasimon* (596 ff.) comes after the scene between Ajax and Tekmessa. The chorus have accepted the probability that Ajax will commit suicide, and sing of their home in Salamis, the miseries of Troy, and the grief of his father and mother. The first pair is largely aeolo-choriambic, long, stately lines with twice a word of three long syllables to end the line (as in the *parodos*).[1] The second pair starts and ends in aeolo-choriambics, but two periods in the middle (629–31) pick up the 'asclepiads' of the *parodos*.

The second *stasimon* (693 ff.) expresses their joy when they believe Ajax has changed his mind. Their appeal to Pan to join them in Mysian and Knossian dances shows that they must dance, and dance excitedly, although the short strophe, which starts iambic and is mostly aeolo-choriambic, contains two longish periods, one two linked glyconics (695) and the other (698b–700) an aeolo-choriambic ennea-syllable plus hendecasyllable (phalaecean).

The search for Ajax's body and its discovery is another lyric dia-logue (886). The two halves of the chorus enter by different *parodoi*. The introduction is partly in short iambics, partly in trimeters. Then they join in a strophe (880). The first part is mainly dochmiac but inter-spersed with dactylic and single-short, and ending with an aeolo-choriambic dodecasyllable. Tekmessa enters from the central door and discovers Ajax's body behind the bush. The long section of iambic trimeters and segments of trimeters from both Tekmessa and the chorus

1. Cf. *L.M.*[2] 154.

is broken at 900 by a short lyric section by the chorus in dochmiac, dactylic, and syncopated iambic, and rounded off at 908 by another in dochmiac changing into dactylo-epitrite for the conclusion. Then after ten trimeters from Tekmessa the whole long and varied system repeats (925) so that it must be reckoned as an antistrophe to the foregoing strophe.

The third *stasimon* (1185 ff.) separates the Menelaos scene from the Agamemnon scene, and echoes the first *stasimon* in theme and metre. Both pairs start with a long asclepiadic line. The first moves into aeolo-choriambic and ends with an enneasyllable with a final word of three long syllables, the effect noticed before in the first stasimon. The second pair continues with another asclepiadic line, then goes into aeolo-choriambic.

Most of the metrical elements present in the *Ajax* are found again in the *Antigone*, which was produced in 441. The general principles are the same but the results are very different. The *parodos* is used not only to give the feeling of the elders of Thebes on the morning after the victory but also to describe briefly the assault of the Seven. The two pairs of strophe and antistrophe are extended by seven lines of recitative anapaests after each stanza. The first pair is in aeolo-choriambic with a first period of 16 syllables, glyconic plus glyconic (23 syllables, if the succeeding pherecratean is added to them, which it probably should be), and in 104–5 a period of 17 syllables, glyconic plus hipponactean, so that this victory song is in slow time. The second pair starts prosodiac with two praxilleans, dddsx, goes over into aeolo-choriambic, and ends with a magnificent long asclepiadic period, d'd'd'dxdx (22 syllables).

The first *stasimon* (332) gives the chorus's reflections on the discovery that someone has buried the body of Polyneikes. The first pair starts with two aeolo-choriambic periods (16 and 25 syllables), then has an iambic period (15 syllables), and ends with what may be regarded as an immensely extended praxillean, dddddddddssx (33 syllables).[1] This pair is in slow time; the second is in dance time, starting with three enoplians xdd, xdd, ʌdddsx (the last is a kind of headless variant of the prosodiac close of the first pair), and continuing in iambic, two dimeters, a trimeter, three dimeters, and a very compressed clausula, sx.

The second *stasimon* (582) follows the first meeting between Antigone

1. On l. 341, see A. M. Dale, *Wiener Studien* 77, 1964, 33 = *Collected Papers*, 205.

and Kreon, and places the disasters of the Theban royal house in a setting of divine law. The first pair starts in stately dactylo-epitrites, and then goes into iambics, including one period of 19 syllables, a syncopated dimeter plus a full trimeter. The second pair is probably in dance time since the only long period is the easy opening glyconic plus hipponactean (17 syllables): this is followed by two asclepiadic lines with a telesillean between them. Then the metre changes to ionic for two periods (609 ff.), and then after telesillean and ithyphallic ends with another asclepiadic period.

After the scene with Haimon Sophocles embarks on a responding system which is longer and more varied than the system starting after the suicide in the *Ajax* (866). It starts with the little hymn to Eros (781), then the long lament with Antigone, which consists of two pairs of strophe–antistrophe and an epode; this leads up to the iambic scene in which Antigone makes her last defence, and the whole is rounded off by the chorus's song of consolation. The little hymn to Eros has a single pair of strophe–antistrophe in aeolo-choriambic.[1] Brief introductory recitative anapaests announce Antigone's arrival. Her first pair of strophe–antistrophe is aeolo-choriambic in long periods; the clausula (814–16) has 25 syllables and ends with a prolonged hipponactean, giving a close of three long syllables, a phenomenon noted already in the *Ajax*. The chorus comment in recitative anapaests. Her second pair starts in aeolo-choriambic and ends in iambics; there are two long periods; 844–6, three dochmiacs plus again a prolonged hipponactean, and 848–9 an iambic tetrameter. This is therefore a stately lament but the chorus are moved to respond in sung iambics. Antigone's epode starts with an iambo-choriambic tetrameter, then two cretics, then four dactyls running into a trochaic dimeter, then two trochaic dimeters, the second syncopated. Here the tempo is more agitated and in the long period the trochaic dimeter is a climax to the four dactyls.

The chorus make no response because Kreon interrupts with spoken iambic trimeters, and Antigone's defence follows. The scene ends in recitative anapaests by the chorus, Kreon, and Antigone, and the

---

1. Colometry is not certain: 782–4 is probably a single period, chor. dim. B plus glyc. plus hippon., but the single-syllable overlap may mean that it is danced as a rush to a climax rather than that it is in slow time. 785–8 I take as 'asclepiadic' recalling the second *stasimon*.

chorus start their song of consolation (944). The first pair has six asclepiadic periods followed by two iambic dimeters and a syncopated catalectic trimeter. The second pair starts with three near-dactylo-epitrite lines[1] (recalling the second *stasimon*), then an asclepiadic line, and ends again in iambics. Nothing here is too long for dance time.

After the Teiresias scene the chorus sing a prayer to Dionysos to come with healing foot as the whole city is in the grip of a violent disease (1140). It is often compared with the prayer to Pan in the *Ajax* (693). Both summon a god; before both the action seems to have taken a turn for the good. But there the chorus ask Pan to dance with them in their joy, here they pray for healing. This song is a *paian* to avert evil. The first pair starts in a kind of headless dactylo-epitrite and then modulates into aeolo-choriambic, which has a number of dragged openings and closes, intentionally gloomy. Agitation can justifiably be seen in the dochmiac and hypodochmiac elements in the second pair. The first period is dochmiac plus choriambic dimeter B, the third (1140) hypodochmiac plus choriamb plus glyconic, the last (1144–5) iambic penthemimer plus choriamb plus hypodochmiac plus hipponactean, a 23-syllable close to an urgent prayer.

Kreon's long lament at the end of the play (1261) is almost entirely dochmiac (the variations are the two cretics in 1263 and the long hexasyllable dochmiac in 1275). The first pair of strophe–antistrophe is punctuated by a single spoken iambic trimeter and both strophe and antistrophe are followed by a block of trimeters. The second pair is punctuated by a block of trimeters, and strophe is separated from anti-strophe by two trimeters.

The *Trachiniae* and the *Oedipus Tyrannus* are not firmly dated but there would be general agreement for placing them not far from each other, slightly before and slightly after 430. In both the *parodos* has no anapaest recitative either before it or in the intervals of the stanzas. It is in fact a *stasimon*, and the chorus presumably did not start to sing until they had taken up their place in the orchestra. In two pairs of strophe–antistrophe and an epode the girls of Trachis reflect on the absence of Herakles, the misery of Deianeira, and the mutability of human fortune. The first pair is dactylo-epitrite, the second follows

---

1. See A. M. Dale, *Wiener Studien*, 77, 1964, 25 f. = *Collected Papers*, 197.

two periods of dactylo-epitrite with aeolo-choriambic, and the epode is iambic. The first pair is certainly in slow time.

After the messenger has given the news that Herakles is coming, the chorus burst into an astrophic song of wild rejoicing, which they call a *paian* to Apollo and Artemis (205). This is in dance time and perhaps much of it in excited dance time, particularly the frequent iambic dimeters and syncopated dimeters (including resolved bacchiacs). The first section has a long climax (212): iambic penthemimer plus catalectic dactylic heptameter, followed by ithyphallic. This is a danced climax, and recalls in an extended lively form the dactylo-epitrites of the *parodos*. The later part twice has a double syncopation (219 and 221).

The first *stasimon* (497) is not sung until Deianeira and Lichas have gone into the house after Lichas has been forced to reveal the truth about Iole. The chorus sing a triad about the power of love and the battle between Herakles and Acheloos. It may be that the narrative content suggested dactylo-epitrites here. The first, third and fifth periods of the strophe–antistrophe are in rising dactylo-epitrites (anapaest–iambics). This is slow time, and so are at least the first two periods of the epode: the first of these is aeolo-choriambic followed by dactyls, the second dactylo-epitrite. The rest is largely in syncopated iambic with aeolo-choriambic close.[1]

The second *stasimon* (633), sung when Lichas has gone back to Herakles with the robe, promises music and rejoicing when Herakles returns. The first pair is in free dactylo-epitrite with long periods ending in a catalectic iambic dimeter. The second pair starts with two enoplians which recall the earlier anapaest–iambics, then has an iambic pentameter catalectic (19 syllables), then shorter iambic periods; the end is corrupt.

The third *stasimon* (821) follows Hyllos' report and Deianeira's silent exit, and comments sadly on the news. The first pair begins in dactylo-epitrite, then switches to iambic trimeters. It ends with four cretics, the second and fourth dragged, and then a dochmiac plus a catalectic iambic dimeter. The three long syllables of the dragged cretics have the gloomy effect that we have noticed before in dragged or prolonged closes. The text of the second pair is difficult, but probably it starts with a choriambic dimeter B, then an enoplian, then iambic and glyco-

1. See commentary by A. M. Dale in *B.I.C.S.* Supplt. no. 21, DE 10.

nic, then four cretics, as in the first pair, and a dragged pherecratean, and finally a long asclepiadic clausula, xd'd'd'ds. Immediately after this the nurse enters, and there follows before her report of Deianeira's death a lyric dialogue between her and the chorus. Essentially this has the form of the opening dialogue between the messenger in Aeschylus' *Persians* and the chorus, but this is not antistrophic. The text here is doubtful; what is certain is that the nurse speaks iambics and the chorus answer in lyric, much of it iambic or syncopated iambic, but a glyconic in 883 and a dochmiac followed by an archilochean in 886 f.[1]

As the nurse finishes her messenger speech the chorus can see Deianeira's body on the *ekkyklema*, and Hyllos comes out to await the procession bringing Herakles' body. The chorus sing while the procession approaches, first a short pair of two iambic dimeters followed by a choriambic dimeter A with a dragged close, then a longer pair (in which they pray for escape) which starts with a telesillean, then goes on in iambic, and finishes (959 ff.) in the rising double-short which we have seen so often in this play and which anticipates the long anapaestic dialogue which follows. Here Hyllos opens in sung paroemiacs (with slight alteration of 972), the old man goes on in recitative anapaests, Herakles picks up in sung anapaests. Then in a more complicated pattern Herakles sings (*a*) two dochmiacs and a glyconic, (*b*) two anapaestic lines and an iambic dimeter, (*c*) five recitative dactylic hexameters, (*a'*) as (*a*); (*c'*) as (*c*) but by the old man, (*d*) Herakles sings four dochmiacs, (*b'*) as (*b*), (*c''*) as (*c*), (*d'*) as (*d*). The pairs of strophe–antistrophe are interwoven round the three groups of recitative dactylic hexameters, the first by Herakles, the second from the old man, and the third by Herakles again. This is a more complicated pattern than anything preserved except the great *kommos* of the *Choephoroe*. Clearly Sophocles has somehow to create sympathy for this monstrous Herakles and the metrical–musical pattern is one way of doing it.

The *parodos* of the *Oedipus Tyrannus* carries on the feeling of the prologue by emphasizing still more the horror of the plague; so it is built as a great *paian* (the word is used twice, 154 and 186, and the ritual cry is referred to twice, 154, 173) to the gods in three pairs of strophe–antistrophe. The first two pairs certainly have long periods in

---

1. In the probably early *Eurypylos* (210P) Astyoche and the chorus comment on the messenger speech in dochmiacs and lyric iambics but there Astyoche has a singing part.

slow time: this cannot be proved for the third pair, but there is no feeling of a change of tempo. The first pair is largely dactylic with at the beginning something of the stately movement of the *parodos* of the *Agamemnon*. The exceptions are the iambic second period, which anticipates the iambics to come, and the enoplian fourth period for the ritual, *iêie Dalie paian*. It ends with an immense dactylic period, tetrameter plus tetrameter plus dimeter plus tetrameter plus dimeter; these 47 syllables have no metrical break but each section ends with a word and this gives the necessary breathing space. The second pair starts iambic, and then oscillates between rising enoplia and falling dactyls which run at the end into an iambic conclusion. The third pair is wholly iambic except for a single enoplian (196).

The first *stasimon* (463) comes after the Teiresias scene, and the pairs are very different from each other in subject matter and metre. Both have long periods, but the first is brilliant description of the lonely fugitive named by Delphi and the second reflection on Teiresias' attack on Oidipous. The first is aeolo-choriambic but has two marching anapaestic dimeters inserted to describe the pursuit of Apollo (469–70). The second pair starts with two pure choriambic tetrameters, which have the same effect as the asclepiadic lines noticed elsewhere in Sophocles. Then the chorus voice their hopes in ionics, and perhaps this exotic metre is meant here to express their agitation.

The transition between the scene with Kreon and the scene with Iokaste is made by a lyric dialogue (649) with nine iambic trimeters, the dismissal of Kreon, between the strophe and antistrophe. It starts in iambics, syncopated tetrameter from the chorus, dimeter from Oidipous (Iokaste in the antistrophe), dimeter and syncopated trimeter from the chorus, spoken trimeter shared by Oidipous (Iokaste) and the chorus, then four dochmiacs from the chorus, two trimeters from Oidipous, then from the chorus syncopated trimeter, four dochmiacs, syncopated tetrameter, dimeter, trimeter. Cretics appear repeatedly in the syncopated iambics of the chorus and emphasize the solemnity of their appeal, as in the rather similar appeal in Aeschylus' *Suppliants* (418).

In the next *stasimon* (863) the chorus are deeply disturbed by the story of the death of Laios and Iokaste's scepticism, and they reflect on divine government. The first pair of strophe–antistrophe is in long heavy iambics but goes over into aeolo-choriambic, ending with an asclepiadic line followed by an aeolo-choriambic hendecasyllable.[1] The second pair starts with an alternation of iambo-trochaic and enoplian rather like Alkman's *Partheneion* (*P.M.G.* 1) and then goes over into heavy iambics (889) to end with a reizianum, xdx, which here picks up the earlier enoplians (xdsx).

After the discovery that Oidipous is not the son of the king of Corinth the chorus (1086) believe that Oidipous will prove to be the son of Apollo, Pan, Hermes, or Dionysos; only for a moment do they cast this into the form of a *paian*: '*iêie* Phoibos, may this please you' (1096). The metre of the single pair is free dactylo-epitrite in dance time. In the next scene the truth comes out, and when Oidipous has rushed into the palace, the chorus reflect on the mutability of human fortune (1186). The first pair is wholly aeolo-choriambic, glyconics, and obvious variants. The last period certainly, and the first probably, has three cola, making 22 syllables. This then is in slow time, a consolatory *threnos*.[2] The second pair starts with four iambic periods, then (rather as *Ajax* 401 f.) three hypodochmiacs and a short enoplian, and ends with two linked choriambic dimeters (16 syllables) and an iambo-choriambic trimeter. The whole tone of this contrasts sharply with the *kommos* when Oidipous comes out of the house blinded (1296). The chorus start in recitative anapaests, Oidipous starts in sung anapaests and they comment in an iambic trimeter. Then he sings two pairs of strophe–antistrophe, which they answer with two iambic trimeters at the end of each stanza and a single iambic dimeter in the middle of each stanza of the second pair. In the first pair Oidipous starts iambic, goes into dochmiac and ends in iambic. In the second he starts in dochmiac and then varies between iambic and dochmiac to the end. Technically this is like the final lyric dialogue of the *Antigone*.

For the Euripidean production of 438 we have two choral fragments of the *Alkmaion in Psophis* and the *Telephos*, as well as the complete *Alcestis*, which Euripides substituted for a satyr play. The fragment of

1. The text of the transition between iambics and aeolo-choriambics is doubtful in strophe (866) and antistrophe. Cf. L.P.E. Parker, *C.Q.*, 18, 1968, 253. On the last line (872) see *L.M.*[2] 141. 883 is probably are solved enoplian.

2. Cf. above, pp. 90, 138. The *Tereus*, which was produced shortly before 431 B.C., has three fragments in long dactylo-epitrites (591–3P) which could well come from such a threnos.

the *Alkmaion* (79N²) is in free dactylo-epitrite, xdd, ddsx, xs's. The fragment of the *Telephos*[1] is in a very Euripidean mixture of prosodiac-enoplian and aeolo-choriambic. In the *Alcestis*[2] too he appears to mix his metres more within the stanza than Sophocles (but with more actual repetition of identical metrical units), and to have already formed new types of lyric dialogue. The actual range of metres in early Euripides is much the same as in Sophocles, but in the four preserved early plays he does not use aeolo-choriambic so much but prosodiac and particularly enoplian much more. It is perhaps chance that not a single song in excited time survives. The new form of lyric dialogue, which is found again and again, is the lyric dialogue between actors with the chorus taking no part. The only astrophic song in early Sophocles is the choral song in the *Trachiniae* (205) welcoming the first news of Herakles' victory. Euripides' *Hippolytos* has three astrophic songs: the chorus's dochmiac lament at the news of Phaidra's death (811), their hymn to Aphrodite in mixed metres (1268), and then the long lament of Hippolytos at the end (1347). Both the choral astrophic song and the actor's astrophic song had a great future.

Of course the very individual shaping of the early part of the *Alcestis* is due to the situation, the chorus of old Pheraians come for news and Alkestis is brought out by the *ekkyklema* to die.[3] According to the scholiast and the manuscripts the *parodos* was sung by semi-choruses, but it is not clear how far we should follow them. Recitative anapaests precede the first strophe, and follow each strophe and antistrophe. The first pair, which ends with an appeal to Paian to appear, starts with an iambic tetrameter (16 syllables) and then is largely enoplian. The second pair starts iambic, then a long dactylic period (19), then prosodiac (ddx), iambic again, and finally, an asclepiadic close.

The first *stasimon* (213) follows on the report of the servant who tells the chorus about Alkestis, and invokes Zeus and again Paian (220). The single pair starts dochmiac and changes between dochmiac, iambic, enoplian, and aeolo-choriambic. At the end Alkestis and her children are brought out. The chorus have recitative anapaests before the lyric dialogue, which is entirely between Alkestis and Admetos and has no

---

1. Cf. Handley–Rea, *B.I.C.S.* Supplt. 5, 1957, 11 = Page, *G.L.P.* no. 3.
2. Cf. A. M. Dale, *Euripides Alcestis*, Oxford.
3. On the staging, see my *Tragedies of Euripides*, 49.

part for the chorus. Her first short pair of strophe–antistrophe is prosodiac and Admetos responds in two iambic trimeters. Her second pair starts with a long enoplian period, then iambic, and then a long aeolo-choriambic period; Admetos again has two trimeters. In the epode again she varies between iambic, aeolo-choriambic, and enoplian, and Admetos now answers in recitative anapaests.

After her death (393) the two children lament her (probably in fact they mime the lament and the actor who has taken Alkestis sings). The single pair is chiefly dochmiac and enoplian. Admetos speaks two trimeters after the strophe only. Before he goes into the house to prepare the funeral, Admetos calls on the chorus to sing a *paian* to Hades (424), and this is the second *stasimon*, which the chorus sing in praise of Alkestis. Both pairs are largely in prosodiac–enoplian with long periods of 16 and 17 syllables in the first pair and 37 at the end of the second pair. Herakles arrives and Admetos offers him hospitality; so the third *stasimon* (568) describes Admetos' hospitality. The first pair starts in free dactylo-epitrite and moves into aeolo-choriambic. The second pair is in dactylo-epitrite with a long prosodiac line in the middle and an iambic close. This again is in slow time with several long periods.

The transition between the Pheres scene, after which Pheres and Admetos with the body of Alkestis exit different ways, and the entrance of the servant, who has been attending Herakles, is marked by six lines of recitative anapaests from the chorus. When Herakles has gone off, Admetos enters and a long lyric lament follows (861). Admetos starts with recitative anapaests, then the first strophe of the chorus, partly iambic, partly dochmiac, and one iambelegus (xsxdd); during this and its antistrophe he is given extrametric interjections and recitative anapaests after them. The second strophe and antistrophe of the chorus are iambic and prosodiac-enoplian; Admetos again has recitative anapaests between them but after the antistrophe goes straight into iambic trimeters, and the chorus round the whole sequence off with their *stasimon* (962) on the power of necessity, which is in fact a *threnos*. Both pairs are mainly in aeolo-choriambic, but the second begins with two asclepiadic periods. This sequence has rather the same shape as Antigone's last entry (802–987) but is simpler.

Of the plays produced in 431 the *Medea* is complete, but no choral fragments survive of the other two tragedies. Like the other early plays, it has a very individual *parodos*, which starts with Medeia singing anapaests from inside the house and the nurse reciting anapaests on stage. The chorus enter (131) to melic anapaests, then a long dactylic–iambic period.[1] Medeia and the nurse continue their anapaests, and the chorus sing the first strophe. This starts in melic anapaests, then they go into aeolo-choriambic, but twice they introduce an aristophanean by a dochmiac (which foreshadows the far distant fifth *stasimon*). The strophe is followed by anapaests again from Medeia and the nurse, and the antistrophe by anapaests from the nurse. The epode starts enoplian and iambic and then goes over into dactylo-epitrite ending with a pherecratean.

This *parodos* sets the themes for the rest of the lyric in the play. Medeia makes her defence and then the chorus have recitative anapaests again to mark Kreon's departure. In the first *stasimon* (410) the chorus comment on Medeia's position: the first pair is dactylo-epitrite with long periods. The second is aeolo-choriambic, repeating the choriambic enoplians of the *parodos*, but has a praxillean as second period. After the first scene with Jason the second *stasimon* (627), the dangers of excessive love, again has a dactylo-epitrite first pair with long periods; the second pair starts with an asclepiadic period, then a long dactylo-epitrite period, then an enoplian, then a very long aeolo-choriambic period.

In the next scene again the chorus have a brief passage of recitative anapaests to mark Aigeus' departure. The third *stasimon*, in praise of Athens (824), has a first pair of dactylo-epitrites in dance time; the second pair starts enoplian, then goes into aeolo-choriambic, again repeating the choriambic enoplians of the *parodos*. After the second Jason scene the fourth *stasimon*, despair for the children (976), is again dancing dactylo-epitrite in the first pair, and in the second pair enoplian–iambic which is a sort of rising dactylo-epitrite. The long penultimate period could be danced as a climax.

The chorus mark the transition between the report of the old man that the gifts brought by the children have been received and the messenger speech of Kreousa's destruction by thirty-five lines of recitative anapaests. After the messenger speech they sing the fifth *stasimon* (1251)

1. Text as A. M. Dale, *Wiener Studien*, 77, 1964, 26 f. = *Collected Papers*, 198.

while the children are being murdered. The first pair is almost pure dochmiac (once a cretic is added, twice an iambic metron is added). The second pair is dochmiac, interrupted by two pairs of iambic trimeters, and ending with an iambic dimeter plus a dochmiac. In the strophe the iambic trimeters are spoken by the children offstage; in the antistrophe they are spoken by the chorus and fit into the sentence construction of the dochmiacs. The contrast between this last dochmiac *stasimon* and the preceding *stasima* which are all dominated by dactylo-epitrite or similar rhythms is very striking.

In the *Herakleidai* the old men of Marathon answer Iolaos' summons for help when he is attacked by the Theban herald, so that dochmiacs broken by trimeters is as natural a structure for this agitated *parados* as for the last chorus of the *Medea*. There is only one pair of strophe–antistrophe and the trimeters are given to the chorus, Iolaos, and the Herald, with Iolaos dominating in the strophe and the Herald in the antistrophe. The chorus mark the Herald's departure with recitative anapaests (288). In the first *stasimon* (353) they sing defiance of Eurystheus. Both strophe–antistrophe and epode are in a mixture of aeolo-choriambic and enoplian in long periods. The second *stasimon* (609) is conventional consolation after Makaria has been taken off to die, a *threnos* in long dactylic periods coming to rest on the spondaic endings; perhaps it is meant to sound old-fashioned. The next scene is broken by recitative anapaests when the chorus try to dissuade Iolaos from going into battle (702). The third *stasimon* (748) is a *paian* addressed to the various gods who may help Athens in the battle, again long periods of aeolo-choriambic, prosodiac, and enoplian in both pairs of strophe and antistrophe. Essentially the same elements occur again and again in long periods in the victory song, which forms the fourth *stasimon* (892).

The *Hippolytos* of 428 is more complicated. In the prologue Hippolytos leads on the subsidiary chorus of huntsmen and sings an aeolo-choriambic hymn to Artemis. This is in dance time; he certainly sings the first three lines and probably sings the rest with them, but it is curious that there is no clear differentiation between leader and chorus. The *parodos* (121) is a lovely decorated song in two pairs of strophe–antistrophe and an epode, sung by the main chorus, the Troizenian women, who wonder about Phaidra's sickness. It is in long periods except for a brief interlude of hypodochmiac in the first pair. Otherwise the first pair is in prosodiac, enoplian, and aeolo-choriambic, the second pair is wholly aeolo-choriambic, and the epode is enoplian and prosodiac with an iambo-trochaic beginning and end. The first pair has an extra long syllable at the end, and the second pair makes the same gloomy effect with dragged glyconics and a syncopated choriambic dimeter. Phaidra and the nurse enter on the *ekkyklema* and hold a dialogue with recitative anapaests for the nurse and sung anapaests for Phaidra, so that the whole shape of the *parodos* is not unlike that of the *Medea parodos* in reverse.

When the nurse extracts the truth from Phaidra, the chorus sing their horror in a strophe (362) which is mainly dochmiac; in two places the dochmiacs are associated with cretics, and they are twice punctuated by iambic trimeters. (The corresponding antistrophe is sung much later by Phaidra after the scene between the nurse and Hippolytos (669).) The nurse has overpersuaded Phaidra and gone to find Hippolytos when the chorus sing the first *stasimon* (525). This hymn to Eros has two pairs of strophe–antistrophe almost entirely in aeolo-choriambic, probably in dance time in spite of the 19-syllable period at the end of the second pair. Phaidra stops the chorus because she can hear the nurse and Hippolytos inside. She speaks iambics, and the chorus breaks in with short runs of dochmiacs; this is essentially the technique often used when a messenger arrives with bad news. Then after the scene between the nurse and Hippolytos Phaidra sings her dochmiac antistrophe (669).

Phaidra proposes suicide and the chorus sing the very lovely escape chorus, the second *stasimon* (732). The first pair is unique, and intentionally unique, in that after an opening choriamb the chorus sing three periods of ionic before reverting to aeolo-choriambic (with one long period) and ending with an ionic clausula. The second pair begins in aeolo-choriambic and then goes into long enoplians and dactylo-epitrites with a long closing period. There is no lament when the nurse announces Phaidra's death because Theseus arrives immediately. The chorus sing dochmiacs with a little iambic as the *ekkyklema* brings out Phaidra's body (811). Theseus sings a long dochmiac strophe and antistrophe with inserted pairs of iambic trimeters. The chorus speak two iambic trimeters after the strophe and sing dochmiacs after the antistrophe. In the following iambic description of the fatal tablet which leads up to Hippolytos' arrival both the chorus and Theseus have patches of agitated dochmiac.

The third *stasimon* (1102), sung when Hippolytos has started for exile, is a consolatory *threnos* in long dactylic periods with an iambic close, a sort of Aeschylean grandeur. The second pair opens in the same way but goes into shorter lines with dactylic and iambic alternating. The epode continues in dance time, aeolo-choriambic, iambic, and prosodiac enoplian. Then the messenger enters.

After the messenger speech the chorus sing an astrophic hymn to Aphrodite (1269), which is mainly dochmiac but varied with enoplians and dactylo-epitrite. Artemis enters to recitative anapaests, and after her iambic speech to Theseus the chorus greet Hippolytos in recitative anapaests. His monody starts in recitative anapaests (1347), then moves into melic anapaests (1370), then (1379) into syncopated iambic, which continues to the end punctuated by dochmiac, enoplian, and choriambic. This is the first example of a new kind of free, astrophic lamentation.

There are a few choral or lyric fragments from the lost plays of this period. In the *Kretes* Euripides revives the anapaestic entrance of the chorus, perhaps because this is a very special chorus of Mystics, which needs to present itself (472N²); in the same play they greet Minos' revelation with what are probably dochmiacs (Page, *G.L.P.* no. 11). In the *Theseus* the young Athenians who are being sent to the Minotaur lament their fate in ionics (385–6N²), and if the lyric dialogue in *P.Oxy.* 2452, fr. 5, belongs, it has typically Euripidean dochmiacs. The *Alope* has a long asclepiadic line (103N²). The chorus on the destructiveness of women from the *First Hippolytos* (429N²) has a very Euripidean run of three choriambic dimeters A, the last two linked. Two fragments from the *Bellerophon* read like different verses from a consolatory *threnos*, the first (303N²) in free dactylo-epitrites with two long dactylic lines, dddddx, and ddddx, and the second may be aeolo-choriambic but the text is difficult (304N²). Bellerophon has a monody in recitative anapaests, when he goes to heaven on Pegasos (307–8N²). Finally, a dactylo-epitrite fragment from the *Aigeus* (11N²) probably comes from a consolatory chorus when Theseus has been sent to capture the bull of Marathon.

When we turn to the fragments of comedy, we can fairly confidently assign Kratinos, Pherekrates, Teleklides, and Hermippos to this period. We are not concerned here with the obvious recitative metres like anapaestic dimeters and tetrameters and trochaic tetrameters, which we have reason to believe were already used by pre-comedy. We are concerned with lyric metres when we have enough evidence to see how the poets used them. Odysseus' sailors in Kratinos' play *Odysses* came on to paroemiacs, used as in the Spartan embateria (144K, cf. above, p. 62). In the *Archilochoi* and in other plays (10, 57, 323K) he uses the archilochean as a repeating line, xddxssx. He has also other varieties such as dddx and ∧dddx which he puts in front of the terminal ssx (325, 239K). And his own name was given to another long metre, choriambic dimeter A plus lekythion, dss'sss. Presumably these were all used in rather the same way as the anapaestic tetrameter and the trochaic tetrameter. The *Ploutoi* preserves a good specimen of dancing iambic dimeters (Page, *G.L.P.* no. 38b) and the *Cheirones* a parody of high-style lyric starting with an Aeschylean iambo-dactylic line and ending with dactylo-epitrite (240K). Pherekrates also has a dactylo-epitrite fragment (2K). His version of the long line used stichically seems to have been the priapean, normally glyconic plus pherecratean but he allowed the choriamb in each half to slide forward or backward to first or last place (109, 131K). He also used, as a short repeating line, the line which is called after him the pherecratean, but in his hands, or at any rate in the form in which he claimed it as his 'new invention' (79K), it is not an aeolo-choriambic line, sdx, but an anapaestic line with no possibility of anceps, $-- - \cup\cup --$: he called it 'folded [i.e. contracted] anapaests', and presumably used it as a substitute for the anapaestic dimeter. In another fragment he uses a string of choriambic dimeters B, the last one running out into a lekythion clausula (96K). Similarly Hermippos has a string of telesilleans, xds, running in a catalectic clausula, xdx (58K).

In the absence of complete comedies we cannot say much about choral technique. What we can see, is a variety of different long and short recitative metres alongside the older ones, an occasional flight into high-style lyric, and some sign of short-line lyric in iambic dimeters, eminently suitable for excited dancing.

7 · FREE PERIOD, 425-370 B.C.

Non-dramatic lyric in the free period falls into two classes, traditional and revolutionary. Traditional are, for instance, Euripides' victor-hymn for Alkibiades and Sophocles' *paian*. Alkibiades won first, second, and third (or fourth) prizes for the chariot race in an Olympiad shortly before the Peloponnesian war, and Plutarch quotes a short section of Euripides' victor-ode (*P.M.G.* 755). It is a quite ordinary piece of free dactylo-epitrite. The Paian to Hygieia by Ariphron of Sikyon (*P.M.G.* 813)[1] is also in free dactylo-epitrite, but opens with three periods in rising double-short. Like many late dactylo-epitrite poems it consists of a single stanza. Likymnios of Chios seems to have copied metre and phrasing of Ariphron in his hymn to Hygieia (*P.M.G.* 769) and has left another fragment in regular dactylo-epitrite (771). Likymnios is quoted by Aristotle and therefore wrote in the earlier part of the fourth century, and Ariphron may have been the Ariphron who was victorious in Athens about 400 B.C. All these were stately slow poems.

Sophocles' *paian* (*P.M.G.* 737) is preserved in an inscription: he wrote a *paian* to Asklepios, but the inscriptional *paian* is addressed to Asklepios' mother Koronis, and the suggestion[2] that the *paian* to Koronis was sung on the way to the altar of Asklepios is attractive. The text is so badly preserved that it is difficult to be sure of the metre, but it looks as if it were long dactylo-anapaests of Stesichorean kind. Both this and the *paian* to Asklepios were still sung in Athens in the imperial period. All that is known of the *paian* to Asklepios is that the god was called 'famed in counsel'. The adjective is applied to Paian (here Apollo) at the beginning of a *paian* which was inscribed at Erythrai in Ionia in the early fourth century and in Egypt, Athens, and Macedonia in the imperial period (*P.M.G.* 934).[3] The text is a very simple list of Asklepios' parents and children, and an appeal that 'my city' may see the light of the sun in joy and glory with the help of Hygieia (health). It seems to be generally assumed that this is too artless for Sophocles and that the writer borrowed an adjective from Sophocles' *paian*, but whatever our judgement of its merits it was

1. For colometry and dating, see Paul Maas, *Epidaurische Hymnen*, 148.
2. J. H. Oliver, *Hesperia*, 5, 1936, 109 ff.
3. Cf. also Oliver, loc. cit.; Powell, *Coll. Alex.* 136. The versions differ considerably and the colometry as well as the text is doubtful.

remarkably popular. In its original form it seems to have had three stanzas, each with the same short refrain (in one version *ie, o, ie paian*; in the others *ie paian*) near the beginning and the same long refrain calling on Asklepios at the end; the long refrain alone breaks the sequence of double-short, it runs xsxs, dd, ʌdx. Apart from the refrain the song is in long dactylic periods, a catalectic octameter before the short refrain, and a decameter between the short refrain and the long refrain. Another *paian* of the same period was the *paian* sung to the Spartan Lysander after the Peloponnesian War: this was in the simplest dancing enoplians, ending with the refrain, *o, ie paian*; xdd, xddd, xddx (*P.M.G.* 867).

The Hymn to the Kouretes[1] opens with a three-period iambo-trochaic refrain in dance time, praying Zeus to come to Dikta and rejoice in the song. This is repeated after each of the stanzas, which have two long stately periods; they start with a description of the chorus singing a song round the altar to the accompaniment of lyres and flutes, then tell how the Kouretes received the infant Zeus and how the world prospered, and finally pray that Zeus may leap into their pools, flocks, cities, ships, young men, and social order. The metre varies strangely between the stanzas. In the sixth (29 f.) it is clear: anacreontic, ionic dimeter, anacreontic, contracted ionic dimeter. But in the other stanzas, though the pattern seems to be 'major' ionic tetrameter with the last metron contracted (so as to make a molossus), a trochaic metron may always be substituted for an ionic metron. This is very strange but not necessarily late: something like it appears in Korinna (see above, p. 97). A date in this period is certainly not impossible.

In the preceding period Melanippides had introduced *anabolai*, astrophic preludes, not necessarily solos, into choral poetry. In this period the movement towards a more emotional music based on a lyre with a greater number of strings continued. The names of which we hear are Phrynis, Timotheos, Krexos, Telestes, and Philoxenos.[2] Phrynis has left no fragments but he is said to have had 'twelve harmonies on seven strings'. He won a Panathenaic victory, probably

1. Diehl, II, VI, 279; Powell, *Coll. Alex.* 160; Bowra in *Essays in Honour of Francis Letters*, 31; West, *J.H.S.*, 85, 1965, 149.
2. On these, see Pickard-Cambridge, *Dithyramb, etc.*[2], 43 ff.; on Timotheos, my *Tragedies of Euripides*, 17 ff. On Philoxenos *Cyclops*, see my *Later Greek Comedy*, 20 f.

in 446, in spite of great opposition, but was himself defeated by the revolutionary Timotheos of Miletos between 420 and 415. Timotheos was born about 450 and lived until at least 360. He used a twelve-string lyre. Philoxenos was born in 436 and lived until 380; according to Aristophanes he introduced songs into dithyrambs; again the meaning may be astrophic passages rather than solos, but not confined to the beginning like the 'preludes'. When the scholiast to the *parodos* of Aristophanes' *Plutus* says that 'Philoxenos the tragic poet introduced Polyphemos playing the lyre and holding a wallet' (*P.M.G.* 819–20), he is only getting confused: this was description, not a solo by a costumed performer, but the confusion does suggest that the new dithyramb was dramatic in a new way, and both the 'songs' of Philoxenos and the 'recitative' ascribed to Krexos were moves in the same direction. Our best evidence is the very realistic stretches of direct speech in the *Persae* of Timotheos.

Timotheos is the one poet of all these of whom we can form some impression. Very little survives of Philoxenos: three lines of the *Cyclops* appear to be catalectic iambic trimeters (or parts of them) (*P.M.G.* 823–4), and one long enoplian period, xddddsssx (*P.M.G.* 821), but we cannot tell how it fitted together. Rather more remains of Telestes, who was writing at the end of the fifth century. His *Argo* (*P.M.G.* 805) seems to have been in dactylo-epitrite with occasional enoplian or prosodiac lines, such as ddddsx. The fragment of the *Adklepios* (806) shows only the dactylic elements of dactylo-epitrite. Another fragment (810) has an ionic trimeter to describe Asiatics in the middle of epitrite lines. In the *Hymenaios* (808) three cretics intervene in the middle of melic anapaests. This is the sort of unexpected mixture which we associate with the new music, but the background seems much more stable than with Timotheos.

The shorter fragments of Timotheos sometimes seem not unlike Pindaric 'aeolic' (*P.M.G.* 780–1, 802), but we also find proceleusmatic anapaests (799), ionics (796), prosodiac–enoplian (800), and anapaestic–paroemiacs (803). The *Persae* (*P.M.G.* 788–91) shows his composition on a larger scale. It can be dated between 420 and 415. Euripides after Timotheos' initial hostile reception in Athens helped him in writing the prologue, and with the *Persae* Timotheos succeeded in defeating Phrynis. This means that Euripides was open to the influence of

Timotheos from at least his second period, i.e. after the *Hippolytos*. The *Persae* is a *nomos*, which was usually performed as a solo, and therefore does not strictly concern us; but, as we have seen, there is no hard division between solo and choral music and song, and it would be artificial to omit the solo songs of tragedy. The *Persae* begins with a hexameter (788), which is quoted by Plutarch in recounting a revival in 205 B.C.; it is, of course, possible that the opening was added then, but more probably the hexameter opening was traditional for a *nomos*, and Timotheos followed (or was persuaded by Euripides to follow) the tradition. The papyrus does not start until the battle of Salamis is nearly over. Two book fragments belong to the preliminary exhortation of the Greeks; one is bacchiac and cretic (789), the other iambic (790). In the papyrus (791), with no antistrophic responsion and a text that is both difficult and badly preserved, scansion and colometry are often uncertain. The earlier section seems to be in long iambic lines, many of which are catalectic tetrameters, permitting choriambic substitution occasionally, plenty of resolution and a good deal of syncopation. Some iambic periods are longer: 31–2 is a syncopated hexameter, 60–3 is a catalectic octameter. This is the beginning of the description of the swimmer and his speech. Here the iambics are broken by three dochmiacs, a cretic, a bacchiac, and another dochmiac (66–9). He starts his speech with an iambic heptameter followed by two dochmiacs (72–6). In 86 the flight of the Persian army begins with a long iambic period with double syncopation at the end; this spondaic rhythm anticipates an anapaestic trimeter, followed by four linked choriambic dimeters. It continues mainly iambo-choriambic to 99. Another section of direct speech starts at 105 and apparently goes into trochaics followed by a considerable run of cretics (116 f.). Towards the end (128 ff.) this speech goes into aeolo-choriambic punctuated by long runs of dactyls. Then a passage in iambics, mostly dimeters (140 ff.) leads into another speech in broken Greek of a captive appealing to his captor. The next description leads us, largely in trochaics to Xerxes' own lament (178 ff.). His opening iambic dimeter leads in long periods, largely aeolo-choriambic; then another iambic dimeter (187) leads in another section of the same length, aeolo-choriambic, dactylic, and dochmiac. Finally a brief section (196–201) dactylic, glyconic, and iambic with aristophanean clausula, describes the Greeks setting up their trophy, singing and dancing a *paian*. Then Timotheos appeals to Apollo '*ieie Paian*' to come to the help of his own song. The transition here is very like the end of Bacchylides' *Theseus* (see above, p. 101). The long autobiographic section (202–36) is in alternating glyconics and pherecrateans mostly linked, but ending with a hipponactean, which is repeated twice in the short final prayer for Apollo's blessing on Athens.

The last section is regular and readily intelligible; the new, self-confident art of Timotheos is expended on the description of the battle and the direct speeches inserted in the story. Here what we seem to see is a basic very free use of long iambic periods, varied at particular points by longer or shorter sections of other metres, sometimes in long periods, sometimes in short periods, sometimes fairly uniform and sometimes very mixed. It is an immense development of the free astrophic song with mixed metres on an iambic framework, of which our earliest example is the lament of Euripides' Hippolytos (*Hipp.* 1379 ff.) and that may, of course, be the first sign of the new music influencing tragedy.

On a much smaller scale than in the *Persae* something of the same speedy switching from metre to metre can be seen in the hymn of gratitude to Poseidon ascribed to Arion (*P.M.G.* 939). The speaker purports to be Arion, and he addresses first Poseidon and then the dolphin who saved him. Bowra[1] thinks of it as a solo introduced into a choral song sung by men dressed as dolphins (hence they can be said to throw their feet lightly). This is an engaging idea, and there is evidence for dolphin choruses on earlier vases (no. 163); the dolphins always have riders, and so a chorus of Arions on dolphins is not impossible. The song certainly seems to be astrophic, but it is not necessarily a solo. The only two lines in the same metre are the two glyconics (10, 10), and the writer rings the changes on various kinds of aeolo-choriambic, dactyls, dactylo-anapaests, enoplians, iambics, and trochaics. It is a simple and pleasing composition which one would gladly ascribe to comedy. An Attic polychrome oinochoe (no. 279) dated 400–390 shows a man rowing a large blue fish, probably a member of a comic chorus.

The three late Sophoclean tragedies, *Electra*, *Philoctetes*, *Oedipus Coloneus*, can be dated 413, 409, and 406.[2] In time therefore they belong to the end of Euripides' third group and the beginning of his fourth

---

1. *Mus. Helv.* 20, 1963, 121.   2. See below ,n. 173 n. 1.

group. It is therefore easier to consider the whole of Euripides' production first. His second group which runs from the *Andromache* to the *Electra*, 427–417 B.C., shows some new developments. The *parodos* of the *Andromache* starts with an elegiac lament by Andromache: Page may well be right that this is in the tradition of the early Argive laments by Sakadas.[1] This solo sets dactylic metre as the dominant for choruses which deal with the heroic past of the Trojan War rather than the sordid present. The women of Phthia come to console Andromache; the metre is dactylic varied with iambo-trochaic, a kind of free dactylo-epitrite; the end of the second pair of strophe–antistrophe is iambic. The long hexameters, picking up Andromache's lament, make this a stately chorus. In the first *stasimon* (274) the chorus go back to the Judgement of Paris. Here long prosodiacs and enoplians are interspersed with iambics and syncopated iambics. The first pair may perhaps be in dance time, but the second begins with a 19-syllable prosodiac, ddddsss, and ends with a 22-syllable period in free dactylo-epitrite.

The second *stasimon* (465) comes after Menelaos has tricked Andromache off the altar. The chorus sing of the evils of double marriages. This is in iambics with a lot of resolution, except for one period of enoplian and one period of prosodiac in the second pair of strophe–antistrophe. The final period of iambic trimeter plus catalectic trimeter is 21 syllables long but should probably be regarded as a climax so that the whole is in dance time. Then six lines of recitative anapaests mark the entrance of Andromache and her child, ready for death. In the following lyric dialogue strophe and antistrophe have a sung part for Andromache and the child (in fact, probably, the actor who takes Andromache sings the child's part as well as Andromache's, as in the similar child's lament in the *Alcestis*), followed by recitative anapaests for Menelaos. The sung part is glyconic with interspersed pherecratean.

When Peleus has rescued Andromache and the child, the chorus are back in the heroic past again for the third *stasimon* (766). Strophe–antistrophe are in straightforward dactylo-epitrite in dance time; only the latter part of the epode which starts with long dactylo-epitrite periods changes into resolved iambics with an aeolo-choriambic

1. *Greek Poetry and Life*, 206 ff.; cf. also above, p. 67.

clausula. In the next scene the nurse reports Hermione's attempted suicide; Hermione dashes out and a lyric dialogue follows (825). The nurse speaks iambic trimeters and so divides Hermione's song into sections. Hermione sings an astrophic song (some rhythms are repeated in the earlier part, but it should not be forced into strophes and anti-strophes): dochmiacs mixed with other metres, two long dactylo-epitrite lines (826, 830), a good deal of prosodiac and enoplian, catalectic iambics, and anapaests later. This is rather the technique of Hippolytos' final lament but on a larger scale.

For the fourth *stasimon* (1009) the chorus go back to the Trojan War and dactylo-epitrites in long periods. After the messenger speech the antistrophic lament of Peleus over the body of Neoptolemos (1173) starts in long dactylic periods; Peleus belongs to the heroic period rather than to the sordid present. The chorus speak two iambic tri-meters after the first pair of strophe and antistrophe. In the second pair they lead off in resolved iambics and then interject iambic trimeters twice into his sung iambics.

In the *Hecuba* also the heroic Trojan War is a sort of foil to the present disaster and finds expression in the *stasima*. The *parodos* starts with Hekabe being helped out of the door after she has seen the ghost of Polydoros in her dreams. Her long monody begins in recitative anapaests, which are punctuated by two dactylic hexameters (74–5). She moves into melic anapaests at l. 85, and these again are broken by two dactylic hexameters (90–1). The chorus of captive Trojan women enter to a very long section of recitative anapaests. Hekabe sings a long passage (which should not be forced into correspondence with 197–215) of melic anapaests broken at 165 by a dochmiac, which opens with a dactyl and is taken up by ddd and then a long dactylic line fading into iambics.[1] Then she returns to melic anapaests. Polyxene then comes out and sings in lyric dialogue with Hekabe; this again is lyric anapaests interrupted six times by dochmiacs or dochmiac equivalents. Then Polyxene sings alone a stretch which has a rough correspondence to Hekabe's earlier solo. The whole passage from 154 has a large number of spondaic lines: dimeters, paroemiacs, hexamakra, and anapaestic dochmiacs. This is a new characteristic which becomes common.

After Polyxene has been led away to die the chorus sing the lovely

1. Cf. above, p. 101.

decorated first *stasimon* in which they wonder where in Greece they will be sent (444). Both pairs are aeolo-choriambic and both have long stately periods. After the description of Polyxene's death the chorus go back to the Judgement of Paris (629) in a triad of mixed metre in dancing time, iambic, aeolo-choriambic, enoplian, and dactylo-epitrite. The arrival of the maidservant with the body of Polydoros causes another lyric dialogue of the kind commonly found when bad news is brought (681). The maidservant and the chorus speak occasional trimeters; Hekabe sings largely dochmiacs but interspersed with short iambics. Then when the maid has gone to fetch Polymestor, the chorus sing another decorated ode about the last night in Troy. This third *stasimon* (905) is again in mixed metre, enoplian, dactylo-epitrite, aeolo-choriambic, and iambic, but dactylo-epitrite predominates; both of the pairs of strophe–antistrophe and the epode have long stately periods.

When Polymestor goes into Hekabe's hut, the chorus sing an excited, gloating astrophic song (1024) which is pure dochmiac except for an iambic dimeter and trimeter in the middle (1030–1). When Polymestor comes out blinded he sings a long lament (1056), only broken by two trimeters of the chorus (1085–6). His dochmiac song is broken by anapaests at 1065, 1070, 1076, and by four cretics followed by an anapaest dimeter at 1081. After the chorus's two trimeters the song varies more from dochmiac: 1091, iambic penthemimers and iambic, glyconic; 1099, epitrites, cretics, and two lines of dactylo-epitrites before the dochmiac close. This mixture is a clear sign of the new technique.

The *Supplices* is quite different because it follows the traditional pattern of a suppliant play, and the chorus, the mothers of the seven champions who attacked Thebes, are engaged in the action as the mothers of the fallen champions. The *parodos* is an appeal to Aithra, the mother of Theseus, in two pairs of strophe–antistrophe in long ionic periods and one in iambo-trochaic dance time, describing their gestures of lament. Later after Adrastos has failed they appeal again (271) with four recitative hexameters, then a lyric run of fifteen dactyls ending blunt, followed by a lyric pentameter, and closing with four recitative hexameters again. This sequence is unique. When Theseus goes off to get the decision of the Athenians, the chorus sing the first *stasimon* (365), wondering what the city will decide. The two pairs are in dancing iambics with a good deal of resolution and an epitrite close.

After the debate between Theseus and the Theban herald, the second *stasimon* (598) starts in dactylo-epitrite, but is largely iambic in both pairs. Both are in dance time but the first ends in a long climax. The mothers ask what is happening and how they will get home. Then the messenger describes the battle and announces the return of the dead. The mothers sing a single iambic pair introduced by an enoplian (778), then anapaestic dimeters (recitative) mark the arrival of the corpses and are followed by a triad of lyric lament (798) shared by Adrastos and the mothers. This is largely iambic but in the strophe–antistrophe Adrastos has a single dactylic hexameter before the clausula; the epode starts with an iambic–cretic–dochmiac period and has a dactylo-epitrite period before the end. (The whole from 778 is probably in dance time in spite of the single long period (826–7) in the epode.)

A little astrophic iambic stanza follows Adrastos' funeral speech (918). When Adrastos and Theseus have agreed on the burial arrangements for Kapaneus and the rest, the mothers sing of their misery in an aeolo-choriambic triad with a first long period of glyconic plus glyconic plus aeolo-choriambic decasyllable (955). The epode has some irregular resolutions, and three (and perhaps four) successive choriambic dimeters B. Recitative anapaests mark the *ekkyklema* rolling out with Evadne perched above the tomb of Kapaneus. Her lament (990) is a long strophe and antistrophe in aeolo-choriambic introduced by two bacchiacs and with four bacchiacs in the middle: the long series of glyconics and choriambic dimeters B pick up the aeolo-choriambics of the preceding triad by the mothers. Finally the mothers announce in recitative anapaests the arrival of their grandchildren with their fathers' ashes. The final lyric dialogue (1123) consists of three pairs of strophe and antistrophe in iambics sung by the mothers and the grandchildren; probably the main chorus sang the whole dialogue and the grandchildren mimed their parts. This is the second song in this play with three pairs of strophe–antistrophe. Both are lamentation (the other is the *parodos*), and Euripides is keeping alive the old tradition of very short stanzas in laments.

In the *Electra*, which belongs late in this group, Euripides consciously contrasts his very individual conception of the story with Aeschylus. This Elektra is not bringing libations from the palace for Agamemnon's tomb but returning with the household water from the spring below her cottage, lamenting her miserable fate. She enters with three periods of lyric anapaests describing her slow walk, which are repeated before the antistrophe. The rest of the first pair is aeolo-choriambic, very largely glyconic. The strophe has a tailpiece of glyconic plus iambic dimeter (unless the second line should also be taken as glyconic resolved) which is not repeated at the end of the antistrophe. The second pair has a long dactylic period at the beginning but then again is almost entirely aeolo-choriambic. Again a short aeolo-choriambic mesode separates strophe and antistrophe. The mesodes and the alien openings of both pairs give this monody something of the complication of earlier laments (e.g. the *Choephoroe kommos*), and the continually repeated glyconics drive home Elektra's misery.

Then the chorus of Mycenaean women enter to invite Elektra to a festival of Hera, and the *parodos* proper consists of one very long pair with both the strophe and the antistrophe divided about half-way between the chorus and Elektra. After the opening enoplian periods it runs through in aeolo-choriambic to the end; the periods are, some of them, too long for dance time; free correspondence between choriambic dimeter B and glyconic is extremely common here. Again in the first *stasimon* (432) the chorus sing of the glories of the Trojan War in a stately, decorated song with two pairs of strophe–antistrophe and an epode. Most of this is aeolo-choriambic, but the second pair and the epode start with a long dactylic line, and the second pair has a long asclepiadic period near the end (460).

After the recognition the chorus sing a short stanza (585) mostly dochmiac but with three enoplian insertions. The second *stasimon* (699) comes after the making of the double plan. The chorus sing of the Golden Lamb in another stately decorated ode, the two pairs are mostly aeolo-choriambic but again there is quite a lot of enoplian. After the messenger speech they sing a victory song (859), a single strophe and antistrophe in danced dactylo-epitrite (they compare themselves to a fawn leaping lightly to heaven), with seven iambic trimeters spoken by Elektra between them. Their next song leads up to the murder of Klytemnestra and the repentance of Orestes and Elektra. They have greeted Klytemnestra's pompous arrival with recitative anapaests (998). Then when she goes into the house they sing (1147) strophe, antistrophe, and epode in dochmiacs interspersed with a little iambic. The epode is punctuated by Klytemnestra's cries off. Then after five spoken trimeters the brother and sister appear. The lyric dialogue (1177) is iambic all the way through after Orestes' opening dochmiac to the chorus's final alcaic decasyllable close at the end of the third pair. Orestes begins and the chorus ends each of the six verses; Elektra has two spoken trimeters in the middle of the first two, and two sung dimeters after Orestes in the last two. The simplicity of this contrasts obviously with the much more complicated *kommos* of the *Choephoroe*, and gives the kind of matt close that Euripides desires.

There are a few choral fragments of other plays of this period, but they do not show anything startling. The most interesting is the new fragment of the *Erechtheus*;[1] it is desperately corrupt but it is fairly clear that the chorus at the beginning, which may be an excited close to the preserved enoplian fragment (369N²), has a lot of cretic and ends with four dochmiacs; Praxithea's lament and the succeeding choral comment on the earthquake is dochmiac with admixture of other metres, iambic, anapaest, and bacchiac. The same sort of mixture also occurs in the very corrupt new fragments of the *Second Phrixos*,[2] which seems to be the lament of Athamas, when he hears that Phrixos must be put to death; there dochmiacs apparently lead into dactyls.

The second group does not show any startling change in the use of metres; the sample is too small for the falling off in dactylo-epitrites and aeolo-choriambics or the rise in iambics and iambo-trochaics to be significant. In fact the repeated choriambic B dimeters in the *Supplices* and *Electra* look forward to the future. The remarkable ionic *parodos* of the *Supplices* may perhaps intentionally recall the last chorus of Aeschylus' *Supplices* (1018); these are also women in distress. The development of astrophic monodies continues. The most advanced in this group are Hermione's suicide song in the *Andromache* and Polymestor's lament in the *Hecuba*.

The third group of Euripides' plays can be taken in the probable order of production.[3] The *Phaethon* was probably produced before 415. The very simple and beautiful dawn *parodos* has a first pair of strophe–antistrophe in the simplest dancing aeolo-choriambics. The second pair

1. P. Sorbonne 2328, *Recherches de Papyrologie* IV, 1967.
2. *P.Oxy.* 2685. Cf. my *Tragedies of Euripides*, 134.
3. See *Tragedies of Euripides*, 163.

is in anapaestic enoplians, which change to a long dactylic period followed by an iambic clausula. The epode is iambic punctuated by a single prosodiac and a single trochaic tetrameter catalectic. The chorus then announce the herald in anapaests, and he opens his proclamation, with four dactylic hexameters. The little marriage song sung by Merops and the subsidiary chorus is in free dactylo-epitrite. The song of the main chorus when Merops rushes into the house appears to be astrophic; it is mainly dochmiac with iambic, enoplian, and dactylo-epitrite interspersed, in what is now the common manner.

From the production of 415 a choral fragment of the *Alexandros* (52N²) is iambic; a choral fragment of the *Palamedes* (586N²) is in very simple aeolo-choriambic, and two dactylo-epitrite lines are preserved of what is probably Oiax's lament for his brother (588N²). The third play, the *Trojan Women*, recalls the *Hecuba* in having a very long anapaestic dialogue *parodos* and decorated *stasima* which act as a foil against the present misery. Here too Hekabe starts the *parodos* in recitative anapaests. Her melic anapaests have many spondaic paroemiacs and dimeters and one line with remarkable light anapaests.[1] The chorus enter from either side and continue her melic anapaests. In the first pair of strophe–antistrophe their more regular anapaests are followed by freer anapaests from Hekabe; the second pair (197) is entirely theirs, and much more spondaic than the first. They then greet Talthybios in recitative anapaests. He ushers in one of the common lyric dialogues which follow bad news (235). Talthybios speaks single trimeters and Hekabe asks her questions in dochmiacs, introduced, followed, or interrupted by iambics, enoplians, prosodiacs, and dactylo-epitrite. Only sixteen trimeters separate Hekabe's commentary on her future as the slave of Odysseus and Kassandra's lyric entry waving torches, singing her marriage song (308). She starts in dochmiacs and then goes into iambics with glyconic for the refrain to Hymen and a short aeolo-choriambic section near the end. This is all in dancing time and much of it in excited dancing time, as 'hurl your foot high, lead the dance up to heaven' (325) implies. It is cast as a pair of strophe (308–24) and antistrophe (325–40).

The first *stasimon* (511) is a stately, decorated description of the last

---

1. 136, cf. *L.M.*² 58, 65. Lines 124–5 are taken as free glyconics, but perhaps they are dactylic ddd, both opening with a light dactyl, and doing duty for paroemiacs.

night of Troy. The strophe–antistrophe starts in dactylo-epitrite and goes over into iambic. The epode is iambic with a dactylo-epitrite clausula. Recitative anapaests lead over to the lyric dialogue between Hekabe and Andromache (577); in the two short pairs of strophe–antistrophe (which recall Aeschylean laments) the metre is almost entirely syncopated iambic; in the epode (which should not be made into a pair) dactylic hexameters and tetrameters in recitative are followed by lyric dactylic hexameters (rather like the appeal of the mothers in *Suppl.* 271). When Andromache and Astyanax have been taken off, the short dialogue in recitative anapaests between Talthybios and Hekabe is followed by the second *stasimon* (799), a stately decorated ode about the first Trojan War in dactylo-epitrite with iambo-trochaic insertions in the second pair.

After the Helen scene the third *stasimon* (1060) is the last decorated ode about Troy. The first pair starts aeolo-choriambic, goes on iambic, and has a prosodiac clausula. The second pair starts with a hemiepes, then goes into iambic, and has five hemiepe before the iambic clausula. Each pair has a single long period, but the rest is in dance time. The end of the play is lamentation: the chorus respond to Hekabe's lament for Astyanax with short iambics and dochmiacs (1216). The great lament for Troy (1287) is almost entirely iambic with a good deal of syncopation and resolution, except for a little dochmiac in Hekabe's first song.

The next production probably included the *Iphigenia in Tauris* and the *Hercules Furens*. The *Iphigenia* also has an anapaestic *parodos*, a lyric dialogue between the chorus and Iphigeneia. These are melic anapaests many of them spondaic, with occasional light anapaests (197, 213, 220) and proceleusmatics (183, 231, 232); besides the more normal lengths, five and six long syllables occur, both the equivalent of dochmiacs. These are 'the barbarian songs of Asiatic hymns', 'the muse of lamentation which has nothing to do with *paians*' (179 f.). The first *stasimon* (392) is a stately decorated song sung after the herdsman has reported the capture of Orestes and Pylades and asking who the strangers are; the first pair is free dactylo-epitrite and the second simple aeolo-chori-ambic with two long periods, one of three and one of four linked cola.

There is no more lyric until the short lyric dialogue between the chorus, Orestes, and Pylades while Iphigeneia fetches her letter (644). The choral part is in dochmiac with Orestes and Pylades speaking a trimeter each. The following recognition duet (827) is much more elaborate. Orestes' iambic trimeters[1] punctuate Iphigeneia's lyrics, which are basically dochmiac but have considerable insertions of cretic, iambic, and enoplian. For us this is the first long astrophic song in the new technique, which is not a lament. When the escape plan is made, the chorus sing the second *stasimon* (1089) in which they wish that they too could go to Greece, another stately, decorated aeolo-choriambic song with a prosodiac insertion in the first pair and a long dactylic insertion before the end of the second. The third and last *stasimon* about Apollo (1234), sung after Iphigeneia and Orestes have gone to their escape, consists of a single very long pair of strophe-antistrophe. This is free dactylo-epitrite with some prosodiac, enoplian, and aeolo-choriambic, and three long periods.

The chorus of the *Hercules Furens* are old men who have come to visit the family of Herakles. They struggle slowly in, leaning on sticks, to iambics which they call a lamentation (109). The pair of strophe-antistrophe is very short and has a short epode in which dochmiacs and cretics mingle with the iambics and a choriambic heptasyllable introduces the clausula. The first *stasimon* (348) follows Lykos' condemnation of Herakles' wife and children. It is a stately *enkomion* of Herakles with a simple dancing aeolo-choriambic refrain (with different words each time) after each of the three pairs of strophe-antistrophe. The first pair is aeolo-choriambic, the second pair starts aeolo-choriambic, goes over into dactylo-anapaest and ends in iambo-trochaic, and the third pair is iambic. The second *stasimon* (637) is a song of rejoicing after Herakles' return. Both pairs are aeolo-choriambic, but the second has an insertion of ionics.

The third *stasimon* (735) begins when Amphitryon has gone into the house to see Lykos die. In the first pair excited dochmiacs are broken by iambic trimeters, including Lykos' cries off. The second pair (763), in which the chorus rejoice at Herakles' victory, are aeolo-choriambics followed by iambics. The third pair is pure aeolo-choriambic. Then the chorus see the *mechane* with Iris and Lyssa; their fear is expressed in iambics and in dochmiacs. When Lyssa has gone into the house they comment (875) in dochmiacs with long insertions of other metres, iambic, aeolo-choriambic, enoplian, prosodiac, and dactylo-epitrite.

---

1. 832 must not be given to Iphigeneia, *L.M.*[2] 109.

Amphitryon's cries off, once in dochmiac, otherwise in iambic, punctuate and direct their commentary.[1] Then the messenger comes out, and his announcement is met with the customary choral lamentation (911) in iambics shared with him and dochmiacs.

After the messenger speech the chorus have a long astrophic song (1016), which leads up to the rolling out of the *ekkyklema* (1028) with Herakles and the bodies of his children, and so to the entrance of Amphitryon and the long lyric dialogue ending with Herakles' awakening (1086). The framework of the whole is dochmiac, but as so often in these late astrophic songs it is interspersed with other metres. The chorus has a dactylo-epitrite period near the beginning and then a pair of enoplian plus prosodiac; and in the latter slower part, the lyric dialogue with Amphitryon, there are periods of aeolo-choriambic, iambic and enoplian. A similar lyric dialogue follows when Theseus arrives (1178), but here the chorus has no part. Theseus is restricted to iambic trimeters and sections of iambic trimeters, but Amphitryon embroiders his dochmiacs with dactylo-epitrite, prosodiac and enoplian periods.

The next production was in 412, *Andromeda* and *Helen* certainly, and probably *Ion*. The *Andromeda* opened with the startling spectacle of Andromeda chained to a rock, alone in the night, answered only by Echo and visited at dawn by the chorus of friendly Ethiopian women. Enough can be reconstructed from the parody in Aristophanes' *Thesmophoriazusae* to show that she started in recitative anapaests (114–6N[2]) and that the dialogue with the chorus began with a curious pendant iambo-trochaic dimeter[2] and then continued in iambo-trochaic (117–120N[2]). The epode (122N[2]) was perhaps basically dochmiac and varied with iambic and prosodiac but here the Aristophanic parody may be misleading.

In the *Helen*, Helen opens the *parodos* with two dactylic hexameters and a dactylic pentameter, then she sings the two strophes and the epode and the chorus of captive Greek women sing the antistrophes. All are in iambo-trochaic with short periods and much resolution. Exceptionally in this play the chorus go into the house (with Helen to consult

---

1. The final lines, 906 ff., belong to the chorus, not to Herakles. Cf. A. M. Dale, *W.S.* 69, 1956, 101 = *Collected Papers*, 124.
2. On this, see A. M. Dale, *W.S.* 78, 1964, 33 = *Collected Papers*, 206.

Theonoe), so that Menelaos can be presented to the audience without either Helen or the chorus. They go in with a lyric dialogue (330); this long astrophic passage starts iambo-trochaic, but Helen has one hexameter in 356. This anticipates the long tailpiece about Kallisto (375), in which Helen sings long runs of dactylic only returning to iambo-trochaic for the ithyphallic clausula (these dactylic runs become increasingly common in the late plays). When they come out of the house (515), the chorus tell what Theonoe has said in a single stanza of simple aeolo-choriambics.

In the recognition duet (625) Menelaos is slightly less bound to spoken iambic trimeters than Orestes in the *Iphigenia*. He has in addition catalectic trimeters (636), dochmiacs (659), and a long enoplian (692). Helen's part is basically dochmiac but she varies them with the usual range of other metres used in this free style. When the two have made their plan to escape, the chorus at last sing the first *stasimon* (1107), a decorated stately ode about the Trojan War. The first pair of strophe–antistrophe are in free dactylo-epitrite going over into enoplian. The second pair is dactylo-epitrite going over into iambic. The second *stasimon* (1301), which marks the pause while preparations are being made for the 'burial at sea', is the decorated song about the Great Mother; both pairs are almost entirely in the late, simple aeolo-choriambics (B dimeters and heptasyllables). The third *stasimon* (1451) sung after the departure of Helen and Menelaos is another decorated stately aeolo-choriambic song in two pairs of strophe–antistrophe; the second pair has a small admixture of prosodiac–enoplian.

The *Ion* may be the third play of this trilogy. The *parodos* starts with the long solo of Ion while he sweeps the temple. He begins in recitative anapaests, then has a strophe–antistrophe in simple aeolo-choriambics; both have a brief refrain prayer in molossi to Apollo as Paian. He goes on in melic anapaests with occasional cola (148–50, 178) which are indistinguishable from dochmiacs. Then the chorus of Athenian women enter to inspect the temple in two stately pairs of strophe–antistrophe; both start in aeolo-choriambic, the second goes into iambic towards the end. The second antistrophe is unique in being interrupted six times (once in the middle of a colon) by the anapaests with which Ion answers the question put by the chorus; presumably the dance stops while Ion makes his points in recitative.

The first *stasimon* (452) is a decorated ode in dance time, a prayer to Athena for children to continue the line of Erechtheus. It consists of a single triad; in the strophe–antistrophe the periods are almost equally divided between aeolo-choriambic and enoplian. In the epode the chorus are agitated by Kreousa's story and sing short lines mostly aeolo-choriambic, but with an occasional dochmiac,[1] and ending up in enoplian–anapaests. The second *stasimon* (676) also consists of a single triad. The chorus are distressed by the news that Xouthos and not Kreousa has been given a child. They sing agitated dochmiacs, interspersed with iambic, prosodiac, and enoplian as in the astrophic songs. When Kreousa and the old man hear the news (here given by the chorus instead of by a messenger) they launch into a lyric dialogue (763) where he has iambic trimeters and segments of iambic trimeters, and she sings dochmiacs and twice a hemiepes to make an iambelegus with his iambic penthemimer. After a stretch of dialogue, in her utter misery at the loss of her child she sings a long anapaestic monody (859): first three melic paroemiacs, then recitative to 880, then melic again including short lines indistinguishable from dochmiacs, actual dochmiacs (894–6), light anapaests (889, 900), proceleusmatics (883, 905), returning to melic dimeters at the end (916). (This is the style of Hekabe in the *parodos* of the *Trojan Women* and Iphigeneia in the *parodos* of the *Iphigenia in Tauris*.)

When the plot has been put into execution, the chorus sing a stately prayer to Hekate as the third *stasimon* (1048). The first pair starts in dactylo-epitrite and then switches to aelo-choriambic. The second pair is also mainly aeolo-choriambic. After the messenger speech the chorus sing in their despair a short astrophic song in dance time (1229) in aeolo-choriambic with two short inserts of ionic. They end in recitative anapaests as Kreousa appears. There are no more lyrics before the long recognition duet (1439) which takes the usual form with Ion speaking iambic trimeters and segments of trimeters and Kreousa singing dochmiacs, dactylo-epitrites, prosodiacs, enoplians, bacchiacs, and cretics.

Euripides' next production was probably the *Antiope*, *Hypsipyle*, and

---

1. 503 (with the MSS. order ἵνα τεκοῦϲα τιϲ παρθένοϲ, ὦ μελέα), and 505 are certainly dochmiac; I do not feel certain that the five long syllables of 498 and 501 are not better here taken as contracted reiziana to suit the context, but they may be dochmiacs.

Phoenissae. In the *Antiope* Amphion started the *parodos* with a monody to his lyre which at least began in hexameters (182N²). We probably have fragments of the chorus commenting in recitative anapaests (910N²) and then of the *parodos* proper in dactylo-epitrites (911N²). In the papyrus fragment (Page, *G.L.P.* no. 10, 45 ff.) the chorus sing excited dochmiacs while Lykos is in the cave and as the *ekkyklema* rolls out to show him between the twins.

The *Hypsipyle* papyrus[1] preserves much of the *parodos* and the final recognition scene. The *parodos* consists of a stately pair of strophe–antistrophe in each of which Hypsipyle sings the first part and the chorus of Nemean women the second part. Both parts start in very simple aeolo-choriambic and end with a rush of dactylic tetrameters leading to, in the first part, an ithyphallic clausula. The metre of Hypsipyle's epode is not clear at the beginning; it may be choriambic rather than ionic, but it certainly ends in pure anapaests leading up to an ithyphallic clausula. At the end of the play there is a short section of comment in dochmiacs on Hypsipyle's discovery of her children (it may be sung by her or by the chorus) before Amphiaraos makes his farewell. Then the recognition duet takes the usual form with one of the sons speaking iambics or segments of iambic and Hypsipyle singing dochmiacs and the other metres associated with dochmiacs in these duets.

The same technique of dochmiacs and associated metres (including here anapaests and dactyls) is used again in the *Phoenissae* for the lyric dialogue which precedes the *parodos*. Here the old man speaks and Antigone sings as they describe to each other the seven champions seen from the walls of Thebes. The *parodos* itself sung by the Phoenician women, explaining their presence in Thebes on the way to Delphi, consists of one triad in very simple aeolo-choriambic with some long periods and a second pair of strophe–antistrophe in very simple iambo-trochaic. Polyneikes arrives and the chorus (291) supplicate him and summon Iokaste in dochmiacs. She enters and sings a long monody (301), basically dochmiac but much iambic and cretic insertion, a little enoplian, and a long dactylic run just before the end. After the debate between the brothers the first *stasimon* on Theban history (638) is a single triad in dancing trochaic except for one long iambic period

1. See G. W. Bond, *Euripides Hypsipyle*; Page, *G.L.P.* no. 12.

(653) near the end of the strophe–antistrophe. The epode is an appeal to the gods for help. The second *stasimon* (784) sung after Eteokles has gone to war is a stately decorated ode, again on Theban history, in long dactylic periods. These continue in the epode after a paeonic opening, then are broken by two periods of dactylo-anapaests. The epode ends with an anapaestic hexameter followed by an aeolo-choriambic decasyllable as a clausula. The third *stasimon*, on the Sphinx (1019), sung after the Menoikeus scene is in dancing iambo-trochaics again. A series of three hypodochmiacs (1023 ff.) ending with a catalectic iambic dimeter is to be reckoned as iambo-trochaic rather than dochmiac. (It seems to be followed by eleven linked iambic metra plus an ithyphallic and this could perhaps be danced as a climax.) The fourth *stasimon* (1284) after Antigone and Iokaste have gone out to try and save the brothers is a single very short pair mostly dochmiac; here for the first time the chorus comment on the present disaster instead of singing the past history of Thebes.

When the messenger brings back the news (1335), Kreon greets him or rather his news with dochmiacs and they are carried on by the chorus. After the messenger speech they greet the arrival of Antigone and the corpses in recitative anapaests. Antigone breaks into a long lament which starts with long runs of dactyls (1485–1537), then goes on in varieties of iambic and aeolo-choriambic, including runs of nine choriambs and five cretics, and after returning to dactylic ends with her summons to Oidipous in six bacchiacs and an adonean. Oidipous enters to ionics and dochmiacs, but the ensuing lyric dialogue with Antigone has much dactylic. After the scene with Kreon the play ends with another long lyric dialogue between Antigone and Oidipous (1710), which oscillates between iambic and trochaic and ends after a lone anapaestic dimeter (1755) with what seems to be a trimeter version of the ithyphallic repeated. In both these long exchanges the chorus have no part at all, and there is no distinction between a singing and a speaking actor as in the recognition duets. Antigone has the more important singing part, but there is no doubt that Oidipous has a singing part with much the same range of metres as Antigone. This is a new development, which points forward to the last group starting with the *Orestes*.

As against the preceding period the remarkable developments in this period are first the increase in aeolo-choriambic, particularly runs of choriambic dimeter B, and in dochmiac. With this goes, of course, the use of dochmiac as a dominant among a number of other metres in astrophic songs, whether sung by the chorus alone or by the chorus and actors or by actors alone. The recognition duets are a notable example, but the technique is not essentially different in Kassandra's marriage song, Antigone's inspection of the Seven, or the chorus's commentary when Lyssa enters the house of Herakles. The end of the *Phoenissae* shows a new free use of metre in Antigone's lament and the first dialogue with Oidipous.

Euripides' production in 408 certainly included the *Orestes* and probably the *Auge* and *Oidipous*. No lyric fragments survive from the *Auge*; from the *Oidipous* there is a fragment in dactylo-epitrite (546N²) and a fragment in dochmiac (555N²). The chorus of the *Orestes* are Mycenaean women who come to comfort Elektra. The *parodos* is a lyric dialogue between them and Elektra, who is afraid that they will awake Orestes. The first pair of strophe–antistrophe is pure dochmiac, including a final run (149) of 32 short syllables ending with two recognizable dochmiacs. In the second pair the dochmiacs are more varied by insertion of cretic, bacchiac, iambic, trochaic, and they have three linked enoplians near the end (181). The first *stasimon* (316) when Elektra has gone into the house is a single pair of strophe–antistrophe in almost pure dochmiac, the chorus speak of the Furies who harass Orestes. In the second *stasimon* (806), when Orestes and Pylades have gone off to the trial, the chorus sing a triad about the house of Pelops in regular aeolo-choriambics with several long periods; many of the lines are choriambic dimeter B. The messenger reports the trial to Elektra, and she follows it with a single triad of monody (960). This is a lament, and she tears her hair and cheeks. The strophe–antistrophe are in iambics, mostly in trimeter length. The epode starts in iambics in shorter lengths, but has a patch of hypodochmiac (992), a patch of trochaic (1001), and finally a long run of dactyls before a single-short clausula.

After the plan to murder Helen has been made (1246) Elektra remains outside singing a lyric dialogue with the chorus, who are divided to watch the approaches from left and right. The strophe and antistrophe are mainly dochmiac, punctuated by iambic trimeters, with a prosodiac

beginning, and towards the end enoplian plus prosodiac and iambelegus. The epode to this triad includes Helen's cries off. The metres are
the same, but Elektra has a long prosodiac on either side of Helen's
cry. When Hermione has been driven in, the chorus has a dochmiac
strophe (1353) with one long enoplian; the answering antistrophe
(1537) comes after the monody of the Phrygian slave.

The monody of the Phrygian (1369) has a near-echo of Timotheos'
Persae[1] and has long been recognized as an example of the new music.
It has more pattern than the *Persae* because it is divided into seven
sections by iambic trimeters from the chorus. Otherwise it is largely
polymetric except for eight runs of identical lines: 1382 ff. dochmiacs,
1403–6, anapaests, 1419 ff. cretics, 1426 ff. anapaests, 1437 ff. bacchiacs,
1444 ff. iambic dimeters, 1483 ff. anapaests, 1490 ff. dochmiacs; but in
the intervening sections it has a tendency to return to iambic or
dochmiac with iambic dominant. The technique is not unlike that of
Antigone's lament in the *Phoenissae* (1485), but this is on a much larger
scale and has a different dominant metre.

The only lyric fragment of any interest from the Macedonian trilogy
of 407 is a dactylic run (263N[2]), perhaps from the lament for Kisseus
in the *Archelaos*. The first play of the posthumous trilogy was the
Iphigenia in Aulis, which opens with the anapaestic dialogue between
Agamemnon and the old man. The chorus of Chalkidian women
arrive cheerfully to see the army. Their first triad is mostly simple
aeolo-choriambics with some long periods, including in the strophe–
antistrophe a long run (172 ff.), which is perhaps asclepiadic rather than
ionic, and a long enoplian, and in the epode at the end a dactylic run.
A dull catalogue of ships follows in two pairs of strophe–antistrophe
and an epode, all in trochaics. The first *stasimon* (543) is a single triad in
simplest aeolo-choriambics with a long run of choriambic dimeters B,
which should perhaps be run together.[2] The second *stasimon* (751) is
very similar, except for an extended glyconic and an extended choriambic dimeter in the epode (792–3). The third *stasimon* (1036) is also an
aeolo-choriambic triad but is much less regular. The strophe–antistrophe starts with a pure choriambic trimeter followed by a similar
dimeter. Later the aeolo-choriambics are broken by a long dactylo-
epitrite line, ddxdd, by an ithyphallic, and by an enoplian. The epode

1. Cf. 1397 with *Persae* 147.   2. Cf. *L.M.*[2] 151, 200.

starts with an iambic metron plus a heptasyllable B, and then continues choriambic. Iphigeneia's first despairing monody (1279) rings the changes on a variety of metres, dochmiac, iambic, dactylic, cretic, melic anapaests each in short sections, seemingly without any basic metre to bind them together, but perhaps there is enough iambic to perform this function. Her final triumph song (1475), however, is in iambics with occasional dochmiacs.

Two fragments, one certain, one probable, remain of the *parodos* of the *Alkmaion in Corinth*: the first is iambic (74N²), the second asclepiadic (1084N²). The *Bacchae*, our one surviving maenad play, has a great deal of ionic in the *parodos* and the first two *stasima*. The use of ionic is interesting in view of the connection which has been suggested above between maenad dances and ionic.[1] Euripides is probably writing in a tradition, and maenads with tympana (59) and pirouetting maenads are attested long before the *Bacchae*. Even the prelude to the *parodos* is in ionics instead of in anapaests. The first pair of strophe–antistrophe is ionic, except for the opening dragged choriambic dimeter A, which repeats after four ionics (74); it is probably in dancing time in spite of two long periods. The second pair starts with the same dragged choriambic dimeter followed by an enoplian, then goes on mostly aeolo-choriambic but with two breaks made by a prosodiac, the first leading in ionics, and the second dactyls. The epode has a thread of dochmiac but with prosodiac, ionic, and aeolo-choriambic insertions, and at the end a long run of dactyls: this is the free style of the late monodies.

The first *stasimon* (370) is a stately ode in two pairs, the first ionic with a choriambic clausula, the second acolo-choriambic. The second *stasimon* (519) is a stately triad, ionic except for the aeolo-choriambic ending to the epode. This is followed directly (576) by the lyric dialogue with Dionysos singing from inside the palace, a wild dialogue in mixed metre, aeolo-choriambic, dochmiac, trochaic, iambic, and dactylic: Dionysos sings pherecrateans and dactyls. The third *stasimon* (862) is an aeolo-choriambic triad with long periods in the strophe–antistrophe and a repeated refrain after strophe and antistrophe. In the fourth *stasimon* (977), when Dionysos has led Pentheus out to his death, the chorus sing a triad of excited dochmiacs. Again a refrain

1. Cf. above, p. 83.

consisting here of iambic trimeter, bacchiac trimeter, and three dochmiacs is repeated after strophe and antistrophe. The short epode prays for Dionysos to appear in dochmiacs and kindred metres.

The chorus greet the messenger with dochmiacs (1034) but here the excited dochmiacs of joy, not the sorrowing dochmiacs of lament. After his speech they sing a triumph song (1153) in which the dochmiacs are varied with cretics and iambelegi. Then they see Agave coming. The lyric dialogue consists of a single pair of strophe–antistrophe, dochmiac except for two iambelegi, two iambic dimeters, and three pairs of bacchiac. It is a dialogue of triumph but metre and partition between singers belong to the technique of lament.

The *Bacchae* is unique in its ionic *stasima*. Here Euripides may well be writing in a tradition of maenad choruses which goes back to the time of Anakreon. The switch to dochmiacs for all the latter part of the play suits the subject matter (until the switch the maenads are much more concerned with the Dionysos legend and their cult than with the present situation), and is paralleled by the much earlier *Medea*. Otherwise the epode of the *parodos*, the dialogue with Dionysos, the dialogue with Agave are in the now familiar polymetric technique of which the most advanced examples, because they almost seem to do without a basic rhythm, are the song of the Phrygian in the *Orestes* and Iphigeneia's despairing song in the *I.A.*

The last three plays of Sophocles date from probably 413,[1] 409, and effectively 406. In the *Electra* the *parodos* is a lyric dialogue as in many plays of Euripides; it starts with a long monody by Elektra in lyric anapaests, preceded by a single paroemiac sung off stage (77). The anapaests are less spondaic than in Euripides and are in regular dimeters. The chorus are Mycenaean women who have come to console Elektra, and they sing the first part of the three strophes and antistrophes and epode, which form the *parodos*. The first two pairs certainly have the long periods of slow time. In the first they start aeolochoriambic, go into dactylic, and end iambic. Elektra's part is dactylic but ends iambic. The second pair is predominantly iambic with insertions of dactylic. In the third pair the chorus sing anapaests with an ithyphallic clausula. Elektra moves from anapaests through dactyls to an iambic clausula. In the epode the chorus starts with three paroemiacs,

1. On the date of the Sophoclean *Electra*, see A. M. Dale, *Collected Papers*, 229.

Elektra takes up with dactyls, moves into anapaests, then has a considerable section of dochmiacs before an iambic close. The dactylic runs are noticeable in this *parodos*, and they are still more a feature of the later plays.

In the first *stasimon* (473) after the first Chrysothemis scene, the optimism of the strophe–antistrophe in dancing time contrasts with the gloom of the epode about the murder of Myrtilos. The strophe–antistrophe start and end aeolo-choriambic but have a long iambic section in the middle. The epode is mainly in iambic dimeters with double syncopation. (In mood they recall the hypodochmiacs in the *Ajax* (401 f.) and *O.T.* (1208 f.).) The periods are short and it is possible that this was danced as a wild lament. Then there is no break in the long scene until after the messenger speech when the chorus sing a lyric dialogue of lamentation with Elektra (823). The first pair of strophe–antistrophe is in stately asclepiadic lines.[1] The second pair is in mixed short periods, dochmiac, anapaest, dactylo-epitrite, and aeolo-choriambic. The second *stasimon* (1058) follows the second Chrysothemis scene. The first pair has long aeolo-choriambic periods, ending with an enoplian. The second starts in dactylo-epitrite and moves into iambic. The chorus pray for Elektra's restitution.

This is the only preserved Sophoclean play with a recognition duet (1232), and if the date is correct it is later than the recognition duet of Euripides' *Iphigenia in Tauris*. Here also Orestes is confined to spoken trimeters (except for a single bacchiac in 1280). Here too Elektra's part is mostly dochmiac, but with considerable iambic insertions. But the Sophoclean singer sings only iambics whereas Euripides is more daring, and the Sophoclean duet is in triad form whereas the Euripidean duet is completely free. Before the murder of Klytemnestra (1384) the chorus has an excited pair of strophe–antistrophe in iambic, cretic, and dochmiac. The second pair, if it should be regarded as a pair, is largely in iambic trimeters spoken by Elektra and the chorus with Klytemnestra offstage in the strophe and Orestes on stage in the antistrophe. Except for Klytemnestra's opening dochmiac the lyrics are given to the chorus: they have two syncopated iambic dimeters, then later two prosodiacs, and finally a syncopated iambic tetrameter and two tri-

---

1. On 823 ff., see *L.M.*[2] 155. I am inclined to take the interjection of 826 as completing the choriamb in 825 and 831 similarly as completing 830 (with γοῦν for γὰρ in 845).

meters, the last syncopated. Apart from the recognition scene this play has a great deal of dialogue between actor and chorus; particularly the lament (849 f.) is not unlike late Euripidean polymetric song but is still strophic.

In the *Philoctetes* again the *parodos* is a lyric dialogue between Neoptolemos and his crew, but here the shape is quite different. The chorus want information about Philoktetes and Neoptolemos gives it in recitative anapaests after the first strophe, after the first antistrophe, and between the second pair and the third pair; otherwise Neoptolemos has only a brief interjection in the first line of the third strophe and antistrophe. After the opening iambic trimeter the first pair is mainly aeolo-choriambic until the final period of dactylic tetrameter plus iambic dimeter catalectic (19 syllables). The second pair is pure aeolo-choriambic with two 16-syllable periods. The third pair after the opening iambic trimeter is aeolo-choriambic, with one period of 25 syllables.

The very long scene after Philoktetes enters is divided by the strophe in which the chorus appeal to Kybele (391) and the corresponding antistrophe (507); they are in iambics, bacchiacs, and dochmiacs in dancing time. The only normal *stasimon* in the play comes at l. 676, when Philoktetes has taken Neoptolemos into his cave and the chorus comment on his fate. Both pairs are predominantly aeolo-choriambic with some long periods, but the first opens with an iambic trimeter followed by a dactylic tetrameter plus a very long enoplian. When Philoktetes falls asleep after his seizure, the chorus pray to Sleep and urge Neoptolemos to leave in a lyric dialogue (827) of rather the same shape as the *parodos*, but here there is only a single triad and Neoptolemos is limited to four recitative dactylic hexameters between the strophe and antistrophe. The strophe–antistrophe are remarkable for the number of long closes to the periods (a special application of a technique already seen in the *Ajax*). After the opening dactylic tetrameter these long closes are sometimes molossi attached to dochmiacs, and sometimes the doubly syncopated endings of iambic dimeters. The opening period has 19 syllables and presumably the whole is in slow time. The epode also has long periods. It starts aeolo-choriambic, moves into dochmiac and dactylic, and goes back into aeolo-choriambic again.

When Neoptolemos and Odysseus leave Philoktetes alone with the chorus (1081), he sings a very long lyric lament with them, two pairs of strophe–antistrophe, and an epode. In the pairs Philoktetes sings first and the chorus only add a sort of refrain, but the epode is true lyric dialogue. In both pairs Philoktetes starts with a long section of aeolo-choriambic and then goes off into dactylic, dochmiac, and iambic, but in the second pair he returns to aeolo-choriambic again at the end. The long, free epode is much more varied. It starts iambic, then goes into ionic, then into aeolo-choriambic, then two long runs of dactylic tetrameters, and then closes with mixed iambic, trochaic, and aeolo-choriambic. The individual sections are entirely clear and the epode works up to the tremendous dactylic run from 1196.

In the *Oedipus Coloneus* the chorus arrive and find Oidipous and Antigone, discover their identity, and listen to Antigone's appeal so that again a lyric dialogue is the natural form. The first pair of strophe–antistrophe are given to the chorus and the dialogue is conducted in recitative anapaests after the strophe and the antistrophe. The chorus start with an enoplian and a dactylo-epitrite, ddxsx, then a glyconic and iambics, then a long period of four glyconics, aeolo-choriambics go on to near the end where an enoplian leads in anapaests to prepare for Oidipous' anapaests. The second pair is true lyric dialogue between the chorus, Oidipous, and Antigone, and is aeolo-choriambic all through.[1] Oidipous has four lines of recitative anapaests between the strophe and antistrophe. The epode starts as lyric dialogue, first aeolo-choriambic, then ionic, then alternating hemiepes plus cretic and paro-emiac; the hemiepe plus cretic give place to anapaestic dimeters as the chorus threaten Oidipous, and the chorus ends with a run of six dactylic tetrameters, which finishes with a dimeter plus an iambic dimeter catalectic. Antigone then makes her appeal, starting in aeolo-choriambic and then mainly long runs of dactylic tetrameters ending in iambic. This is very much the technique of the last lyric dialogue in the *Philoctetes*, and in both the very long epode is out of scale so that it becomes almost an independent astrophic song.

The chorus take up Oidipous' past with him again after Ismene has been sent to pour libations to the Eumenides, so that another lyric

---

1. I take 176–7 as asclepiadic, sd′d′d′dx, rather than anapaestic (but the ambiguity is deliberate), and 186 as glyconic resolved rather than iambic dimeter.

dialogue takes the place that would normally be occupied by the first *stasimon* (510). This has two pairs of strophe–antistrophe. The first is aeolo-choriambic starting with a long asclepiadic period, the second is iambic but ends with a dactylic tetrameter plus an iambic trimeter catalectic. The first *stasimon* has the famous praise of Athens (668). Both pairs of strophe–antistrophe are aeolo-choriambic with long periods; the first has inserted a dactylic tetrameter plus an iambic dimeter catalectic near the end, the second has two iambic periods after the beginning. The strophe and antistrophe of lyric dialogue, while Kreon seizes Antigone (832) and tries to seize Oidipous (876) is dochmiac.

In the second *stasimon* (1044) the chorus wish they were in the battle and pray to the gods for help, so that it is in fact a *paian* in dance time. The first pair is mixed aeolo-choriambic and iambic, the second iambic with one hipponactean and one dactylo-epitrite, ddxssx, inserted. The third *stasimon* (1211) on old age marks the bottom of Oidipous' fortunes. The strophe–antistrophe of the single triad starts in acolo-choriambic with two long periods, then changes through an iambic dimeter into trochaic for the final section. The epode begins in iambic and then continues in aeolo-choriambic except for an enoplian followed by a prosodiac (1244–5); the last four lines, or the last three if 1247–8 should be taken as a single long period, all have dragged closes and so create the same kind of effect as the sleep chorus in the *Philoctetes*.

With the departure of Polyneikes and the beginning of the thunder which summons Oidipous a new lyric dialogue (1447) begins with two pairs of strophe–antistrophe in dochmiacs and iambics. Five lines of spoken iambics follow each strophe and antistrophe, and the first three groups are given to Oidipous with Antigone speaking the central line. The last group is Theseus' opening speech on arrival. When Oidipous leads Theseus off, the chorus pray to Hades and the nether goddesses for him (1556). The single pair of strophe–antistrophe, in dochmiac, cretic, enoplian, and iambic, is in dance time like the lyric part of the preceding lyric dialogue. The final lament (1670) is shared by Antigone, Ismene, and the chorus. In the first long pair of strophe–antistrophe Antigone ranges from iambic through dactylic back to iambo-trochaic, Ismene starts in iambo-trochaic and ends with an iambo-choriambic tetrameter, and the chorus finish the system with aeolo-choriambics. The shorter second pair is a true lament dialogue with the short iambic and trochaic periods shared between the singers. This play has more lyric than either of the other two late Sophoclean plays, but the *Bacchae* is equally out of scale in the last group of Euripides. It is a reasonable guess (partly confirmed by the preserved *Iphigenia in Aulis*) that the other plays in the same productions were not so rich. In the late plays of Sophocles as a whole lyric dialogues are more frequent than before, and Sophocles has taken over melic anapaests from Euripides but he uses them in a more regular form – usually in pairs and without proceleusmatics or light anapaests. He maintains his love for aeolo-choriambics and particularly for asclepiads. Dactylo-epitrites are not so frequent now, but there is a great increase in runs of dactyls. But he keeps his shapeliness, and even the long epodes are not nearly so free as Euripidean astrophic songs.

One other tragedy probably belongs to this period, the *Rhesus*.[1] Its strangeness is partly due to its unknown author, partly to its being a camp-play of a type we do not otherwise know. The chorus enter at the beginning to recitative anapaests to rouse their commander Hektor. He answers in anapaests. The chorus sing a brief strophe in aeolo-choriambics, dactyls, and dactylo-epitrites with long periods. Hektor answers again in recitative anapaests and the chorus sing their antistrophe. Except for the fact that this play has no prologue but instead the chorus arrive to anapaests, the lay-out of this *parodos* might be described as a simpler version of the *parodos* of the *Philoctetes*.

The chorus support Aineias' speech in the debate with a strophe of mixed iambic and dochmiac (131). The antistrophe comes after Dolon has stated his terms (195). When Dolon has gone, they pray to Apollo for his safety (224); the first pair of strophe–antistrophe is in dactylo-epitrite with one long period, the second in iambo-choriambic, dactylo-epitrite, and aeolo-choriambic. The second *stasimon* starts as a prayer to Adrasteia after the arrival of the messenger who describes Rhesos (342); the first pair is in aeolo-choriambic with a dactylo-epitrite ending, the second is aeolo-choriambic;[2] both have long periods.

Rhesos' speech again is greeted by the chorus with a short strophe (454), which starts iambic and then goes into dactylo-epitrite of various

1. Perhaps by the younger Euripides, cf. my *Tragedies of Euripides*, 6.
2. I take 363 ff. to be asclepiadic rather than ionic.

lengths. The antistrophe does not come until 820, when the chorus defend themselves against Hektor's charge that they let the Greek spies through. The third *stasimon* (527) is the very pretty dawn-watch song. Strophe and antistrophe are in dactylo-epitrite. Each is followed by seven lines of recitative anapaests, ending with a call for their relief, whom they in fact go to find. They (or does the chorus now take the part of the Lycian relief?) re-enter chasing Odysseus (674) in dochmiacs, trochaics, and cretics, a brief, wild, astrophic song, followed by a dialogue in trochaic tetrameters with Odysseus, when he gives the password and escapes. They then sing an excited strophe and anti-strophe in dochmiacs with insertions of iambics and bacchiacs (692).

Rhesos' charioteer enters to a catalectic iambic tetrameter (728). Then after two trochaic tetrameters shared between him and the chorus, he makes his lament in recitative anapaests divided into three sections by the iambic trimeters of the chorus. When Hektor enters and accuses them, they answer with the antistrophe (820) to their much earlier strophe. Finally they greet the arrival of the Muse with Rhesos' body in recitative anapaests. She speaks five trimeters and then sings a short strophe (895) in enoplians; the second has an ithyphallic attached to it, and the last period is a dactylic heptameter. The chorus speak two iambic trimeters before her antistrophe. In choral technique the *Rhesus* remains unique.

Euripides' *Cyclops* is the only satyr-play which survives complete, and it has reasonably been dated to 408, the year of the *Orestes*.[1] The chorus seem tamer than in the earlier satyr-plays of Aeschylus and Sophocles; they sing no proceleusmatic anapaests and have dochmiacs only in their last song, but as in earlier satyr-plays most of the songs are short and astrophic. Only the *parodos* has strophe, antistrophe and epode. Strophe and antistrophe are aeolo-choriambic; epode changes in the latter part to hemiepe and anapaests. The strophe has a 'refrain' in a mixture of aeolo-choriambic and enoplian which may repeat after the antistrophe (but is not given there by the manuscripts). This is probably excited dancing and the one 16-syllable period (47–8) could be danced as a climax. Their second song (356), which describes the Cyclops, is astrophic and in dance time, mostly iambic but with dactylic

---

1. On the date of the *Cyclops*, see A. M. Dale, *W.S.* 69, 1956, 109 = *Collected Papers*, 129.

and anapaestic insertions. The next song is a drinking song in anacreontics with a long ionic period at the end (495), sung in three identical strophes by a semi-chorus, the Cyclops, and another semi-chorus. In the next astrophic song (608) the satyrs sing of the future blinding of the Cyclops; the short song contains two dactylic tetrameters alternating with lekythia; it must be in dance time and here, as the whole song is very short, the diairesis at the end of the dactylic tetrameters is evidently pause enough; two other catalectic dactylic lines are followed by iambic dimeters and here there is no question of joining the two elements. Finally, as in the vase illustration (no. 263) the satyrs shout encouragement to Odysseus' crew in an excited little song (656) in dochmiac, cretic, and aeolo-choriambic.

For this period and for this period only we have complete comedies, and complete comedies of one man, Aristophanes. What we know of earlier and contemporary comedy[1] suggests that much of his art was traditional, but within the traditional form there was plenty of room for variety, as the plays of Aristophanes themselves show. Many of the choruses themselves were traditional in the sense that earlier comedy and pre-comedy had choruses of knights and birds, like Aristophanes, and the double chorus of men and women in the *Lysistrata* has an ancestor in the choruses of komasts and nymphs on the Attic padded-dancer vases (nos. 82–3). Old Comedy has a peculiar shape: iambic scenes, *parodos*, *agon*, parabasis, iambic scenes, *exodos*. It is usually assumed that the iambic scenes were added, probably on the analogy of tragedy, to an original structure in which the basic elements, repeated in the fully developed *parodos-agon*-parabasis, were four – strophe, antistrophe, epirrhema, and antepirrhema; strophe and antistrophe were sung; epirrhema and antepirrhema were corresponding sections of recitative tetrameters, anapaestic, trochaic, or iambic. It was perhaps the addition of the spoken iambic scenes to the recitative and sung formal structure which marked the transition from pre-comedy to comedy. The recitative metres are all old: we are only concerned with the sung parts of the formal structure and the songs dividing the iambic scenes before or after the formal structure.

Chronologically the preserved plays run from the *Acharnians* of 425

1. Cf. above, pp. 150 ff., and on contemporaries, Pickard-Cambridge, *Dithyramb, etc.*[2], 159 ff.

to the *Plutus* of 388. There is a considerable time break between the *Peace* of 421 and the *Birds* of 414 and between the *Frogs* of 405 and the *Ecclesiazusae* of 391. The first period down to the *Peace* coincides with the second group of Euripidean plays, and the second period from the *Birds* to the *Frogs* coincides with the last two groups of Euripidean plays. This relationship is important because some of Aristophanes' most exciting lyric effects are achieved in parodying Euripides. The absence of this incitement may be part-cause of the metrical poverty of the two fourth-century plays.[1] The *Ecclesiazusae* is still named after the chorus, and they still have some interesting songs, but the practice of the chorus singing choral interludes which were not written for the particular play had already begun, and in the *Plutus* only the *parodos*, which is in the simplest iambics, and the excited dochmiacs which greet the news that Ploutos has regained his sight (an obvious echo of the chorus's reactions to the arrival of the messenger in tragedy) were written for the play.

In the formal parts of the play (and elsewhere when the poet uses tetrameters) the tetrameters often end with a string of dimeters of the same kind.[2] In the tetrameters themselves all three kinds – anapaestic, trochaic, and iambic – tend to have word division between the full dimeter and the catalectic dimeter. This is not an absolute rule in Aristophanes and is more strictly applied in anapaestic tetrameters than in the other two kinds. The dimeters also avoid word-overlap. In fact the few trochaic dimeters which follow tetrameters have no instance of word-overlap; anapaestic dimeters occur in every play and in many more than once; the only form of overlap is elision between dimeters and that only occurs three times.[3] Genuine word-overlap, however, occurs quite frequently in iambic dimeters which come after iambic tetrameter scenes, and they seem therefore to obey a different rule; perhaps the term *pnigos*, 'choke, sung without drawing breath', which ancient authors use of the anapaestic and trochaic dimeters found after the tetrameters of the parabasis, should not be extended to include all runs of dimeters after tetrameters (or, indeed, not after tetrameters), as it often is, but should at least be confined to anapaestic and trochaic

1. On the chorus in fourth-century comedy, see my *Later Greek Comedy*, 15, 58 ff.; *Hellenistic Poetry and Art*, 267 ff.
2. References are easily found in Pickard-Cambridge, *Dithyramb, etc.*[2], 203 ff.
3. *Equ.* 828, *Vesp.* 629, *Ran.* 1078.

dimeters after tetrameters because they almost universally observe the word-break between each dimeter. It is this word-break allowing for a minimum taking of breath, as we have supposed for the runs of dactylic tetrameters in tragedy, which makes delivery 'without drawing breath' possible.

The frequent dimeters which survive in fragments of comedy may or may not belong to these dimeters which come after tetrameters. We have not usually enough context to decide. In the formal part of the play these tetrameters and dimeters are given both to the actors and to the chorus. In these long scenes they are presumably recitative rather than sung; they were not spoken in the sense that iambic trimeters were spoken, because they had a flute accompaniment.[1] Where recitative tetrameters are given to the chorus, it seems probable that the leader of the chorus delivered them in recitative and the rest of the chorus stood silent, but there is no clear evidence apart from probability.[2] But within the formal part itself the *parodos* and the *exodos* were of course sung and danced (or marched or run) by the chorus. The chorus of old Acharnians run on to trochaic tetrameters, and the old jurors of the *Wasps* with their slaves walk on to iambic tetrameters. We have already seen instances of anapaestic *parodoi* in Kratinos.[3]

Between them anapaests, iambics, and trochaics account for a great many of the sung choruses of Aristophanes, and the very common cretic–paeonics can be associated with the trochaics because they often rise out of trochaics or sink back into trochaics. Of the tetrameters anapaests are in any case a marching metre (so also anapaestic dimeters), trochaics with their regular diairesis may, as we have seen, be a running metre, as in the entry of the Acharnians; iambics are on the borderline between walking and dancing, but the slow and slippery progress of the old jurors in the *Wasps* is surely walking. The dimeters can be taken in dance time or even excited dance time if they have word-break between them, but the linked iambic dimeters and the linked cretics of, for instance, the *Acharnians parodos* (210 f.) must have been taken quite slowly. Every play, except the two fourth-century plays, has more than one chorus or lyric dialogue in each of the three times, walking, danc-

---

1. E.g. *Av.* 659–60, 682–4.
2. Cf. A. M. Dale, *Collected Papers*, 289.
3. Cf. above, p. 70.

ing, and excited dancing, and this variation of tempo is much more noticeable in comedy than in tragedy.

If we regard anapaests, trochaics, and iambics as Aristophanes' inherited stock-in-trade, we need only mention songs in these metres when they are of particular interest. In the *Acharnians* (263) Dikaiopolis' song in the procession with the phallos-pole is in long iambics throughout and, like so many religious songs in Aristophanes, probably repeats a ritual song fairly closely. The chorus burst into excited dochmiacs after Dikaiopolis' speeches (358, 490, 566); individual words are parody, but of choral lyric rather than tragedy, and essentially Aristophanes is using the metre as it is used in tragedy and satyr-play to register the excitement of the chorus. One chorus (1150) is metrically very like a tragic chorus, long choriambics leading into iambics, and perhaps the audience were meant to draw the contrast between the tragic metre and the absurd content. Lamachos' final entry (1190) in resolved iambics of various lengths and an occasional dochmiac is a parody of a tragic sung lament, contrasted with Dikaiopolis' antiphonal song of joy which follows the same metrical pattern. (Even in tragedy the same metres are used for joy and sorrow.)

The Knights enter to trochaic tetrameters. It is not clear where they dismount if they do dismount; perhaps their steeds remain in the orchestra, as 595 ff. would certainly be more effective in their presence. In the second pair of strophe–antistrophe of the *parodos* the normal cretic–trochaics are varied by a run of dactyls in the middle (328). After the anapaests of the parabasis (551) the chorus sing the first of several kletic hymns in Aristophanes, which are not so very different from cult hymns as we know them in earlier poetry.[1] Here the strophe invokes Poseidon and the antistrophe Athena. Aristophanes starts with two long periods of choriambic dimeters, then shifts to an asclepiadic period, and ends with glyconic–pherecratean. He uses glyconics and pherecrateans again for a later chorus (973), and the lyric dialogue between the knights and Demos (1111) is in long periods of linked telesilleans. The last preserved choral utterance (1264) is in long dactylo-epitrites taking off from a quotation of Pindar in the strophe and from a quotation of Euripides in the antistrophe.

The *Clouds* is more interesting metrically than either of the two earlier

1. Cf. above, p. 72.

plays. The Clouds enter to long dactylic lines (275). Their dialogue
with Strepsiades goes from trochaic and prosodiac into dactylo-
epitrite (457). The kletic hymn (563) starts in aeolo-choriambic for
Zeus and Poseidon, goes into dactyls for Aither, and back to aeolo-
choriambic for Helios, but within the aeolo-choriambic sections each
god has his own variety. Aristophanes clearly feels that the Clouds
should dance in the high style of tragic lyrics, and this continues in the
mixed aeolo-choriambic and dactylo-epitrite of their next song (700),
followed by anapaestic dimeters from Strepsiades, which are a blatant
parody of Euripides' *Hecuba*. Strepsiades' song of triumph (1154) is
also a parody of tragic monody in mixed metre.

The *Wasps* has an interesting opening and an extremely interesting
end. After the entry in iambic tetrameters the chorus begin the first
pair of strophe–antistrophe with a long ionic period (273). This rare
metre is used again at the end of the first pair and then all through the
second pair. The intervening section of the first pair is in aeolo-
choriambic, trochaic, and dactylo-epitrite.[1] Philokleon's monody (316)
parodies tragic monodies in mixed metres with anapaestic dimeters at
the end. In a later lyric dialogue (526) the chorus sing aeolo-choriambic,
and the two actors break in with iambic tetrameters. The chorus use
mixed iambics and dochmiacs to persuade Philokleon to give in (729).

The end of the play has some important but extremely difficult
allusions to dancing which have been much discussed.[2] The slave
Xanthias (1478) reports that the elderly Philokleon 'does not stop
dancing the ancient dances with which Thespis used to compete, and
says that he will dance down the modern *tragoidoi* and show them up as
useless'. (It is presumably possible that Philokleon can be imagined as
having had an elderly schoolmaster who taught Thespis' dances from
the days of his youth.) Philokleon then comes out and describes his
dance. There is no necessary relation here between the recitative
anapaests and the steps of the dance because he is trying out steps in

---

1. On the very curious free responsions, see A. M. Dale, *L.M.*[2] 125, 189.
2. See particularly Erwin Roos, *Die tragische Orchestik im Zerrbild der altattischen Komödie*,
1951; E. K. Borthwick, *C.Q.* 18, 1968, 44. Karkinos himself was a tragic poet, cf. *Nub.*
1263, and his son Xenokles, victorious in 415. Whether the other two played in the chorus
of tragedy, as the scholiasts assert of all three is unknown (Schol. *Pax* 781, *Vesp.* 1500); it
may be false inference from the context. The word *tragoidoi* was used for tragic poet,
tragic actor, and member of the tragic chorus.

slow motion. He bends his sides; 'Phrynichos crouches like a cock, kicking his leg heaven-high.' The bending appears to be sideways, and that our schematized profile-pictures of dancers never show us. Phrynichos is presumably the early fifth-century tragic poet as Philokleon has been dancing Thespis before. The high-kick will be our posture B (forward), and the crouching is the forward-bending of the torso which may accompany it. It has nothing to do with the Asiatic dance with joined hands, which is probably rightly called *oklasma*[1]: that is the dance described by the late fifth-century comic poet Auto-krates (fr. 1K) as performed by the Lydian girls in honour of the Ephesian Artemis, 'clapping their hands', which is the distinctive gesture (cf. also Ar. *Nub.* 600). Philokleon has now limbered up (1494) and invites *tragoidoi* to compete with him, and he will destroy them with a 'knuckle-*emmeleia*' – i.e. a tragic dance which will knock them out. The three sons of Karkinos appear. The chorus then stand aside in order that they may have room 'to turn themselves into tops in front of us'. The chorus then sing an excited song in enoplians and ithyphallics while the dance goes on. The dancers are told to swing the foot quickly and kick the Phrynichan kick. The play ends with recita-tive Archilocheans (xddxssx)[2] from the chorus, which after more instructions tells the dancers to lead the chorus out. All this seems to be addressed to the sons of Karkinos, and Philokleon is not mentioned, so that perhaps the sons of Karkinos lead the chorus off in three files. The Phrynichan kick is posture B again. New in the instructions to the sons of Karkinos are belly-slapping and pirouettes – 'tops', 'whirls', and 'advancing circularly' (1516, 1523, 1529 f.). Pirouettes we only know from maenads, and they are new a little before the time of this play (no. 235). Belly-slapping and posture B are found in satyrs, and of course are in the komast tradition. But all along Philokleon has talked of tragic poets, and both maenad dances and satyr dances were composed by tragic poets. What surely is funny is to see a drunk old man and three tragic poets dancing these wild dances at all, and we need not look for any complicated explanation. This of itself made a brilliant finale to the play.

The opening of the *Peace* is dominated by parody of Euripides' *Bellerophon*, but the dactyls of Trygaios' child (114) actually parody

1. Cf. J. D. Beazley, *J.H.S.* 59, 1939, 31.
2. Cf. now *P. Oxy.* 2743, 8.

another play, the *Aiolos*; the long anapaestic monody to the beetle (154) is certainly parody of the *Bellerophon*. The chorus of farmers enter to running trochaics (301). They pull the image of Peace up to excited palimbacchiacs, cretics, and anapaests (459). (It would be interesting to know what metre Aeschylus used when the satyrs hauled the chest ashore in the *Diktyoulkoi* since the stage arrangements were the same in both cases.)[1] The chorus's song while Trygaios returns to earth (775) is in dactylo-epitrite, starting from a quotation of Stesichoros; this is the familiar use of high lyric metre to convey everyday content. The next three choruses are all cheerful, the joys of peace; 856 is mixed telesillean and iambic, 939 mixed iambic and enoplian, 1127 cretic and trochaic. The *Peace* ends with a long marriage song sung by Trygaios and two half-choruses as he conducts his bride to his farm. This is all in telesilleans and catalectic telesilleans; this is surely meant for excited dancing, and the few cases where the lines are joined by word-overlap could be taken with a rush. The refrain *Hymen, O Hymenaie*, appears in the form *Hymen Hymenai'O,* which makes it into a catalectic telesillean.[2]

The *Birds* comes after a gap of seven years by which time we believe that the new music was already influencing Euripides. Aristophanes shows himself at his most inventive in this play and at his most skilful in parodying. The hoopoe's call (227) summons the birds in a long monody, which associates different metres with different sorts of birds, shifting through iambics, dochmiacs, dactylo-epitrites, trochaics, ionics, anapaests, cretics, and dactyls. The recurrent dochmiacs seem to be a sort of theme which holds the whole together.[3] Light anapaests (242) and proceleusmatics (241, etc.) are particularly characteristic of Euripides' polymetric monodies, and Aristophanes has brilliantly adapted the new style to his own valid and beautiful ends. Much of the dialogue between the birds and the humans is in excited dochmiacs or resolved anapaests. But the birds settle down to stately dactylo-epitrites when they make peace (451). The mood of the hoopoe's call is carried on in the birds' summons to the nightingale before the para-

1. Cf. my *Greek Theatre Production*, 18 f.
2. Cf. p. 73 f. above on earlier marriage songs.
3. Apart from 230, dochmiacs recur 234, 236, 239, and I am inclined to take 254 not as a paroemiac but as spondee (ending the preceding dactyls) + dragged hypodochmiac: $-\,-\,'\,-\,\cup\,\widehat{\cup\cup}\,\overline{\times}\,-$. I see no justification for lengthening the first alpha of ταναοδείρων.

basis (676), which is in aeolo-choriambic, and the strophe and antistrophe in the middle of the parabasis (737), but they are in mixed metre,
resolved anapaests, free dactylo-epitrite and trochaic. This is the style
of choral lyric rather than monody. It is found also in later choruses,
the spondaic anapaests of 1058, and the rising dactylo-epitrites of the
lyric dialogue with Peithetairos in 1313 ff. Much of the later part of the
play consists of the monodies of various Athenian professionals who are
trying to get themselves a place in Cloud-cuckoo-land, and they all
parody high lyric. At the end of the play Peithetairos comes out holding
the thunderbolt of Zeus with Basileia as his bride. The chorus greet
him first (1720) with a prelude in trochaics, choriambics, and anapaests,
and then with a strophe–antistrophe of telesilleans as in the *Peace*.
Peithetairos asks them to hymn the thunder and lightning, which they
do in dactyls, ending again with the marriage refrain (a pherecratean in
this form). Peithetairos and his bride lead them off in iambic dimeters.
Their final utterance combines the refrain of the *paian* (*ie, paion*) – it
will be remembered that Sappho (44LP) described the men as singing a
paian at the wedding of Hektor and Andromache – and the refrain of
Archilochos' hymn to Herakles (*tenella kallinikos*), an anticipation of
Aristophanes' own victory.

The *Lysistrata* is the only play preserved which has a double chorus
of men and women. The men come on first to iambic tetrameters
and sing two pairs of strophe–antistrophe in dancing iambo-trochaics;
the women come on to two iambo-choriambic tetrameters and then
sing a long pair of strophe–antistrophe, starting with very Euripidean
choriambic dimeters B and going over into longer choriambic metres.
The men enter, notionally at any rate, with loads of fire-wood and
jugs holding burning coals (255, 297); the women have water-pots on
their heads (327); (the much earlier skyphos in Thebes (no. 167) had a
chorus of old men running on with flaming torches). The women's
song ends with a prayer to Athena to help them. After that in every
song the men sing the strophes and the women sing the antistrophes
until 1042, when having come to an agreement, the men announce that
they will both sing together. After the opening there is nothing exciting
metrically until the end.

How much of the end was realized and how much imagined is
difficult to say. The Laconian delegation, which arrives in 1072, is

plural, and they are met by a similar Athenian delegation (1082). Lysistrate then comes out. The first difficulty is her final line (1186), 'and then each of you shall take his wife and go away'. It would be natural to take this as both the Laconians and the Athenians, but the only Laconian wife we have heard of is Lampito, who went back to Sparta (242) to persuade the Spartan wives to behave like the Athenian wives. Perhaps then Lysistrate only means the Athenians and more particularly the chorus. But unfortunately for this suggestion she mentions both Spartans and Athenians in 1274; presumably Aristophanes does not worry about the inconsistency and can provide some extra mutes for the final procession. The Laconian calls on a flute-player to play the Laconian flute, and he will sing and dance (1242); the Athenian says that he likes seeing them dancing: 'take then the Laconian flute'. We must therefore suppose that a Laconian flute-player comes out with the Laconians, rather as in *Birds* the chorus ask to have the nightingale to play with them (660). In both cases a mute probably mimed the extra flute-player; flute-players were expensive professionals, and it is unlikely that two were provided for any comedy. The Laconian sings and dances himself; he starts with an iambo-choriambic trimeter and then goes into iambo-trochaic with three double-short insertions. The fact that the Athenian says 'I like seeing *you* [plural] dancing' does not necessarily imply that the other Laconian ambassadors dance: it may merely mean Laconians in general. Then Lysistrate says that Laconians and Athenians should take off their respective wives; 'and let man stand by woman and woman by man, and then let us dance in honour of the gods to win good fortune'. The second part of the instruction can at least be carried out by the two semi-choruses of the ordinary chorus rearranged so that men and women alternate, and they sing an Attic hymn to the gods (1279), largely resolved trochaic, but with some dactylic and prosodiac. This is a *paian* (1291), thanksgiving for averted evil. Lysistrate then tells the Laconian to sing again (her imperative singular outweighs the manuscripts' attribution of the song to a chorus of Laconians). Text and scansion are difficult, but this seems to be largely iambic. This is unlikely to have ended the play, but the final march off is lost in our manuscripts.

The *Thesmophoriazusae* opens with Euripides visiting Agathon.

Agathon is brought out on the *ekkyklema*. He is leading a chorus of girls in a hymn to Apollo, Artemis, and Leto (101). Although some of the details are difficult, this song is certainly mainly in ionic, and the ionics are remarkably free, showing syncopation, contraction of the short syllables, and even resolution of the long syllables. The song ends with a run of dactyls plus a catalectic iambic dimeter and finally a line which should probably be taken here as a free ionic dimeter.[1] It is the ionics which produce Mnesilochos' reaction, 'how sweet and feminine, kiss-like, and almond-like'. Aristophanes has probably exaggerated Agathon's tricks, but essentially this is the kind of development to be expected when the basic metre is well established in the tradition and the poet can exploit the knowledge of his chorus. We have noticed the remarkably free use of ionics in the hymn to the Kouretes, which is a cult hymn probably of this period.

There is no reason to suppose that Aristophanes used a subsidiary chorus here; Agathon sang both parts (leader and chorus) himself.[2] The main chorus of women enters with a kletic hymn (312), when the scene has changed to the Thesmophoreion, brought forward by the *ekkyklema*. They start in iambic and then invoke Zeus and Apollo in dactylic running into iambic, Athena in trochaic, Artemis in dactylic, Poseidon, the Nereids, and the Nymphs in dactylo-epitrite. Their actual prayer (352) is in iambic with an aeolo-choriambic middle section. In 655 the chorus propose to themselves an energetic search; they carry it out in running trochaics (659), which change into dancing trochaics (663). The following strophe–antistrophe (668) has much corruption, and in any case the strophe is modelled on the antistrophe (707), which is a lyric dialogue accompanying Mnesilochos' arrest, in anapaests, trochaics, and dochmiacs. A great deal of the rest of the play is parody of Euripides' *Palamedes*, *Helen* and *Andromeda*. But in 947 the chorus say: 'Let us dance as is the custom here' (at the Thesmophoria). They then start in very simple dancing iambo-trochaics a circular dance, hand on wrist (953). This is followed by three short stanzas in trochaic. The next pair of strophe–antistrophe (969) is in

---

1. 129: ‒‒ — ⏔ ‒‒ — —, ionic dimeter with first syllable of both metra contracted and last syllable of first metron resolved. This process produces the rare form known as the major ionic, as in the hymn to the Kouretes (above, p. 152). Cf. *L.M.*[2] 122.

2. I.e. as Van Leeuwen suggests, the scholiast rather than the MSS. is right here.

dancing iambics; they sing to Artemis, Hera, Hermes, Pan, and the Nymphs, and they call their dance a *diple*, perhaps a circular dance in two rows.[1] Another brief interlude in iambics demands an excited ring dance in honour of Dionysos, and this follows in a corrupt pair of strophe–antistrophe (990), which is largely aeolo-choriambic but ends syncopated iambic. The last chorus is again a kletic hymn (1136) to Athena and the two goddesses of the Thesmophoria and is almost entirely in double-short: ibyceans, glyconics, pherecrateans, dactyls, and a final praxillean (the song should not be forcibly made into strophe and antistrophe).

The *Frogs* again is immensely versatile metrically, and also has a good deal of cult song and a great deal of parody. The chorus of frogs is mostly simple iambics and trochaics, but near the beginning (216) has a pair of linked telesilleans and two dactylo-epitrite periods to describe Dionysos. The entrance song of the main chorus of mystics is the most elaborate cult hymn in Aristophanes (312 ff.).[2] They enter to the flute, carrying torches, and first address Iakchos in danced ionic. Then the leader in recitative anapaestic tetrameters warns all unsuitable people to keep away, while they raise the night songs suitable for this feast (*pannychis*, 371). In the second pair of strophe–antistrophe in spondaic melic anapaests the chorus exhort the mystics to enter the meadows and extol Soteira. She is perhaps best interpreted as Athena, as the scholiast says. The leader then asks for another form of songs to Demeter (384). This third pair consists of iambic dimeters and should perhaps be taken slowly, as in the antistrophe the first three dimeters are connected and the fourth is linked to the clausular catalectic dimeter. The leader changes from anapaestic to iambic tetrameters to ask the chorus to summon Iakchos (396), and they sing three identical stanzas of dancing

---

1. *Diple.* Perhaps a double line in a round dance, cf. no. 181. Cf. also Lawler, *T.A.P.A.* 76, 1945, 59, and above, p. 119, on Aeschylus, *Theoroi.*

2. Mystics. It is perhaps best to admit that we do not know whether Aristophanes is echoing the Eleusinian mysteries or some other mystery cult: cf. M. Tierney, *P.R.I.A.* 42, 1935, 199; G. Hooker, *J.H.S.* 80, 1960, 112 f.; J. A. Haldane, *C.Q.* 14, 1964, 207. There is, as I see it, no trace of criticism either of the Mysteries in these songs or of the gods in Aristophanes' other kletic hymns. Some editors assume that the *Frogs* had a chorus of men and women and that the women were dismissed in 447. I suspect 447 alludes to the proverbial *P.M.G.* 881 and so can be used proleptically 'I will go to be with'; then this is the first mention of women and they are *not* present. Van Leeuwen may be right in assuming that the *koryphaios* now retires because he is no longer needed, but this is, in any case, curious.

iambics, mainly trimeters. Probably the comments of Dionysos and Xanthias after this should be regularized as two iambic trimeters, and then the chorus sing five stanzas of excited iambics, two dimeters and a trimeter, in which they abuse Archedemos and others (420). Dionysos frames his question in the same shape, and the chorus answer him in another verse, and finally Dionysos gives his instructions to Xanthias in an eighth verse. The leader tells the chorus to enter the holy circle of the goddess, but he will go with the girls and women to light their night festival. The final dance of the chorus is in telesilleans after an iambic beginning (449). The contest between the poets is heralded by two songs, one with a single pair of strophe–antistrophe (675), the other with four stanzas (814), both in stately dactyls or dactylo-epitrite of the Stesichorean–Aeschylean kind; this continues in the astrophic 875. In the parodies of Euripides the choral parody (1309) mocks his fondness for glyconics, particularly irregular glyconics, and choriambic dimeter B; the monody (1331) is a wonderful new style polymetric monody, based to a certain extent and possibly more than we know on quotation, combining every sort of metre but returning again and again, like the hoopoe's call, to dochmiacs which, though they are themselves very free, yet give the whole a sort of shape. The actor who played Aeschylus needed all the vocal technique of a tragic actor.

In the *Ecclesiazusae* the chorus apparently enter one by one to meet Praxagora (30 ff.). Then the *parodos* is their preparation to leave the orchestra. This is, of course, conditioned by the plot. They are assembled in their male disguise, and Praxagora tells them to lean on their sticks and sing the sort of song that old countrymen sing (278). They start in iambic tetrameters and then sing a pair of strophe–antistrophe which begins iambic and then goes into telesilleans; as there are two periods with two linked telesilleans plus a catalectic telesillean (21 syllables), the whole song is probably walked. They re-enter at 479 to iambic tetrameters. They then take off their beards and put them down by the wall of the skene in the shadow of the central door (496). At 571 they have an astrophic song in free dactylo-epitrites. At the very end of the play they say that they are going to sing a before-dinner song (1153), and call on Blepsidemos and themselves to move their feet in Cretan fashion, i.e. excitedly. Then they describe the monstrous dish in a run of very free dactylic tetrameters.[1] Whether the dish was actually brought on the stage we do not know, but two contemporary vases are relevant: Blepsidemos with his torch (1150) recalls the picture of a comic actor dancing off with a torch followed by a boy carrying a large cake (no. 275). And the polychrome oinochoe from the Agora (no. 280) has two men running with a long cake on a spit: such Obeliaphoroi (spit-cake carriers) gave the name of a fourth-century comedy by Ephippos.

The *Ecclesiazusae* still has something of the old lyrical Aristophanes. The *Plutus parodos* (290) advertises itself as a parody of the *Cyclops* of Philoxenos, but Aristophanes only gives us the simplest iambics.

8 · LATER

Both the literary and archaeological sources produce much less material after 370 B.C. On the archaeological side the cessation of red-figure vases in Athens and South Italy by the end of the fourth century has a great deal to do with this. On the literary side we have seen that in the last comedy of Aristophanes only the entrance song of the chorus was specially written for the play; when we next have moderately complete texts of comedy, with Menander, not even the first song was specially composed. The two reliefs from the Agora (nos. 282a, b) show the chorus dancing out of the orchestra behind their flute-player, doing the old step BC, and we must suppose that in the third quarter of the fourth century two comedies at least had *exodoi* to excited metres, cretics or trochaics perhaps; this is not unlikely, as we have a little evidence that new choral lyric was sometimes written for comedy after the time of Aristophanes.[2] In tragedy Aristotle tells us that they sang *embolima* from the time of Agathon, and *embolima* probably means choral interludes transferred from another play. Agathon's first victory was in 416, and he probably went on writing into the early fourth century. Drama still had its chorus,[3] but what they sang we do not know. Similarly the many forms of religious chorus went on, and some texts survive, but there are no great names

1. Cf. *L.M.*[2] 25. I am inclined to see both resolved dactylic $\widehat{\cup\cup}\cup$ and light dactyls $\cup\cup\cup$ in 1169 ff.
2. See my *Later Greek Comedy*, 61.
3. See G. M. Sifakis, *Studies in Hellenistic Drama*, 1967, 113 ff.

after Timotheos,[1] and in the latter part of the fourth century on monu-
ments recording dithyrambic victories the name of the flute-player
precedes that of the poet. It was the accompanist who was important:
he wove the exciting new improvised musical arabesques round the
sung line.

The dance of women with linked hands on a terracotta relief from
the Agora (no. 287) is a *partheneion*. Two pretty fragments quoted in a
fourth-century treatise on metrics (*P.M.G.* 926)[2] may come from contemporary *partheneia*: the first (a), describing meadows where maidens
dance, is in alternating cretic and iambic periods; the second (e) in
syncopated iambics addresses the chorus of girls. Both are in dancing
time. The beginning of a hymn to Artemis (*P.M.G.* 955) is quoted by
Dikaiarchos and cannot therefore be later than the fourth century but
may of course be earlier. The text is bad, but it was certainly in dactylic
tetrameters with an alcaic decasyllable as clausula: 'Artemis, my soul
desires to weave a lovely song: someone lifts the fair, gilded, bronze-
cheeked castagnets.' At least the author remembers the Homeric hymn
to Apollo (cf. above, p. 55) even if he is not himself writing for the
Delian maidens.

Three reliefs from the Athenian Acropolis (no. 288, fig. 11) show
pyrrhicists doing their traditional dance. There is plenty of evidence for
armed dances in the fourth century and later but none for the words that
they sang. Xenophon in the *Anabasis* (vi, i, 5) speaks of armed dances
performed to entertain the Paphlagonians; in particular, the Mantineans
put on armour 'and sang to the flute in enoplian rhythm, and sang
paians and danced as in processional songs to the gods'. This is an
interesting combination of types that we tend to keep separate, but
clearly an armed chorus proceeding to a temple and singing to avert
evil or in thanksgiving for averted evil could be called a *paian*, and
there is no reason why enoplian should not mean what we mean by
enoplian, since we have noted before its association with pyrrhics.
Athenaeus says that a Macedonian military dance with arms was known
in Greece in the fourth century (629a) and speaks of armed dances at
dinner at the court of Antiochos the Great (155b).

One of the Acropolis reliefs (no. 288c) has a chorus of men muffled

---

1. See the list of dithyrambic poets in Pickard-Cambridge, *Dithyramb, etc.*[2], 54 f.
2. Powell, *Collectanea Alexandrina*, 192; Page, *G.L.P.* no. 88; *P. Oxy.* 2687.

in cloaks. The part of the inscription giving the festival is lost, but the phrase 'chorus of men' implies a dithyramb; this is a stately chorus in walking time. A fragment of what is probably a dithyramb, since it describes Dionysos, survives in the metrical papyrus already quoted (*P.M.G.* 926d); a cretic trimeter is followed by a choriambic pentameter, so that this is certainly in walking time.

The muffled men on the Acropolis relief give us a picture for a number of stately songs that have survived from this period. Aristotle's praise of Hermeias of Atarnai (*P.M.G.* 842)[1] is written in regular dactylo-epitrites ending with a 26-syllable period. It is an address to Arete giving heroic examples of which the last is Hermeias. It is a single long stanza. The ancients disputed whether it was a *paian* or a *skolion*, but this was a religious question: was Aristotle setting up Hermeias as a god? It was agreed that he sang the song at symposia. It was therefore a solo, but as we have seen before there is often no distinction metrically between solo and choral song.[2] A choral *paian* of the late thirties or early twenties of the fourth century is preserved on an inscription in Delphi.[3] The inscription gives the text of a *paian* to Dionysos by Philodamos of Skarpheia. The song is monostrophic with twelve stanzas. Each stanza has first three full choriambic dimeters A and one catalectic linked together, then an ionic trimeter as a first refrain (*Euoi, O Iobakche, O ie Paian*), then a glyconic linked to a phalaecean hendecasyllable, then two glyconics and a pherecratean linked together, and finally a longer refrain consisting of an ionic dimeter and a glyconic linked to a pherecratean (*ie Paian*, come saviour, kindly preserve this city in the happiness of good living). The linked lines make it certain that this is a stately song in slow time. The actual prayer is contained in the repeated refrains and in the opening of the first stanza: 'Come hither with ivy in your hair, Dithyrambos, Bakchos, Bromios, in this holy spring season.' The rest tells of the spread of Dionysos' worship and ends with Apollo's rules for the cult in Delphi including this hymn, which is to be sung in the streets by ivy-crowned choruses.

1. Cf. Bowra, *C.Q.*, 31, 1938, 182.
2. Two curious and pompous poems, one about Dolon, one to Mnemosyne, both in free long dactylo-epitrites, are preserved on papyrus and are not later than the fourth century, *P.M.G.* 917b, c; Powell, op. cit., 191, 19, and 20; Page, *G.L.P.* 86.
3. Powell, op. cit., 165; Webster, *Hellenistic Poetry and Art*, 1 ff.

About the same time as Philodamos' *paian* at Delphi is Isyllos' *paian* at Epidaurus.[1] Isyllos has had a vision of Asklepios, who had cured him after saving the Spartans from Philip of Macedon. In return Isyllos arranged that the best men of Epidaurus, wearing their hair long and dressed in white, should go in procession, some with wreaths of laurel to Apollo Maleatas and some with branches of olive to Asklepios, and pray for the health, peace, and wealth of Epidaurus. The prayer is the paian. It is written in long periods of free ionics, free in the sense that either long can be resolved and the first short can be lengthened.[2] Most of the text is a simple genealogy of Asklepios, but it opens 'Sing of the god, *ie paian*, dwellers of rich Epidaurus', and ends '*ie, Paian, ie Paian*, farewell Asklepios, patron of our mother-city Epidaurus, and send health clear to see for our minds and bodies, *ie paian, ie Paian*'.

In 306 B.C. at the City Dionysia in the Procession (*pompe*) celebrated by Demetrios of Phaleron as archon the chorus sang in his honour a poem of Kastorion of which Athenaeus preserves a fragment (*P.M.G.* 845): it runs s'd'd'dxs'sx, probably a single long period changing from double- to single-short. Metrically this is not unlike the two preserved fragments of Lykophronides, who was probably contemporary (*P.M.G.* 843–4) but there is no evidence to show how or if they were ever performed. The first states that modesty is better than a pretty face, and the second quotes a goatherd in love dedicating his gear to the Graces. Like the epigrammatist Anyte, who also wrote lyric poetry, he represents mainland Greek pastoral.

For the third century we can quote the beginning of a song inscribed at Erythrai in honour of Seleukos as son of Apollo, and therefore dated 281–0; it is in long dactylo-epitrites.[3] The two hymns[4] of Aristonoos of Corinth which survive in inscriptions at Delphi date from 230 to 220. The hymn to Hestia is a single strophe in long dactylo-epitrite periods, and asks that she in return may grant 'us to have much prosperity and dance about her altar'. His hymn to Apollo ends with a very similar prayer: 'Rejoicing in our hymns grant us prosperity, save us and look

---

1. Powell, op. cit., 132; Wilamowitz, *Isyllos von Epidauros*, 19; Webster, *Hellenistic Poetry and Art*, 6 f.
2. This seems the only way of explaining metra like — ∪ — ᴖᴗ, i.e. it is not anaclasis in the ordinary sense as in anacreontics (see Wilamowitz, loc. cit.).
3. Powell, op. cit., 140. Cf. Roztovtzeff, *S.E.H.W.* 431.
4. Powell, op. cit., 162; Audiat, *B.C.H.* 56, 1932, 299 ff.

after us.' But the hymn to Apollo consists of six stanzas; in each the third line is a pherecratean ending *iê ie Paian,* and the sixth and last line is also a pherecratean ending *o ie paian.* The other lines can be either glyconics or choriambic dimeters B; these seem to be interchangeable and no pattern emerges. The lines of the first half of the stanza are all found linked in one stanza or another so that this must be regarded as a single long (31-syllable) period; the second half is probably the same, but the only actual case of word-overlap is between the sixth and seventh lines.

From the beginning of the second century we have the end of a *paian* in long dactylo-epitrites sung to Titus Flamininus by a chorus in Chalkis.[1] The maidens who are asked to sing here are probably the Muses, and the *paian* was sung by men as is implied by Plutarch's masculine. Melinno's hymn to Rome[2] has with some probability been dated in the second century as a time when the celebration of the festival of Rome was popular in Greece. Her five stanzas in sapphics could have been sung at a Romaia, but we have unfortunately no evidence. For 128–7 we have the two well-known Delphic hymns recorded with their music.[3] We know that 39 singers, 2 flute-players, and 7 lyre-players were involved. The first song is called 'song with lyre to the god' and was composed by an Athenian whose name is lost. It is entirely in cretic-paeonic. The colometry is uncertain, but word-overlap shows that it contained periods of six and seven cretics, so that it must have been a stately song. The Muses are summoned to sing of Apollo, and the present festival with its sacrifices, songs to the flute and songs to the lyre, is described; the end is partly damaged and partly lost so that there is no means of knowing if it ended with a prayer.

The second hymn is described as '*paian* and processional' (*prosodion*) to the god, which Limenios, son of Thoinos, Athenian, composed and accompanied with his lyre. The song has two parts, the first in stately cretic–paeonics like the other hymn, and the second in aeolo-choriambic, again as with Aristonoos, either glyconic or choriambic dimeter B, ending with a pherecratean as clausula. In the fourteen lines of this second part the first three lines are linked; so also are the fourth and

1. Powell, op. cit., 173.
2. Diehl, *Anth. Lyr.,* VI, 315; Bowra, *J.R.S.* 47, 1957, 21.
3. Powell, op. cit., 141; Webster, *Hellenistic Poetry and Art,* 245; Sifakis, *Studies in Hellenistic Drama,* 88.

fifth, the seventh, eighth, and ninth, and the eleventh and twelfth, so that there is no doubt that this part too was in slow time. It is perhaps dangerous to say anything about the music. The editors established that no unaccented syllable in a word is given a higher note than the accented syllable (whatever the accent is). So far the music agrees with the pitch accent, but a 4-syllable word can be sung on one note. The notes indicate pitch but not duration so that a long or short syllable may have the same sign. But long syllables may be sung to two notes, and when this happens the text reduplicates the vowel or vowels (e.g. *Phoioibon*). The cretic–paeonic parts of both hymns are remarkably alike in subject matter. Both summon the Muses to sing Apollo in Delphi; both mention the Athenian Artists of Dionysos (who gave this festival as a gift to Delphi); Apollo both slew the snake and disposed of the Gauls (this is clear from the fragments at the end of the first hymn). Then the aeolo-choriambic part of the second hymn goes over to a prayer: save Athens, look after the people of Delphi, bless the Artists of Dionysos and glorify the Romans. It is probably right to take the aeolo-choriambic part as the processional and the paeonic part as the *paian*, although there is no prayer in the paeonic part. Paeonic is the traditional rhythm for *paians*, and the only allusion to the traditional refrain *ie, paian* is in the paeonic part where it is explained as the echo of the rocks in Athens when Apollo played a duet with Athena, lyre and flute.

A final late-Hellenistic example of a stately song is the hymn to all the gods of which the end is preserved in an inscription at Epidaurus.[1] The concluding prayer prays for 'safety for this temple of Epidaurus in the populous orderliness of the Greeks'. The writer has not felt it incongruous to insert two hexameters from the eighteenth book of the *Iliad* (484 f.) before his conclusion. The metre is not regular dactylo-epitrite but composed of separate double-short ('anapaestic dimeter', hexameter, catalectic hexameter) and single-short elements (iambic trimeter, ithyphallic).

A few examples of songs in dancing time survive. The Pan hymn from Epidaurus,[2] which is probably early Hellenistic, is in trochaic

1. *P.M.G.* 937; Maas, *Epidaurische Hymnen*, 128. The stone is third to fourth century A.D. The odd word applied to the gods, *hierokallinikoi*, may suggest the date; it is obviously formed on *hieronikes*, which seems to be Hellenistic.

2. *P.M.G.* 936; Maas, *Epidaurische Hymnen*, 130; Webster, *Hellenistic Poetry and Art*, 2.

dimeters: only the last two are linked and they form a climax, contrasting with the syncopated clausula, *o iê Pan Pan*. In 291 Demetrios Poliorketes was greeted in Athens 'by processional choruses and ithyphalloi with dance and song'. The song preserved is almost certainly the *paian* of Hermokles[1] and was sung by the ithyphalloi (see above, p. 71). It is in alternate iambic trimeters and ithyphallics, which are frequently separated by hiatus, so that there is no doubt that they could be danced. It is a *paian* because it is an appeal to a god, Demetrios Poliorketes, to avert an evil, the Aetolian War. The same combination of metres was used by Theokles in his ithyphalloi which were performed in Alexandria on the festival of Ptolemy I.[2] In the late third century Euphronios of the Chersonese wrote songs to Priapos which may have been choral since he addresses a plurality, 'Initiates of the New Dionysos';[3] the metre is choriambic dimeter B alternating with pherecratean; in the six surviving lines there is no overlap between the two. Later, in the second century, Aristokles[4] reports that pyrrhic no longer survives; it has become Dionysiac, and they dance Dionysos in India and the story of Pentheus. It is unclear what this means, it may mean no more than a change in subject matter of the songs sung by pyrrhicists while they danced.

The general picture of choral lyric in the later fourth century and the Hellenistic period is unexciting. There are no great poets and no innovations in metre; the complications and subtleties of antistrophes and epodes seem to have vanished, and the remarkable polymetry of astrophic song found in the late fifth-century poets both for choruses and for monodies seems also to have vanished.[5] Most of what has survived was danced in slow time to uncomplicated metres. The actual amount of choral performance of which we know from inscriptions and other sources is considerable. We have little evidence to tell how much of it was revival of old songs. How should we interpret the inscription of 194 B.C. from Delphi[6] which says that a famous flute-

1. Powell, op. cit., 173; Webster, *Hellenistic Poetry and Art*, 13; Renehan, *H.S.C.P.* 68, 1964, 380.
2. Powell, op. cit., 173; Webster, *Hellenistic Poetry and Art*, 124.
3. Powell, op. cit., 176; Webster, *Hellenistic Poetry and Art*, 140.   4. Athenaeus 631a.
5. In a small way the Grenfell song, a monody with anapaests, iambics, and cretics varying what is basically dochmiac, is a survival (Powell, op. cit., 177; Webster, *Hellenistic Poetry and Art*, 127).
6. *S.I.G.*[3] no. 648; Sifakis, *Studies in Hellenistic Drama*, 96 f., with bibliography.

player Satyros performed 'a song with chorus "Dionysos" and a lyre-piece from the *Bacchae* of Euripides'. Presumably he performed as an accompanist, but the flute-accompaniment, which was presumably the free composition of the flautist, was very highly thought of, as we have seen. As the song with chorus is given a title, it is presumably a known and therefore old piece. But what sort of adaptation of what part of the *Bacchae* was the lyre-piece?

Another text which tells us a little about survival is the account of Arcadian education in Polybios.[1] The Arcadian boys sang and danced the *nomes* of Timotheos and Philoxenos in the theatres to the accompaniment of flute-players who belonged to the Guild of Artists of Dionysos. Where in the two centuries that separate these poets from Polybios the Arcadian performances came we do not know, but the passage has a double interest; in the first place it is evidence for survival and revival of classical lyric poetry, and in the second place it is evidence for choral performance of what was composed as a solo *nome*. Here again it is clear that the boundary between solo and choral is ill-defined.

1. Athenaeus 626a. Cf. Pickard-Cambridge, *Festivals*², 247.

III

Conclusion

The fascination of Greek art and Greek poetry lies in the interplay of the traditional and the original, of the formal and the realistic. This is as clear in the history of the Greek chorus as it is in the history of Greek sculpture or in the history of Greek tragedy itself. Much of the development happens gradually within a traditional framework by skilful adaptation to new needs; every now and again the needs are so different that they demand a new framework and then the new framework becomes in its turn traditional.

The history of the Greek chorus goes back farther than we can trace it. New discoveries may in time make more precise the hints that point back to Mycenaean or even Minoan origins. But for the present we must be content with what we can see happening between the time of Homer and the late Hellenistic period. The illustrations of Greek choruses on the whole show more of tradition than of innovation (although they do show us in the sixth century a new energy in girls dancing and in the fifth new steps for satyrs and maenads). But it is a major gain to have the three tempi, which we have called walking or stately time, striding or dance time, and excited time, clearly distinguished and to know that they were already in existence in the eighth century. The fact that we can construct long series of illustrations which show identical dance steps lasting for centuries, women dancing with linked hands, muffled walkers, pyrrhic dancers, padded-dancers, prancing satyrs, and the rest, is some confirmation of the reasonable conjecture that the survival of rhythms in choral poetry also means the survival of dance steps, that, for instance, an Athenian tragic chorus in the late fifth century would dance what we call an alcaic decasyllable in the same way as Alkman's girls in the seventh century. We can accept, as a provisional formula, that a great many units of dance movement, which are also metrical units controlling the sung words, were traditional and that much of the art of the choral poet lay in finding new combinations of traditional units rather than in inventing new units.[1]

We can also show that once a dance unit is established a later poet can play considerable tricks with the rhythm of the words without upsetting the rhythm of the dance. Several instances of this have been quoted:[2] within drama the development of the dochmiac is an obvious example. A glance at Mr Conomis' useful table[3] shows seven types of dochmiacs in Euripides which Aeschylus never used at all; we have noticed also its shy introduction in the *Persae* and *Prometheus Pyrkaeus* in 472, and the complete confidence with which Euripides in 408 can write a run of 32 short syllables and know that they will be sung and danced as four dochmiacs. After its introduction the dochmiac rapidly became popular: in 467 it dominates the agitated choruses of the *Septem*, and from that time becomes the standard metre for agitated choruses and monodies. It must rank as one of the most successful inventions. The ionic series is longer: in Alkman, Sappho, and Alkaios the metra are separated by word-break so that the rhythm is entirely clear; Anakreon in the mid-sixth century, as far as we know, introduced the metre called after him the anaclastic dimeter in which a trochaic metron is substituted for the second ionic metron; at the end of the fifth century the remarkable free ionics, which Aristophanes attributes to Agathon (*Thesm.* 101), with resolved longs and contracted double-short, can in isolation be paralleled in late Sophocles and Euripides; what is even more interesting is that similar licences occur in the cult hymn of the Kouretes and in the *paian* of Isyllos at Epidauros, so that this development of elements which blur the basic rhythm is not confined to a highly sophisticated centre like Athens and to a highly sophisticated art like drama.

This phenomenon, the spread of a highly sophisticated metrical development to comparatively unsophisticated cult hymns, is not isolated. The several late dactylo-epitrite poems that have survived are lineal descendants of the great dactylo-epitrite of Pindar and his

1. Cf. A. M. Dale, *Collected Papers*, 252.
2. Cf. also the use of 'light' anapaests and dactyls; the variations of the first part of choriambic dimeter B; the free correspondence of glyconics and choriambic dimeters B.
3. *Hermes*, 92, 1964, 23.

contemporaries, and the Pindaric corpus itself shows that metrically there is little to choose between a victor-ode sung by a trained chorus in a great centre and a small family affair like the Daphnephorikon of Pagondas in Thebes (fr. 94b).

This evidence that normal cult hymns were wide open to the influence of great choral poetry makes it difficult to answer two further questions which we should like to be able to answer. One is how much does a comparatively new art like tragedy owe to existing cult hymns. The other is whether we can speak legitimately of traditional forms of lyric (as distinct from traditional metrical units).

The most certain case of borrowing by tragedy is probably the refrain. Here we can trace the marriage refrain and the *paian* refrain through centuries, and we have other early instances in Archilochos' hymn to Herakles and the hymn of the Elian women to Dionysos ('precious bull, precious bull'). The refrain is used to mark sections of the song, but the different forms of the marriage refrain and the *paian* refrain, as we meet them, show that, though the words are traditional, they do not impose an identical metre because the exact formulation can be varied. In tragedy refrains are comparatively rare, and the songs in which they occur often seem to have a rather close relation to cult, such as the Binding Song in the *Eumenides*, the hymn to Herakles in the *Hercules*, and the maenad choruses in the *Bacchae*.

Another very old form which was borrowed by tragedy is the exarchon form in which the chorus responds to a solo leader. The archaeological evidence puts this back into the eighth century, and Homer describes not only solo laments with a responding chorus but also Nausikaa and her girls singing and playing ball and the boy singing the Linos song with the grape-carriers answering him. Later in the seventh century Archilochos' hymn to Herakles is described as having this form, and he himself claims to be able to 'lead' the dithyramb and to 'lead' the *paian*. In tragedy this form is primarily used for laments, but it is capable of development into the remarkable astrophic lyric dialogues of late Euripides. A particular variant is the so-called epirrhematic form of comedy where both the solo (a), normally a recitative by the leader of the chorus, and the choral response (b) are repeated, and the order may be either a, b, a', b' or b, a, b', a'. It is common belief that this form is older than established comedy and therefore was the form of pre-comic choruses, but we have not the evidence to prove this.

How far individual metres were connected with particular forms of cult or performance is difficult to say. Paeonics (cretics with one long resolved) probably were especially the metre for *paians* and we have seen both their use in late *paians* and allusion to them in Pindar's *paians*. But there are plenty of *paians* not written in paeonic, and no one would see an allusion to a *paian* in the paeonics of the binding song in the *Eumenides* or of comic choruses. Ionics may well be eastern and connected with the Kybele cult,[1] and there is a real allusion to this in Sappho's Adonis song, perhaps in the choruses of the *Persae*, and certainly in the maenad choruses of the *Bacchae*; but we have also to remember that what is probably the earliest ionic line that we possess (Alkman 46) appears to be a normal opening of a *partheneion* and to carry no such allusion. Anapaestic dimeters were certainly a marching metre, and it seems to me possible that the melic anapaests of lament in tragedy may be derived from melic anapaests sung in real life while the body was being taken from the house to the pyre or the grave. Enoplia (particularly the paroemiac form) probably got their name from armed dances. But when a poet transfers one of these metres to another genre, we should not see any allusion to its origin unless the situation is such as to demand it. The answer then to the question how much tragedy owes to existing cult hymns is probably a great deal both immediately and through the medium of earlier poets who themselves made the borrowing, but the poet only means us to be aware of this when he has contrived a situation which brings the cult origin to mind; but this is a thing which he is always at perfect liberty to do.

The second question which the writing of cult hymns in new metrical forms suggested was how far it is permissible to speak of traditional forms of choral lyric. In fact it is. We have quoted the survival of the 'leader and chorus' form through tragedy and of its variant, epirrhematic form, through comedy. Whatever the origin of antistrophic form, it is well established by the time of Aeschylus and survives for as long as we can trace tragic and comic choruses. The string of identical stanzas, monostrophic form, goes back at least to Alkman and survives beside triadic form in Pindar and Bacchylides and beside antistrophic

1. Cf. A. M. Dale, *Collected Papers*, 256.

form in comedy, and is still used in the *paian* of Philodamos in the fourth century. Once a successful form is established poets continue to use it for some purposes, whether or not they have themselves adopted a newer form for more exciting purposes.

The origin of forms is lost to us, but we can say something, though much less than we should like, about invention and development from the eighth century onwards.[1] Three forms are certainly very early: stichic, epodic, systematic. Stichic means the repetition of like lines with Pause between. The evidence seems to suggest that both stichic hexameters and iambic trimeters could be sung chorally or solo, but probably long stichic lines were more normally in recitative or spoken. But short lines could be put together like this for dancing or excited dancing, e.g. the six paroemiacs of the Spartan *embaterion* (*P.M.G.* 856).

Epodic form is essentially composed of two separate elements (AB) which are then repeated. The best-known form is the elegiac couplet A, dactylic hexameter B, blunt hemiepes plus blunt hemiepes: it is preserved from the early seventh century and may have been earlier. Archilochos, who surely was one of the great pioneers in Greek rhythm, has a number of varieties, some with A and B similar (as in the elegiac couplet), some with A and B different. The first class (of which the most famous example is the trochaic tetrameter catelectic, consisting of full trochaic dimeter separated by diairesis from the following catalectic dimeter) could certainly be choral; the hymn to Herakles has alternating iambic dimeters catalectic and iambic trimeters. The second class combines a double-short element with a single-short: the line to which Archilochos' name was given is an example; A is an enoplian, xddx, and B is an ithyphallic, ssx. This was later used chorally and stichically by Aristophanes, as we have seen, but its real future was to be an element in a larger polymetric structure such as the dactylo-epitrite triad.

The regular repetition of AB, particularly when A is like B, produces an effect which is not so very different from the regular stichic repetition of identical elements. A slightly more varied effect is obtained if the shape is AABAAAB, i.e. if the second element recurs at irregular intervals. This is called a system. An obvious instance, which is prob-

1. The development is sketched *L.M.*[2] 195, and was treated more fully by A. M. Dale in a seminar in 1961 at the London Institute of Classical Studies.

ably very early, is the march composed of anapaestic dimeters broken irregularly by paroemiacs, which in these contexts are catalectic anapaestic dimeters. We know these best from the *parodoi* of Aeschylus but they are clearly old, and *P.M.G.* 857 is probably a fragment of an early Spartan song of this type. A system of this kind could be produced by a repeated refrain line, whether the refrain line was in the same metre, a kindred metre, or an alien metre.

Irregular systems have a long subsequent history Anakreon's hymn to Artemis (*P.M.G.* 348) is an irregular system of two glyconics (A), a pherecratean (B), four glyconics (A), and a pherecratean (B). Regular systems appear with the Lesbians: instead of the two-structure of the epodic form, AB, the poets write a regular AAB, or AAAB. The Sapphic and Alcaic stanza have both the form AAB, and Anakreon uses the form AAAB, three trochaic dimeters and a catalectic trochaic dimeter (*P.M.G.* 347), three glyconics and a pherecratean (*P.M.G.* 358). In the Sapphic and Alcaic stanzas B is longer instead of shorter than A: in the Sapphic B is A with an added dx, in the Alcaic B is a sort of reduplication of both the single-short and the double-short elements of A.[1]

Technically the Sapphic and Alcaic stanzas should be called regular systems and not stanzas, and the word stanza reserved for more complex metrical wholes which contain at least three different metrical elements. Perhaps a fragment of Archilochos (112D) may be regarded as the original and minimal stanza, dactylic tetrameter B, ithyphallic, iambic trimeter catalectic. The stanzas of the Lesbians are very simple: Sappho 96 is s'xxds, xxds, xxdssx – here xxds (the Lesbian glyconic) is basic: in the first line a cretic is prefixed, in the last line the glyconic is extended to an extra sx, so that the whole could be called A[1], A[2], A[3]. Alkaios 130 is xxd'ds, xxd'ds, xxdsx, xd'ds – the last line is a shorter version of the first two and the third is alien, so that the whole is A, A, B, A[1].

As far as we can see, the man who exploited the potentialities of Archilochos and first built a complex stanza was Alkman, who was writing his *partheneia* before the Lesbians. The first *partheneion* has stanzas of three parts, the first four pairs of lekythion plus enoplian, the second two trochaic trimeters and a trochaic tetrameter, the third a

---

1. See above, p. 76.

dactylic tetrameter B plus a catelectic dactylic tetrameter (or an alcaic decasyllable). It might be called four epodic AB, one system $B^1B^1B^2$, one epode CC^1 (or CD). This is not only the most complex structure which we have seen yet but it also shows for the first time the combination of double- and single-short within a single metrical unit, the enoplians of the first part, xdsx, and the variant close of the last part, ddsx, a combination which is developed by the Lesbians.

The stanzas of Alkman's *partheneion* repeat unchanged (except for the variant close). This is the monostrophic form of song which continues to be used to the end of Greek lyric poetry. The next step forward is to make the stanzas themselves into a pattern. If we assume that the kind of song which consists of unlike pairs of strophe–antistrophe (AA', BB', etc.) was the creation of the dramatists, as seems probable, the first step was the triadic form: the song consisting of like triads, each composed of identical strophe and antistrophe and variant epode. If the dance of the monostrophic song was A, A, A.., the dance of the triadic song was A, A', B, A, A¹, B . . . We are told that Stesichoros invented the triad, and we have no reason to doubt this. The only Stesichorean triad that is partially preserved is the triad of the *Geryoneis*. The strophe–antistrophe consists of five dactylo-anapaestic periods: tetrameter catalectic, octameter catalectic, hexameter catalectic, hexameter, octameter. The epode is shorter by the equivalent of a tetrameter and is also purely dactylo-anapaestic, but the detailed colometry is unclear. Other poems of Stesichoros did not exclude the single-short so rigorously, and some of his long lines anticipate dactylo-epitrite.

Drama, perhaps because the exarchon form was as important a source of inspiration as choral lyric, went its own way. But other forms of choral lyric (and much solo lyric) seem to have been predominantly triadic by the early fifth century: for dithyramb Lasos of Hermione before the end of the sixth century changed the form from monostrophic to triadic. The next step forward is to increase the size and complexity of the dancing units, both the individual periods and often the wholes (single stanzas, strophe–antistrophe, and triad) in which the periods were combined.

If the triads of the *Geryoneis* are more or less typical, early sixth-century choral lyric had stanzas of about five similar periods (in the *Geryoneis* the periods only differ in length not in metre), and this description still fits the *stasima* (as distinct from the lyric dialogues) of Aeschylus' *Persae* in 472 (548 ff. is unique in having nine periods; no other stanza has more than six). This use of short stanzas is one of the reasons for supposing that Aeschylus was working in a tradition of many short stanzas which was fixed by Thespis when Stesichoros still dominated choral lyric. In choral lyric the change came much earlier: the triad of the *Geryoneis* probably had 13 periods in all, but in 498 the triad of Pindar's earliest victor-ode, *Pythian* X, had 18, as does the earliest dactylo-epitritic victor-ode in triads, *Nemean* V. If we look later in the fifth century we find that Bacchylides' *Theseus* (XVII) has a triad of 42 periods, Pindar's First *Olympian* has a triad of 30 periods, and the triads of *Pythian* IV and *Pythian* VIII are respectively 22 and 20 periods long.

In the new long triads each repeated stanza is not only much longer but also much more varied than in the earlier short and metrically homogeneous triad of the *Geryoneis*. Take for instance *Pythian* IV: no single period repeats in strophe or epode and every period except the last two of the strophe mix double- and single-short. What repeats within the stanza are elements like sxdd, sxsx, dddxsx, and these elements may be inverted: ddxs inverts sxdd, xsxddd inverts dddxsx. So the whole long triad is patterned and the pattern would be seen and heard more easily because of the fondness of dactylo-epitrite for dd and sx. In Pindar's aeolic the pattern is less clear because the elements are not so stereotyped. But in the late *Pythian* VIII[1] (which again mixes double- and single-short in every period except the last of the strophe) one would probably recognize sds (glyconic) as a basic element; three occur in the strophe, one at the end of a longer period, and four, all embedded in longer periods, in the epode; and one might feel ds as an echo and xsd as an equivalent. Thus the periodic style in both its more formal and smoother dactylo-epitrite and its freer and rougher aeolic is a form of free composition which is given a shape by the repetition of certain pattern elements with the periods. Each period in strophe and antistrophe is normally unique, and it is quite impossible to express the relationship of one period to another by a simple letter system as in Alkman, Sappho, and Alkaios: one can only hope to see and hear the common elements and their variations.

1. Analysed A. M. Dale, *C.Q.* 1, 1951, 25 = *Collected Papers*, 71.

On our evidence it looks as if Simonides may have been responsible for the popularity of the new style, if he did not invent it. The victor-ode to Glaukos of Karystos (*P.M.G.* 509), which was probably written in 520, is already in regular dactylo-epitrite, and the *skolion* to Skopas (*P.M.G.* 542) shows periodic 'aeolic' before 500.

It is difficult to define the influence of periodic style on tragedy. Two things, however, are clear, the adoption of dactylo-epitrite and the common increase in stanza length. The stately chorus on Dareios' empire in the *Persians* (852) is more like Stesichoros than Pindar, and it is this tradition which survives in the great dactylic stanzas of the *Agamemnon*, but the *Prometheus Vinctus* has regular dactylo-epitrite choruses as well as free dactylo-epitrite. From that time dactylo-epitrite is common, sometimes for whole stanzas, sometimes for parts of stanzas, sometimes regular and sometimes free, in Sophocles down to the *Oedipus Tyrannus* and in Euripides particularly at the end of the first and the beginning of the second group (*Medea* and *Andromache*) but continuing sporadically down to the *Helen* in 412. As a stately metre of high choral lyric he naturally chooses it for foil choruses, which contrast the heroic past with the realistic present.

In length of stanzas the obvious change comes between the typical Aeschylean chorus with six or more pairs of strophe–antistrophe and the choruses of his successors which never have more than three pairs of strophe–antistrophe, very frequently have two pairs, and sometimes have a single pair and an epode. But Aeschylus himself was already writing long stanzas by the time of the *Agamemnon* and so far may be said to feel the new influence; they are, however, much more homogeneous metrically than the stanzas of Pindaric 'aeolic'. The first strophe of the first *stasimon* of the *Agamemnon*[1] (367) can be analysed into ten periods, but they are all iambic except the final aristophanean, dsx. The whole pattern is very simple: A, A, A^1, A^2, A^3, A^4, A, A, A^5, B.

Sophocles' stanzas usually show much more metrical variety. As an early example the first strophe of the first *stasimon* of the *Antigone* (332) is very elegant: the first period is dss'sds; then it is not clear whether sds, sds, xsdx should be reckoned as three or one, but at any rate the sds (glyconic) of the first period is repeated twice and then its catalectic form is tied on by a link anceps: then the single-short element is taken

1. *L.M.*[2] 201.

up by itself xsxsxssx; then in the long last period double-short comes back in strength, ddddddddssx, but with a close that echoes the close of the preceding period. This is something like an immensely elaborated alcaic stanza; it is much clearer and more shapely in spite of its diversity of elements than Pindaric 'aeolic'. The praise of Athens in the posthumous *Oedipus Coloneus* is even clearer in shape: the first period is sds, sdssx; the second sds, sds, sds, sdx; the third sds, sds; the fourth ddd'sssx; the fifth repeats the first; the sixth is sdsx. Everything here is glyconic or variant of glyconic (longer or shorter) except the fourth period which starts with racing double-shorts and ends like the first and fifth periods: this is the familiar dactylic tetrameter B running into an iambic dimeter.

The parallel for this is not the full periodic 'aeolic' of Pythian VIII, but the simpler version adopted by Bacchylides in the *Aigeus* (18): there are eight periods all containing at least one glyconic, the first and second periods are identical with the first period of the O.C. chorus, and the second part (hendecasyllable) repeats as the clausula. The sixth period is like the first but has one syllable more (sds'sdsss). The third period is a variant on this, sds'sds'sss, and repeats without the first glyconic as the seventh period. The fourth and fifth periods are one and two glyconics respectively. Bacchylides does not even allow himself the runaway dactylic tetrameter B to break the glyconic variants.

The long late stanzas of Euripides are difficult to compare because it is often uncertain where the period ends come. The last *stasimon* of the *Helen* (1451 ff.)[1] probably has five periods in the first strophe, (1) xs'dxs'dsx'ds, (2) xs'd'sdx, (3) s'dxs'd'sdx, (4) sds'sxd'sdsxdx, (5) xsd'sxdsx. Here, although it is quite possible to give the parts the traditional names, glyconic, choriambic dimeter B, etc., the total effect is less obviously shapely than either the Sophocles or the Bacchylides quoted above and more like free period construction.

The next step (and, as far as we know, the last step forward in the development of choral lyric) was to free parts of songs or whole songs from the pattern element of triadic form or antistrophic form. It is unfortunate that we have no major example of this development outside drama except Timotheos' *Persae*, which dates very little before Euripides' *Trojan Women*. Melanippides, who started it, seems to have

1. Cf. A. M. Dale, *Euripides: Helen*, on this.

been at least as old as Sophocles, and his successor Phrynis won a Panathenaic victory before the date of Sophocles' *Antigone*. For us the first preserved astrophic song is the beginning of the *parodos* (73 lines) of Aeschylus' *Septem* in 467, and we cannot tell whether Aeschylus was already influenced by Melanippides. This is not simply a system of dochmiacs substituted for the normal system of anapaests for the entry of the chorus because, though dochmiacs are the dominant metre, they are punctuated at irregular intervals by iambic, iambo-choriambic, cretic, and bacchiac. Thus the long line of astrophic songs in dochmiacs and associated metres is begun.

The interesting question is how far there is a stable element in these astrophic songs. In Aeschylus they are predominantly dochmiac and iambic. A new element in *P.V.* 687 ff. is a dragged prosodiac, ddss, which can be regarded as a dochmiac of form ds extended in both directions. The only astrophic song in Sophocles is the little song of triumph in the *Trachiniae* (205) when the news first comes of Herakles' victory. This is mainly iambic and syncopated iambic with a run of dactyls in the middle. Where he shows the influence of the new music is in the lyric dialogues of the later plays, particularly in the long epodes but he doesn't abandon the antistrophic or triadic framework.

Many of Euripides' astrophic songs are in the tradition of Aeschylus, dochmiacs and associated metres, but as time goes on the associated metres become more prominent, particularly enoplian, prosodiac, and the simpler forms of dactylo-epitrite. One might name as stages on this road Hermione's monody in the *Andromache* (825), Polymestor's monody in the *Hecuba* (1056), the recognition scene in the *Iphigenia in Tauris* (827), and the lyric dialogue between Antigone and the old man before the *parodos* of the *Phoenissae* (103 ff.). We do not need to invoke any influence outside drama in this development once Aeschylus had given the signal with the *parodos* of the *Septem*, whether he himself was influenced by Melanippides or not.

But there are some Euripidean astrophic songs which stand outside this tradition, where an outside influence may be at work. The first is the very remarkable lament of Hippolytos (*Hipp.* 1370) in 428: he moves from melic anapaests through dactylo-anapaests to iambics varied by dochmiacs and aeolo-choriambics. Probably we can here speak of iambics as dominant, but they are much less obviously dominant than the dochmiacs in the series which we have just reviewed. Then there are the astrophic songs in melic anapaests like Hekabe's opening to the *parodos* of the *Trojan Women* in 415 and the whole dialogue *parodos* of the *Iphigenia in Tauris*. It may be that melic anapaests are an old lament metre, as has been suggested above, but these anapaests are remarkable for their variations in length (some are dimeters, many are paroemiacs, some have four, five, or six long syllables, all of which are the equivalent of dochmiacs), their predominantly spondaic character, but also (the reverse of this) their admission of proceleusmatics and even light anapaests of three short syllables. Proceleusmatics are found in Timotheos (*P.M.G.* 799) and notably in Pratinas' *hyporcheme* (*P.M.G.* 708), which may, as we have seen, be attributed to a lyric poet of about 430–20, so that Euripides may here be influenced by contemporary lyric poetry.

Finally there are the few songs which can reasonably be said to show the influence of Timotheos: Antigone's lament in the *Phoenissae* (1485), the lyric report of the Phrygian in the *Orestes* (1369), and Iphigeneia's lament in the *Iphigenia in Aulis* (1283). In Antigone's lament the dominant is dactyls, but after the initial run the song is largely polymetric returning to dactylic occasionally and particularly before the end. The Phrygian's messenger song has an actual echo of Timotheos *Persae* (1397): in both one could probably say that iambic is the dominant but both are very largely polymetric; Euripides more than Timotheos gets occasional stability by short runs of identical lines in different metres, but this element is also present in Timotheos. These short runs in different metres are particularly clear in Iphigeneia's lament where one can hardly speak of a dominant metre, only that the song ends in iambics and iambics have appeared sporadically before. One other example of this style is interesting because of its early and well attested date, the hoopoe's monody in Aristophanes' *Birds* (227) which was produced in 414. Here the different kinds of birds have each their own section in a different metre, but there is a thread of recurrent dochmiacs and dochmiac anapaests which holds the whole together. The beauty of the song is manifest, but it is also a parody of the new music.

With this kind of polymetric lyric, free of the patterning of strophe, antistrophe, and epode, Greek choral and solo lyric and dance seem to have reached a sort of end. The last dance development which we can detect, the pirouetting maenads, is nearly contemporary with the beginnings of Timotheos. Whether there is any connection, we cannot say but one would rather suppose that the long runs of short syllables formed by resolving long syllables which normally remained long gave the kind of variation of rhythm necessary for pirouettes. After the early years of the fourth century we cannot detect any important new development, and it is not unlikely that pure music takes over the lead from choral music, just as in the third century solo dancing takes over the lead from choral dancing, as the new and exciting art.

Glossary of Metrical Terms

ACATALECTIC. See catalectic.

AEOLIC is used in three senses: (i) of the three groups of metres which tend to use *ds*, here divided into aeolo-choriambic, prosodiac, and enoplian; (ii) more particularly, of the use of these metres by Sappho and Alkaios, who put two syllables, which can be either long or short, before, e.g., the *ds* of the glyconic, so that they can only be represented by *xx*; (iii) of the metres used by Pindar and Bacchylides which are not dactylo-epitrite.

AEOLO-CHORIAMBIC. A group of metres: (i) with *ds* as a normal element, e.g. *dss*, choriambic dimeter A; *sds*, glyconic; *dsx*, aristophanean, *xds*, telesillean; *sdsx*, hipponactean; *sd'ds*, asclepiad; (ii) catalectic forms of these, e.g., *sdx*, pherecratean; *xdx*, reizianum; (iii) *d'd*, choriambic dimeter; *sxd*, choriambic dimeter B.

ALCAIC DECASYLLABLE. See prosodiac.

ANACREONTIC. See ionic.

ANAPAEST. Rising double-short rhythm ʌ*ddd*. (i) Recitative anapaests, reckoned in metra and usually used in dimeters or tetrameters catalectic. The metra, ʌ*dd*, are normally separated by diairesis. Dimeters are built into systems, subdivided by a catalectic dimeter (paroemiac). (ii) Melic anapaests. No metron diairesis and irregular lengths, hence the terms hexamakron (six longs), etc. Often spondaic. Long lines of this type, but with little contraction and much dactylic inversion are called dactylo-anapaest.

ANCEPS. A syllable which can be either short or long. Anceps may be either initial or link or final. Distinguish from normal anceps: (i) brevis in longo; (ii) drag: unusual lengthening of enclosed single short. Cf. A. M. Dale, *Collected Papers*, 185 f.

ARISTOPHANEAN. See aeolo-choriambic.

ASCLEPIAD. See aeolo-choriambic.

ASTROPHIC. A song not divided into strophes, strophe–antistrophe, or triads.

BACCHIAC. *xs*, iambic metron, with short omitted and anceps normally short, or *sx*, trochaic metron, with short omitted, long anceps, and first long usually treated as short anceps.

213

BLUNT. Used of a colon or period which ends on a true long, e.g., *sds*, *dd*.

BLUNT JUNCTION. Juxtaposition of units within a period so that true long comes next to true long, e.g., *sds'sds*.

BREVIS IN LONGO. See Pause.

CAESURA. Recurrence of word division at a regular place within the metron. Contrast diairesis.

CATALECTIC. Used of a metron or longer unit which stops short of the last syllable. Thus a pherecratean, *sdx*, is a catalectic glyconic, *sds*, when it serves as clausula after a glyconic. The term acatalectic may be used to mark the fact that the full form is used when the catalectic form is expected.

CHORIAMBIC METRON, *d*.

CHORIAMBIC DIMETERS. See acolo-choriambic.

CHORIAMBIC ENOPLIAN. See enoplian.

COLOMETRY. The arrangement of cola on the printed page so as to show their presumed relation to periods.

COLON. A metrical unit which forms a recognizable subdivision of a period.

CONTRACTION. Substitution of a long syllable for two contiguous short syllables.

CRETIC METRON, *s*. The resolved form is known as paeon or paeonic.

DACTYLIC. Falling double-short rhythm, *ddd* . . . Traditionally the single dactyl is counted as a metron, hence hexameter, etc. Note: (i) A-type hexameter, etc. ending with anceps, *dddddx*; (ii) B-type dimeter and tetrameter, apparently ending with double-short, often with diairesis, but the period must run on into the next colon as it must end either on a long syllable or anceps; (iii) hemiepes, etc., *dd*; (iv) elegiac: A-hexameter followed by *dd'dd*.

DACTYLO-ANAPAEST. See anapaest.

DACTYLO-EPITRITE. A metre which joins *s* with *dd* by link-anceps (usually long). Note *xsxdd*, iambelegus; *ddxsx*, encomiologus.

DOCHMIAC. Colon much used by the dramatists. Basic form, $\cup--\cup-$, but the longs can be resolved and the shorts can be dragged (and then occasionally resolved, provided that the contiguous longs are not also resolved). Cf. *L.M.* 105. Equivalents are the hypodochmiac $-\cup-\cup-$ and the hexasyllable $\cup-\cup-\cup-$ (both of which have resolved and dragged forms), and the tetrasyllable $----$

ELEGIAC. See dactylic.

ENCOMIOLOGUS. See dactylo-epitrite.

ENOPLIAN. Cola in rising rhythm containing double-short. They may start from double-short, single-short, or anceps, and may change to single-short before the end, e.g., ᴧ*dds*, *xddx* (enoplian paroemiac), *xdsx* (choriambic enoplian A), *xsdx* (choriambic enoplian B).

GLYCONIC. See aeolo-choriambic.

HIPPONACTEAN. See aeolo–choriambic.

HYPODOCHMIAC. See dochmiac.

IAMBELEGUS. See dactylo–epitrite.

IAMBIC. Rising single–short rhythm. Iambic metron, *xs*. The penthemimer, *xsx*, is used in compounds.

IAMBO–TROCHAIC. Used of lyrics which alternate between iambic and trochaic, and of those which are dominated by ambiguous cola like the lekythion, *sss* or *sxs*, and the ithyphallic, *ssx*.

IBYCEAN. See prosodiac.

IONIC METRON, ∧*dx*. But the final syllable is never short unless the succeeding syllable is long (as in the anacreontic, ∧*dxsx*). The initial double–short may be contracted; the long and the long anceps may be resolved (contraction of the double–short plus resolution of the long anceps gives the so–called major ionic).

MAKRON. Long syllable. Pentamakron, hexamakron: colon consisting of five, six long syllables or their equivalents.

METRON. Rhythmical unit, dactylic, anapaestic, iambic, trochaic, choriambic, or ionic (*q.v.*), which normally occurs in a longer structure of similar elements: dimeter (2 metra), trimeter (3), tetrameter (4), pentameter (5) hexameter (6), etc.

MOLOSSUS. Bacchiac with long anceps.

MONOSTROPHIC. A song in which the strophes repeat identically.

PAEONIC. See cretic.

PAROEMIAC. See anapaest, enoplian.

PAUSE. The gap at the end of a period when the dance comes to rest. Indications of Pause are: (i) hiatus – an unelided vowel at the end of one period is followed by an open vowel at the beginning of the next; (ii) anceps at the end of one period followed by anceps at the beginning of the next; (iii) brevis in longo, short syllable at the end of a period where the metre demands a long: Pause justifies the admission of the short; (iv) a catalectic colon very often precedes Pause.

PENDANT. Used of a colon or a period which ends with anceps. Contrast blunt.

PENTHEMIMER. See iambic.

PERIOD. A metrical unit bounded on either side by Pause. It may be sub–divided into cola where these are themselves recognizable metrical units. In drama, where Pause is often difficult to establish, sometimes the colon must be regarded as the basic unit.

PHERECRATEAN. See aeolo–choriambic.

PNIGOS, 'choke'. A number of cola in synaphaea, which were delivered in a single breath.

PRAXILLEAN. See prosodiac.

PROCELEUSMATIC. Anapaest consisting of four short syllables.

PROSODIAC. Cola in falling rhythm containing double-short. They start from a long and may change to single short before the end, e.g., *dds*, ibycean, *ddsx*, alcaic decasyllable, *dddsx*, praxillean.

REIZIANUM. See aeolo-choriambic.

RESOLUTION. Substitution of two short syllables for a long; common in iambic, trochaic, iambo-trochaic, cretic-paeonic; in anapaests used with contraction to form dactylic inversion and without contraction to form proceleusmatics; uncommon in ionics and for frame longs in choriambs of aeolo-choriambic.

SPONDEE. Two successive long syllables, formed by contraction in dactyls and anapaests; by double syncopation in iambics and trochaic; by drag in other metres.

SYNAPHAEA. Cola are in synaphaea when there is no Pause between them. This may be indicated: (i) by word-overlap; (ii) if the earlier colon ends in double-short or short anceps. Cf. *L.M.* 27.

SYNCOPATION. An iambic or trochaic metron is syncopated when either the anceps or the short or, less commonly, both are suppressed.

TELESILLEAN. See aeolo-choriambic.

TROCHAIC. Falling single-short rhythm. Trochaic metron, *sx*.

Index

Abdera, 99
Achaios, 135
Adonis, 73, 203
Aegina, 8, 15, 88, 89, 90, 96, 100, 110
Aeschylus, 98, 110 ff., 159 f., 163, 179, 191, 203, 205
  preserved plays: *Oresteia*, xi, 29, 125 ff., 141, 142, 160, 161, 202 f., 208; *Persae*, 25, 32, 110, 113 ff., 121 f., 124, 201, 203, 207 f.; *Prometheus Vinctus*, 130, 201, 208, 210; *Septem*, 113, 120 ff., 130, 132, 201, 210; *Supplices*, 113, 122 ff., 130, 142, 161
  lost plays: *Aigyptioi*, 122, 125; *Danaides*, 73; *Diktyoulkoi*, 119, 186; *Edonoi*, 27; *Glaukos Potnieus*, 118; *Heliades*, 113; *Herakleidai*, 131; *Nereides*, 20, 29; *Phineus*, 25, 113, 118; *Prometheus Pyrkaeus*, 14, 28, 118 f.; *Thalamopoioi*, 24; *Theoroi*, 119, 190; *Toxotides*, 29
Agathon, 189, 192, 201
Alkaios, 72, 113, 201, 205
Alkibiades, 151
Alkman, 49, 53, 56 ff., 61, 66, 69, 79, 97, 116, 143, 201, 203, 205
altar, 16, 20, 22, 26, 152
Amazons, 22, 93, 94
Anakreon, 14, 19, 80, 81, 83 f., 93, 113, 115, 173, 201, 205
Anthesteria, 71, 81 f., 92
Aphrodite, 72, 105, 108
Apollo, 15, 22, 47, 48, 50, 54, 65, 72 f., 92, 97, 99 ff., 102, 194 ff.
Arcadia, 49, 199
Archilochos, 16, 56, 60, 62, 63 ff., 79, 187, 202, 204 f.
Argos, 6, 13, 48, 49, 53, 67, 96, 156
Ariadne, 4, 13, 15, 16, 17, 30, 46

Arion, 67, 112, 155
Ariphron, 151
Aristokles, 198
Aristonoos, 195 f.
Aristophanes, 112, 153, 180, 192, 201, 204; *Acharnenses*, 94, 180, 182 f.; *Aves*, 73, 94, 181 f., 186 ff., 211; *Ecclesiazusae*, 69, 181, 191 f.; *Equites*, 69, 94, 181, 183; *Lysistrata*, 47, 69, 81, 180, 187; *Nubes*, 94, 183 f., 185; *Pax*, 73, 181, 185 ff.; *Plutus*, 181, 192; *Ranae*, 181, 190 f.; *Thesmophoriazusae*, 48, 165; *Vespae*, 69, 181 f., 184 f.
Aristotle, 52, 70, 94, 151, 192, 194
Aristoxenos, 62
Artemis, 9, 21, 48, 63, 68, 72, 84, 94, 100, 193, 205
Asine, 101
Asklepios, 151, 195
astrophic songs, 120, 127, 132, 144, 149, 153, 155, 157, 158, 159, 164 ff., 167 ff., 171, 179 f., 191, 198, 202, 209 ff.
Athena, 72, 75, 84, 95, 151
Athenaeus, 49, 56, 61, 71, 98, 112, 133, 193, 195, 199
Athens, 6, 9, 12, 13 ff., 17, 19, 21, 52, 60, 69 ff., 80, 84, 87, 91 ff., 100, 102 f., 104, 111, 153, 192, 195, 197, 201
aulodia, 56
Aurai, 26
Autokrates, 94, 185

Bacchylides, 66, 73, 80, 84, 87 ff., 95 f., 98, 101 f., 105 ff., 109, 112, 155, 203, 207, 209
Barron, J., 79
Beazley, J. D., 1, 16, 18, 19, 185
birds, 20, 93, 94, 180
Boeotia, 8, 12, 17, 53, 72, 95, 97

Bowra, C. M., 51, 77, 79, 80, 85, 152, 155, 194, 196
Brauron, 16, 22

cakes, 31, 60, 65, 192
Caskey, J. L., 5
Chalkis, 12, 13, 196
chorus, types of, 2; Anacreontes, 11, 14, 19, 21, 23, 24, 25, 27, 67, 70, 83; circular, 47 f., 68, 77, 91; comic, 4, 15, 20, 31, 69 f., 93 ff., 150, 180 ff., 192, 202 f.; laments, 6, 11, 17, 49, 73, 90, 114, 116 ff., 132, 138, 145, 149, 156 ff., 159, 162 ff., 170 f., 174 f., 177, 179, 183, 202 f.; leader and chorus, 5, 12, 15, 47, 49, 51, 61, 64, 111, 189, 202, 203, 206; linked dancers, 5 ff., 8 ff., 21, 25, 32, 47 f., 50, 75, 96, 189, 193; maenads and/or satyrs, 4, 11, 12, 13 f., 18, 26 f., 30, 53, 70, 80; maenads, 'lenaian', 14, 18, 19, 23, 25, 26, 27 f., 30, 53, 81; maenads, tragic, 19, 25, 27, 83, 130, 172, 185; maenads with wing-sleeves, 18, 29, 26, 27, 30; padded dancers, 8, 9, 11 ff., 16, 21, 53, 63, 67 ff., 70; pyrrhics, 7, 11, 22, 26, 32, 52, 55, 62, 193, 198, 203; races, 16, 22; satyr-play, 24, 28, 30, 32, 69, 95, 118 f., 134 f., 179 f., 185; satyrs with lyres, 4, 15, 18, 20, 24, 28, 93, 133; square, 68, 112; tragic, 25, 26, 27, 111 ff.; victory songs, 15, 64, 80, 174
City Dionysia, 20, 32, 70 f., 82, 92 f., 103, 195
Clazomenae, 21
Coldstream, J. N., 10
Conomis, N., 134, 201
Corinth, 6, 9, 11, 15, 16, 17, 21, 48, 50, 51, 57, 63, 67, 70, 105, 108, 112, 115, 195
Crete, 4, 10, 16, 46, 52, 56
Crowhurst, R., 5
Cunningham, M. L., 115, 125
Cyprus, 52
Cyrene, 108

Dale, A. M., xiii, 54, 57, 59, 63, 65, 66, 76, 77, 78, 79, 84, 86 ff., 90, 101, 103, 105 f., 108, 110, 116, 133 ff., 139, 143, 146, 164 f., 171, 173 f., 179, 182, 184, 189, 192, 201, 203 f., 207 ff.
dance-gestures, 2 f.
    arms: backwards, 25, 27, 28; downwards, 7, 12, 13, 23, 24; forwards, 12, 18, 24, 25, 27, 28; greeting, 5, 7, 11, 12, 14,

17, 18, 19, 22, 24, 25, 27, 28, 31, 32; muffled, 11, 12, 17, 19, 20, 21, 22, 26, 27, 28, 29, 30, 31, 32, 93, 94, 132, 193; upwards, 6, 18
    hands: clapping, 7, 9, 10, 50, 51, 64; near forehead, 10, 11; near hip; 10, 12, 13, 19, 24; on hip, 7, 14, 20, 21, 22, 24, 25, 27, 28, 30, 31; to forehead, 11, 13, 24, 25, 27, 29, 32
dance-steps, 2 f.; headstand, 6, 21, 52, 53; jump, 7, 8, 12, 15, 51, 53; kick, backwards, 7, 8, 11, 12, 13, 18, 21, 24, 28, 30, 31, 32, 53, 83, 134, 192; kick, forwards, 7, 8, 11, 12, 13, 14, 18, 20, 21, 25, 27, 28, 29, 30, 31, 32, 53, 134, 185, 192; knees, both flexed, 7, 8, 11, 12, 13, 14, 18, 20, 21, 24, 28, 31, 53; lunge, 18, 23, 24, 25, 27, 28, 30, 31, 32; march, 4, 15, 55, 62, 112, 182, 203; pirouette, 26, 27, 172, 185, 212; prance, 15, 20, 28, 49, 54, 93, 133; run, 13, 15, 16, 22, 25, 28, 29, 31, 69, 75, 93, 118, 182, 186; stride, 5 ff., 10, 14, 16, 17, 18, 19, 21, 22, 23, 24, 25, 26, 27, 28, 29, 53, 55, 182; walk, 6 f., 8 ff., 15, 16, 19, 20, 21, 22, 23, 26, 27, 28, 29, 30, 53, 75, 93, 94, 97, 104, 106, 109, 113, 122, 129, 142, 173, 182, 191, 193 f., 197
Delian maidens, 22, 48, 54, 193
Delos, 6, 48, 50, 51, 54, 60, 99 ff.
Delphi, 14, 50, 52, 80, 87, 96, 100, 102, 108, 110, 194 ff., 198
Demeter, 49, 60, 64, 65, 84, 91
Demetrios (poet), 30
Demetrios of Phaleron, 195
Demetrios Poliorketes, 198
Dikaiarchos, 193
Dionysodotos, 62
Dionysos, 5, 13, 15, 18, 19, 21, 24, 27, 28, 30, 53, 60, 63, 64, 67, 68, 69, 80, 83, 92, 102 ff., 194, 197 ff.
Dioskouroi, 72, 95
dithyramb, 17, 26, 29 f., 32, 63, 68, 70, 80, 82, 90 ff., 101 ff., 112, 132 f., 153, 193 f., 206
dolphin-riders, 20, 29, 93, 94, 155
double-row dances, 12, 15, 22, 47, 61, 190

Edwards, M. W., 18
ekkyklema, 126 ff., 141, 144, 148, 159, 165, 168, 189
Elian women, 59 f., 63, 83, 202
embateria, 62, 65, 150, 204 f.

Index

endymatia, 67
enkomia, 79, 104 f.
Ephesos, 94, 185
Ephippos, 192
Epicharmos, 93
Epidaurus, 195, 197
Epikrates, 94
Eratosthenes, 60
Eresos, 61
Eretria, 9
Erythrai, 151, 195
Eukleia, 63
Eumelos, 50, 54
Euphronios, 198
Euripides, 151, 153, 174 f., 181, 183, 187, 191, 201 f., 209 f.
    preserved plays: *Alcestis*, 143 ff.; *Andromache*, 156, 208, 210; *Bacchae*, 26, 82, 113, 172 f., 178, 199, 202 f.; *Cyclops*, 14, 30, 83, 179 f.; *Electra*, 159 ff.; *Hecuba*, 48, 156, 184, 210; *Helen*, 165 f., 189, 208, 209; *Heraclidae*, 147; *Hercules Furens*, 29, 46, 48, 164, 202; *Hippolytos*, 125, 144, 147 ff., 155, 157, 210; *Ion*, 166; *Iphigenia in Aulis*, 171, 178, 211; *Iphigenia in Tauris*, 163, 167, 173, 210 f.; *Medea*, 66, 145 ff., 148, 173, 208; *Orestes*, 170 f., 173, 179, 201, 211; *Phoenissae*, 51, 168 f., 171, 210 f.; *Supplices*, 125, 158, 163; *Troades*, 162 f., 167, 209, 211
    lost plays: *Aigeus*, 149; *Aiolos*, 186; *Alexandros*, 16; *Alkmaion Kor.*, 172; *Alkmaion Psoph.*, 143 f.; *Alope*, 149; *Andromeda*, 165, 189; *Antiope*, 168; *Archelaos*, 171; *Bellerophon*, 149, 185 f.; *Cretans*, 149; *Erechtheus*, 161; *Hypsipyle*, 168; *Oidipous*, 170; *Palamedes*, 162, 189; *Peliades*, 25; *Phaethon*, 73, 161; *Phrixos B*, 161; *Telephos*, 143 f.; *Theseus*, 149
Europe, 48
exodos, 94, 180, 182

feathers, 47, 58
Flamininus, 196
flower-song, 61
flute, 7, 9, 10, 13, 15, 16, 17, 19 f., 22, 28, 29, 50, 56, 61, 73, 75, 89, 91, 94, 106, 107, 133, 152, 182, 188, 190, 193, 196, 199
Forsdyke, J., 4
Frickenhaus, A., 18 f.
Friis Johansen, K., 92

game-songs, 61
Geranos, 10, 101
Glaukos of Rhegium, 50, 56, 62
Grenfell song, 198
grinding-song, 61
gymnopaidiai, 61 f., 67

Harvey, A. E., 56, 67, 72, 90 f., 97
Helen, 48
Helikon, 48
Hellotia, 48
Hephaistos, 13, 24, 28, 68, 72
Hera, 25, 48, 49, 59, 67, 72
Herakles, 16, 64, 79, 88, 103 ff., 187
Hermes, 58
Hermippos, 94, 150
Hermokles, 198
Herms, 20, 22, 93
Herodotos, 48
Hesiod, 48, 73
Hestia, 195
Himera, 76
Homer, 46 ff., 56, 57, 73, 202
Homeric hymns: *Apollo*, 48, 49, 50, 54, 55, 193; *Gaia*, 48
Huxley, G. R. B., 50, 56
Hyakinthia, 61
Hygieia, 151
hyporcheme, 51, 63, 95, 99, 133

Ibykos, 78, 85
Iobakchoi, 64
Ion of Chios, 135
ioulos, 60
Isyllos, 195, 201
ithyphalloi, 71, 198
ivy, 12, 17, 18, 20, 21, 27, 29, 80, 82, 92, 194

Kahil, L., 22
Kallimachos, 82, 92, 94
Karkinos, 184 f.
Kastorion, 195
kaunakai, 69
Keos, 5, 8, 80, 99, 101, 109
Kephisodoros, 94
Kerenyi, K., 82
Kleisthenes, 67
kletic hymns, 112, 183 f., 189 ff.
Klonas, 56
knights, 20, 93, 180
Knossos, 5, 46

Korinna, 97, 152
Kouretes, 152, 189, 201
Krates, 94
Kratinos, 15, 94, 150, 182
Krexos, 153

Lasos, 80, 91, 111, 206
Lawler, L., xi, 14, 18, 48, 60, 190
Lenaia, 20, 64, 70, 81
Lesbos, 56, 67, 72
Likymnios, 151
Limenios, 196
Linos song, 46, 54, 202
Lloyd-Jones, H., 103, 132 f.
Lucian, 47, 51
Lykophronides, 195
Lykourgos, 53
lyre, 5 f., 9, 10, 11, 12, 13, 15, 16, 17, 22,
    47, 49, 50, 51, 70, 73, 75, 98, 105, 107 f.,
    152 f., 196, 199
lyric dialogue, 29, 111, 114, 116, 120,
    122 ff., 126 f., 130, 135 f., 141 ff., 144,
    156 f., 159 ff., 162 ff., 165 ff., 168 ff.,
    171 ff., 174 ff., 177 f., 184, 202, 207,
    210 ff.
Lysander, 152

Maas, P., 151, 197
maenads, 53, 59, 81 f.
Magnes, 15, 94
marriage-dances, 16, 47, 50, 73 ff., 98, 101,
    162, 186 f., 202
Marsyas, 132
Melanippides, 132, 152, 209
Melinno, 196
Messenian women, 54
metre: xiii f.; alcaic, 72, 76, 87, 205, 209;
    aeolic, 59, 66, 74, 85, 90, 96, 97, 99, 102,
    104 ff., 107 ff., 110, 207, 213; aeolo-
    choriambic, 61, 84, 125 ff., 132, 135 ff.,
    138 ff., 142 ff., 145 ff., 148, 154 f., 156,
    158 ff., 161 ff., 164 f., 166 ff., 169 ff.,
    172 ff., 175 ff., 178 f., 184, 187, 189, 196,
    210, 213; anacreontic, 70, 84, 121, 124,
    152, 180, 201, 215; anapaestic, 15, 20, 60,
    61, 62, 70, 77, 93 f., 112, 113 f., 116 ff.,
    123, 125 ff., 128, 130 f., 133, 134 f.,
    137 f., 141 f., 144 ff., 147 f., 149 f.,
    153 f., 156 ff., 159 ff., 162 f., 166 ff.,
    169, 171 ff., 174 ff., 178 ff., 181 f., 184,
    186 ff., 189 f., 198, 203, 205, 210 f., 213;
    aristophanean, 110, 114, 117, 121, 124,
    125 ff., 129, 131, 136, 146, 154, 208, 213;

asclepiad, 73, 90, 113, 135 ff., 138 f., 141,
    143 ff., 149, 160, 171 f., 174, 176 ff., 183,
    213; bacchiac, 119, 120, 126, 130 f., 154,
    159, 161, 167, 169, 170 ff., 173 ff., 179,
    213; choriambic, 86, 87, 88, 97, 109, 115,
    116, 119, 121 ff., 125, 139 f., 142 f.,
    148 ff., 154, 159 f., 161, 164, 166, 169 ff.,
    172, 178, 183, 187, 191, 194 ff., 198, 209,
    213 f; cretic, 59, 62, 95 f., 120 f., 123,
    128, 131, 133, 135, 138, 140 f., 147 f.,
    153 f., 158 f., 161, 164, 167 ff., 170 ff.,
    173 f., 176 f., 179 f., 182 f., 186, 193,
    196, 198, 214; dactylic, 50, 51, 54, 56 ff.,
    65, 74, 78, 79, 92, 97, 99, 102, 104, 106 f.,
    112, 115, 122, 125 ff., 128 f., 135, 138,
    140 ff., 144, 146 f., 149, 154 f., 156 f.,
    162 ff., 165 f., 168 ff., 171 ff., 174 ff.,
    177 ff., 180 f., 183 ff., 186, 188 ff., 191 ff.,
    206, 209 ff., 214; dactylo-anapaest, 77
    130, 151, 155, 164, 169, 206, 210;
    dactylo-epitrite, 66, 78 f., 84 ff., 88 ff.,
    100, 103, 104 ff., 107ff., 110, 131 ff.,
    135 f., 138, 140, 143, 145 f., 148 ff., 151,
    152 f., 156 f., 158 ff., 162 ff., 165 ff., 168,
    170 f., 174, 176 ff., 179, 183, 185 ff.,
    189 ff., 194 ff., 197, 201, 207 f., 210, 214;
    dochmiac, 114, 116 ff., 119 ff., 122 f.,
    126 ff., 129, 131, 134 ff., 137 ff., 141 ff.,
    145 ff., 148 f., 154, 157 ff., 160 ff., 163 ff.,
    166 ff., 169 ff., 172 ff., 175 ff., 179 ff.,
    183 f., 186, 189, 191, 198, 201, 210 f.;
    elegiac, 54, 56, 65, 67, 156, 204, 214; enó-
    comiologus, 58, 66, 78, 85, 214; eno-
    plian, 46, 55, 57 f., 62, 64, 65, 79, 85 f.,
    90, 96, 98, 99, 102, 121, 123, 130, 137,
    140, 142 ff., 145 ff., 148 f., 152, 153, 155,
    156 ff., 159 f., 162, 164 ff., 167 f., 170 ff.,
    174 ff., 177, 179, 185 f., 203 ff., 210, 214;
    glyconic, 59, 84, 86, 87, 88, 97, 101, 103,
    106, 107, 109, 110, 114, 115, 119, 121,
    123, 134, 136 ff., 139 f., 141, 150, 155 f.,
    158 ff., 162, 171, 176, 183, 190 f., 193 ff.,
    196, 205, 207, 208 f., 213; hipponactean,
    86, 114, 137 ff., 155, 177, 213; hypo-
    dochmiac, 136, 139, 143, 148, 169 f., 174,
    186, 214; iambelegus, 145, 167, 171, 173,
    214; iambic, 16, 59, 60, 61, 62, 64 f., 69,
    79, 102, 104, 115, 117 f., 119 ff., 122 f.,
    125 ff., 128 f., 130 f., 135, 136 f., 138,
    140, 142 ff., 149 f., 153 ff., 156 ff., 159,
    161 ff., 164 ff., 167 f., 170 f., 172 ff.,
    175 ff., 178 ff., 181 ff., 184, 186 ff.,
    189 ff., 193, 198, 204, 208, 210, 215;

iambo-trochaic, 58 f., 64, 65 f., 69, 71, 113 f., 118 ff., 121, 124, 125 f., 128 f., 131, 148, 152, 156, 158, 163 ff., 166, 169, 177, 180, 185, 187 ff., 198, 205, 215; ibycean, 78, 120, 190, 216; ionic, 59, 70, 84, 97, 113, 115, 116, 121, 124, 126, 130, 132, 142, 148 f., 152 f., 158, 161, 167, 172, 176, 180, 184, 186, 189 f., 194 f., 201, 203, 215; molossus, 152, 166, 175, 215; paeonic, 62, 99 ff., 104, 126, 128, 182, 203, 214; paroemiac, 46, 55, 60, 61, 62, 65, 77, 78, 86, 112, 117, 129, 141, 150, 153, 157, 162, 167, 173, 176, 203 ff., 211, 213 f.; pherecratean, 60, 84, 86, 97, 109, 114, 117, 119, 121, 123, 126, 128, 134, 137, 141, 150, 155 f., 172, 183, 190, 194 ff., 198, 205, 213; praxillean, 129, 137, 190, 216; proceleusmatic, 116, 133, 134, 163, 167, 178 f., 186, 211, 216; prosodiac, 79, 85, 96, 99, 100, 102, 104, 121, 123, 127, 130, 137, 144 f., 147 f., 149, 153, 156 f., 161 ff., 164 f., 167, 170, 172, 174, 177, 184, 188, 193, 206, 210, 216; reizianum, 60, 143, 150, 167, 213; sapphic, 72 ff., 76, 196, 205; telesillean, 88, 96 f., 102, 138, 150, 186 f., 190 f., 213; trochaic, 29, 56 ff., 59, 65, 78, 79, 93 f., 118 f., 130, 132 f., 134, 138, 152, 154 f., 162, 168, 170 ff., 176 f., 179 ff., 182 ff., 186 ff., 189 f., 197, 204 f., 216
Minoan dress, 8, 9
Minotaurs, 21, 93
Morelli, 60
Mother of the Gods, 96, 203
Muses, 15, 22, 48, 196
museums, 32–45; Adolfseck, 23; Aigina, 8, 15; Altenburg, 22; Amsterdam, 6, 14, 25; Argos, 6, 7, 8, 13
   Athens: Acropolis, 7, 10, 16, 17, 32, 73, 193; Agora, 6, 7, 8, 9, 21, 25, 31, 102, 192, 193; Kerameikos, 6, 7; National Museum, 4, 5, 6, 7, 9, 11, 12, 18, 21, 22, 28, 31, 32; Vlastos, 7, 9, 11, 17, 29
   Balat, 8; Baltimore, 22; Basel, 26; Berkeley, 21, 23; Berlin, 6, 9, 10, 12, 17, 19, 20, 22, 23, 25, 27, 28, 29, 94, 180; Beziers, 16; Bologna, 24; Bonn, 12, 22; Boston, 6, 20, 23, 24, 25, 27, 29; Brauron, 16; Brooklyn, 20; Brussels, 11, 13; Cambridge (Eng.), 18, 21, 25; Cambridge (Mass.), 20, 23; Castle Ashby, 23; Chicago, 23, 27; Christ-church, 15; Cleveland, 24; Copenhagen, 5 ff., 13, 16, 19, 22, 23, 29, 32, 47, 133; Corinth, 6, 9, 15, 25, 115; Cracow, 23, 27; Delos, 6, 7, 21; Delphi, 68; Dresden, 6, 7, 12, 16; Düsseldorf, 7; Eleusis, 10, 19; Ferrara, 24, 25, 30, 83; Florence, 10, 12, 16, 23, 25, 73; Frankfurt, 22; Gotha, 22; Heidelberg, 15, 20, 21, 31; Heraklion, 4, 5, 6, 10, 16; Karlsruhe, 30; Laon, 27; Leiden, 12; Leningrad, 25; Locri, 22; London, British Museum, 9, 13, 16, 17, 18, 20 ff., 23 f., 25 ff., 29, 30, 31, 83, 93, 155, 180; Madrid, 19; Mainz, 11; Makropoulon, 7; Meggen, 19; Milan, 23, 32; Munich, 7, 12, 17, 18, 19, 21 f., 24; Naples, 19, 28, 30; New York, 6, 12, 13, 15, 16, 19, 22, 27, 28, 74, 133; Nicosia, 20; Orvieto, 20; Oslo, 11, 17, 22; Oxford, 10, 12, 22, 23, 26, 28, 29, 118, 132; Paestum, 22; Palazzolo, 12; Palermo, 18
   Paris: Cab. Med., 17, 18, 27, 28; Louvre, 4, 6, 7, 9, 11, 13, 15, 16, 17, 21, 22, 23, 27, 31, 68, 192; Niarchos, 17; Rodin, 22
   Parma, 32; Perachora, 17; Philadelphia, 9; Providence, 27; Rhodes, 9, 14, 24
   Rome: Mus. Ind., 21; Vatican, 29, 132; Villa Giulia, 23, 25
   Ruvo, 30; Selinunte, 20; Sparta, 6, 56; Stavanger, 22; Stockholm, 19; Sydney, 19, 31; Taranto, 12, 20, 22, 32; Tarquinia, 16, 21; Tegea, 5, 6; Thebes, 20, 187; Toronto, 7; Tübingen, 5; Vienna, 8, 10, 24; Vienna University, 29; Warsaw, 7, 23, 27; Woburn, 27; Würzburg, 8, 17, 20, 23
Muth, R., 73
Mycenae, 4, 6, 52, 53
Myron, 132

Nausikaa, 49, 202
Nereids, 17, 68, 72
Nilsson, M. P., 59, 80, 82
nomos, 56, 153 f., 199

oklasma, 185
Olen, 54
Oliver, J. H., 151
ololyge, 49, 73, 130
Olympos, 50, 56, 62
oreibasia, 18
ostrich-riders, 20, 93

Page, D. L., xiv, 58, 60, 67, 72, 73, 76, 156
paian, 48, 50, 55, 57, 62, 64, 72, 73, 77, 84, 88, 98 ff., 104, 127, 139 f., 141, 143, 145, 147, 151 f., 155, 166, 187 f., 193 ff., 196 ff., 202 f
Pan, 24, 28, 197
Panathenaia, 6, 21, 26, 28, 32, 52, 71, 75, 92 f., 133, 152
parodos, 94, 130, 135, 137, 139, 144, 146 f., 156, 157, 158, 160, 162, 166, 168, 170, 172, 173, 175 f., 178 ff., 181 ff., 184, 191, 205
Paros, 63
partheneia, 49, 56, 67, 96 ff., 193, 205
Pausanias, 49, 50, 54, 59, 69, 80, 96
Pause, 54, 57, 59, 60, 61, 62, 65 f., 74, 76, 114, 204, 215
Payne, H. G. H., 63
periodic style, 85 ff., 90 ff., 110, 113, 207
Persephone, 24, 64
Phaeacia, 51
phallophoroi, 69
Pherekrates, 94, 150
Philippaki, B., 19, 81
Philodamos, 194, 204
Philoxenos, 153, 192, 199
Phrygia, 50, 56
Phrynichos, 29, 111, 112 f., 131, 185
Phrynis, 152 f., 210
Pindar, 58, 66, 78, 79, 80, 84, 86 ff., 90, 91 ff., 95 f., 97 ff., 103 ff., 107 ff., 110, 118, 183, 201, 203, 207
pipes (syrinx), 73
Pittakos, 61, 72
platform, 7, 10, 20, 48
Plato, 85, 94
Plutarch, 59, 62, 65, 67, 133, 151, 154, 196
pnigos, 181
Podlecki, A., 90
Polybios, 199
Poykrates, 78 f.
pompe, 69, 195
Pratinas, 14, 24, 95, 133, 211
Praxilla, 97
Priapos, 198
processional, 8, 16, 17, 22, 26, 29, 46, 48, 49, 50, 68, 73 ff., 77, 93, 97, 195 f.
Proclus, 98
prosodion, 50, 54, 98, 193, 196
Prudhommeau, xi
Ptolemy I, 198
pyleon, 49, 59, 60
pyrrhics, *see* Chorus, types of

recitative, 65, 153, 182
refrain, 50, 99, 123, 152, 164, 172, 179, 194 f., 197, 202, 205
Rhegion, 50, 56, 78
Rhesus, 132, 178
Rhodes, 60
Rome, 196 f.
rope-dance, 6, 47
Rosenmeyer, T., 67
Rumpf, A., 82

Sakadas, 67, 156
Samos, 78
Sappho, 72, 97, 101, 113, 187, 201, 203, 205
Satyros, 199
satyrs, 11, 67 f.
Seeberg, A., 3, 8, 63
Seleukos, 195
Sifakis, G. M., 192, 196, 198
Sikyon, 67, 69, 97, 151
Simonides, 80, 85, 90, 208
Skopas, 85
soldiers, 20 f., 93
Sophocles, 98, 151, 155, 179, 201, 210
   preserved plays: *Ajax*, 135 ff., 139, 143, 174; *Antigone*, 112, 137 ff., 143, 145, 208; *Electra*, 101, 173 ff.; *Oedipus Coloneus*, 101, 176 ff., 209; *Oedipus Rex*, 113, 141 ff., 174, 208; *Philoctetes*, 175 f., 177 f.; *Trachiniae*, 47, 210
   lost plays: *Amykos*, 28; *Dionysiskos*, 134; *Eurypylos*, 141; *Ichneutae*, 69, 134 f.; *Inachos*, 134; *Nausikaa*, 29, 49; *Pandora*, 24, 134; *Tereus*, 143; *Thamyras*, 29, 131 f.
Sparta, 6, 7, 12, 47, 48, 49, 52, 59, 61, 65, 67, 90, 195, 204 f.
sprays, 6 f., 8, 48, 58, 97 f., 195
Stesichoros, 56, 71, 76 ff., 79, 85, 112, 116, 118, 151, 186, 191, 206 f.
stilts, 15, 31
subsidiary chorus, 27, 124, 129, 147, 159, 189
symposion, 14, 64 f., 72, 84, 104, 194
swallows, 60, 65, 69

tambourines, 26 ff., 30, 81, 172
Tegea, 5 f., 47, 56
Telekleides, 15, 150
Telesilla, 96, 103
Telestes, 153
Terpander, 56, 71, 94
Thaletas, 56, 62, 67
Thargelia, 5, 47, 92, 102

Index

Theokles, 198
Theseus, 10, 16, 17, 46, 48, 98, 101, 102
Thesmophoroi, 60, 189 f.
Thespis, 19, 111, 184, 207
threnos, 90, 104 ff., 138, 143, 147, 149
Timotheos, 153, 171, 193, 199, 209, 211 f.
Tiryns, 6, 49
Titans, 15, 70
Tölle, R., 5, 7, 52

victor-odes, 64, 79, 85, 105 ff., 151

West, M. L., 56, 57, 78
Wilamowitz, U., 59, 81, 195
wreath, 6, 26, 48 f., 58, 59, 60, 97 f., 195

Xenokles, 184
Xenophon, 52, 112, 193